MARCO ⊕ POLO

BALI

D1471803

Top Destinations

Lush green rice terraces and an impressive volcanic landscape, endless beaches, sunny palm groves and dense tropical forests, smiling people and mystic temple complexes: Experience fascinating landscapes and the exotic culture of the small Indonesian holiday island Bali.

Royal monuments in the valley of the little Pakerisan River and the sacred spring temple Pura Tirtha Empul
page 233

❼ ✶✶ Besakih
For the Balinese this is the »Mother of all Temples«   page 152

❶ ✶✶ Bali Barat National Park
The national park at the extreme western end of Bali protects many endangered species of animals.
page 139

❷ ✶✶ Singaraja
In the old port city there are still many Dutch colonial style houses.
page 220

❸ ✶✶ Kubutambahan
Unusual stone relief in Pura Meduwe Karang
page 182

❹ ✶✶ Bedugul
A Hindu temple with a Buddhist stupa on a small island in the peaceful Lake Bratan
page 146

❺ ✶✶ Negara
Negara's attraction: water buffalo races à la »Ben Hur«
page 201

❻ ✶✶ Tampaksiring

❽ ✶✶ Amlapura

Former prince's palace and the royal pools Tirtha Gangga
page 136

Do You Feel Like...

... a very special Hindu temple or volcano hikes? Or a relaxing stay in a wellness resort? Experience the world of the gods, spirits and demons; encounter Bali's animal world (sometimes up close) and let Bali's wonderful mountain landscape impress you. Then enjoy the island's culinary diversity.

TEMPLES

VULCANOS

WELLNESS

CULINARY

BALI'S ANIMAL WORLD

Creative crafts are for sale in the Art Market of Sukawati or Bali's »artistic heart« Ubud

Relax on Kuta Beach, Bali's most popular beach

SIGHTS FROM A to Z

PRICE CATEGORIES
Restaurants
(main dish)
££££ = more than £15
£££ = £8 – £15
££ = £4 – £8
£ = up to £4
Hotels (double room)
££££ = more than £120
£££ = £80 – £120
££ = £40 – £80
£ = up to £40

Note
Billable service telephone numbers are marked with an asterisk: *0800

PRACTICAL INFORMATION

On Bali's neighbour island Lombok there are (still) wonderfully peaceful beaches

BACKGROUND

Volcanoes, rainforests and paddy fields, temple festivals, gods and demons: interesting facts about Bali, about the country and its people, its art and culture, its history and everyday life.

Island of the Gods

Once a year thousands of Balinese gather on the beach in Sanur at sunset. The festively-dressed multitude gazes out at the water and, every now and again, people glance over to the small altar adorned with flowers and crowned by a canopy.

As the sun's rays grow weaker and the crowd swells with the arrival of hundreds of people dressed in white and yellow, the first individuals begin standing up and walking toward the ocean. They carry small boats woven from palm fronds with offerings of rice, a few coins, and tropical blossoms: blue ones for Vishnu, red ones for Brahma and white ones for Shiva – the three major deities of **Hinduism**. As if acting on a signal, they lay their offerings down on the sand, pause for a moment in silent prayer, then return to their place and sit down again. It is the eve of **Nyepi**, the Balinese New Year celebration, and the people have assembled on the beach of Sanur to solicit the goodwill of the spirits of the sea for the coming year.

GODS, SPIRITS AND DEMONS

There is sense for the spiritual dimension in everyday life in Bali. All over the island the Balinese live in harmony with the cosmic mandala, honour the gods, and are fully aware that there is something more than just the cares and joys of this present life. Everyone who sets foot on the **tropical island** feels its magical atmosphere. Contributing factors to this are the numerous festivals and ceremonies that enrich village life throughout the whole year and which foreign visitors are welcome to attend. In addition, the Balinese world of dance, often marked by spiritualism, is full of vitality. Bali is the sweet smell of tropical blossoms and incense sticks, and the sounds of gamelan orchestras. And it is also the deep spirituality and exuberant joy of its people, the verdant **rice terraces** that sparkle in the sunlight as well as the many **temples**: in fact more temples have been counted on the island than homes. Bali also means volcanoes and dark lava beaches lined with palm trees, lush tropical vegetation, and a range of hotels that could have sprung out of a catalogue of international furnishings.

BEAUTIFUL LANDSCAPES AND DECORATIVE ARTS

If only for its religion, Bali is different from the other 13,000 or so Indonesian islands. The **volcanoes Batur** and **Agung**, set in enchan-

Visitors will often encounter ceremonially dressed believers with artistic sacrifices

ting landscapes ideal for hiking and trekking, are considered to be the abode of the gods. Tourists appreciate the many seaside resorts and their beaches, from the black lava sand in the north to the mangrove-lined beaches in the south of the island. In point of fact, all of the tourist centres are on the coastline with the exception of the artists' town of Ubud. Visitors are enthralled by the wealth of luxuriant vegetation. Thanks to the heavy rainfall, many varieties of palm thrive, as do lush, blossoming frangipani trees and orchids in all sizes and colours. Dense forests, on the other hand, can only be found in the west of the island, primarily in **Bali Barat National Park**. Numerous rivers flow through the island and contribute to the constant irrigation of the rice terraces. The Balinese are unique craftsmen: for them, the wish to create something stems from their desire for inner and outer harmony. Museums provide a good overview of the diversity of art objects, but only the displays in the shops and a visit to those engaged in the decorative arts can familiarize the visitor with the great variety of woodcarving, painting, weaving art, wickerwork, jewellery and **batik art**. And so it is, at the latest on the return trip home, that every visitor to Bali discovers how a stay on the small Indonesian island only arouses the wish to return again as soon as possible.

Facts

Nature and Environment

Bali, the westernmost of the Lesser Sunda Islands, fascinates its visitors with a unique landscape of volcanic mountain ranges, lavish tropical vegetation and artfully arranged rice terraces.

NATURE

Bali is the westernmost of the Lesser Sunda Islands. It is separated from its much larger western neighbour Java by a strait that is only 3m/2mi wide. While western Bali is now characterized by rugged **mountain ranges** that formed during the Tertiary period, there are four larger **volcanoes** in the east, including Gunung Agung (see below), which erupted most recently in 1963, claiming around 2000 lives. Bali's south consists of fertile **plains**. Bali is located on the **Ring of Fire** that goes all around the Pacific and is known for its severe **volcanic eruptions** as well as its **earthquakes and seaquakes**, which can trigger hugely destructive **tsunamis**, such as in 2004 (off the coast of Java) and in 2011 (off the coast of Japan). The reason for the volcanic and seismic activity on Bali is continental drift. In Bali's case the Sahul Shelf, part of the Australian continental plate, is pushing its way under the Sunda Shelf, part of the Eurasian continental plate, at a speed of several centimetres per year. In the process, the earth's crust is periodically ripped open and magma is able to reach the earth's surface through the volcanic conduits that were formed a few million years ago. This process is illustrated nicely in the Gunung Batur volcano, which erupted four times in the 20th century.

Young island of volcanic origin

During the **last ice age** (Pleistocene), which started around two million and ended around 10,000 years ago, Bali was part of the Eurasian landmass. After the inland ice melted, **sea levels rose**. During that process, the lower-lying land of what was the mainland was flooded, creating the chain of islands that Bali is a part of, along with the straits of varying widths.

The highest mountains in Bali are the volcanoes Gunung Agung (3142m/10,308ft) and Gunung Batukau (2276m/7,467ft), the latter of which has been active again since 1999. On the neighbouring island of Lombok the Rinjani volcano is the highest elevation at

Mountains and rivers

Rice plays a central role in Bali as a food source. Many rituals accompany its cultivation, from sowing to harvest

Island Topography

5561sq km/2147sq mi of land of volcanic origin: Bali, the westernmost of the Lesser Sunda Islands, is located in the Indian Ocean between Java and Lombok. Its highest elevation is the still active volcano Gunung Agung at 3142m/10,308ft. The volcano, which is considered sacred by Hindus, erupted most recently in 1963.

❶ Central Bali

Bali's central region is dominated by four volcano complexes, of which the highest is Gunung Agung in the eastern section of the island. Gunung Batur (1717m/5633ft) marks the transition to northern Bali. It features a large crater lake. Further to the west are the volcanoes Catur (2096m/6877ft) and Batukau (2276m/7467ft).

❷ Western Bali

Deep valleys between mountain ranges that formed during the Tertiary period characterize the narrow western part of the island that is home to Bali Barat National Park. Since this region lies on the protected leeward side of the mountains, it is substantially drier than southern Bali.

❸ Southern Bali

Southern Bali is the most fertile region of the island. It is characterized by the humid plains that are made fertile by volcanic ash. These plains are located on the windward side of the central volcanic mountain range that extends southwards, and benefit from high precipitation all year round. This region is home to the areas used intensively for agriculture.

❹ Eastern Bali

The central Balinese mountains come close to the edge of the island, characterizing the landscape there. Gunung Agung with its foothills, which are oriented north-south, and Gunung Batur, whose massif marks the transition to central Bali, dominate the landscape.

At the edge of Gunung Agung's crater

The ocean water temperature is almost **like a warm bath** all year: the average temperature is around 27.9°C/82.2°F in April and it reaches no less than 29°C/84.2°F in December.

The relatively high **humidity** can occasionally be hard on visitors from less tropical climes. It rises to 80 percent in February, and sinks by only 5 percent in August and September. Those who feel uncomfortable in high humidity conditions should therefore travel to Bali between May–June and September–October; during the other months when the temperature is high the moist air can be almost unbearably oppressive.

Humidity

FLORA

The Wallace Line, a bio-geographical boundary named after the British zoologist **Alfred R. Wallace** (1823–1913) runs between the Asian and Australasian flora and fauna zones along the depths of the strait between Bali and Lombok (Lombok Strait). Wallace explored the islands between 1854 and 1862, finding striking differences in the animal and plant worlds.

Wallace Line

No other island in Indonesia is so intensively cultivated as Bali; wherever you look there are rice fields. Even the smallest patch of earth manages to yield **up to three rice harvests per year** (▶MARCO POLO Insight, p. 20).

Rice and tropical foresta

But there is also another Bali to be found, for the most part in the west of the island in the Bali Barat National Park: **tropical forests** made up in the lower regions of hardwoods such as mahogany, and in the higher elevations of slender, tall-growing pines and various species of dipterocarp (Greek: two-winged fruit). Stretching out in the south are forests of palms, which give way to the large and small rice fields of the harmonious landscape gently rising towards the interior. The southern coastal region, on the other hand, seems at first glance to be quite unimpressive. For its part, East Bali, where the mountains reach close to the coast, still possesses reserves suitable for agriculture. The flora becomes thinner in the mountainous regions, where hardy, low-growing shrubs and plants dominate the landscape. This then gives way to a barren zone of black lava rock.

MARCO POLO INSIGHT

?

Rice colours

Rice is much more than just the Balinese staple food. It is given to the gods during ceremonies in red, black and white. Every rice field, every rice terrace possesses numerous shrines, some even have their own temple. The creation of a new paddy field resembles a ritual celebration.

From the Rice Terrace to the Table

As is true for the whole of southeast Asia, rice is the number one staple food on Bali too. Bali's rice terraces (▶MARCO POLO Insight, p.228) are famous and shape large parts of the island.

Rice fields also surround Ubud, a centre of art and culture. Nobody ever has to go far to see how rice is grown. The view guests get from the restaurant terrace of the »Four Seasons at Sayan« hotel is particularly spectacular. The hotel, which is built in a valley, towers high above the Agung river and the rice terraces that travel up the mountain in their graceful curving forms. There are many other locations outside of Ubud, such as will be passed on walks and hikes, where visitors can experience the rice terraces that appear like natural artworks as they climb up the steep mountain slopes.

On the way to the fields that appear like ladders to heaven, women with baskets on their heads are a frequent sight. They are carrying rice snacks and fruit for the workers on the fields. They walk with a relaxed grace, unperturbed by cars, motorbikes and constantly honking lorries that now clog up the roads even in Bali.

Rich Harvests

The creation of this cultivated landscape follows an old tradition: the soil is compacted and then shaped into pools. Channels guide water from springs and rivers to the fields. Water flows from the upper terraces through openings to lower terraces, some of which are only a few metres wide – it is an ingenious system. Rice plants germinated and allowed to grow elsewhere are planted in the flooded terraces and fields. In just eight weeks the thin seedlings that are reflected in the water have spread so much that the entire hillsides are resplendent in a lush green. Fertile volcanic soils and the tropical monsoon climate encourage rich harvests. The steep fields, some of which are hard to access, are still worked with cows and buffalos. Ducks and geese populate these wet fields, always in search of food.

Dewi Sri

In previous centuries the population's survival and affluence were particularly dependent on the quality of the rice harvest. For that reason, one of the most important deities known to and worshipped by the Balinese is Dewi Sri, the goddess of fertility and protector of the rice fields, depicted as a beautiful, youthful goddess. At the time of the harvest Dewi (goddess) Sri manifests herself in the form of countless grains of rice. In fact, grains of rice are also seen as the embodiment of Shiva, who is believed to be Dewi Sri's husband. Temples and altars are still built for the goddess at the edge of the rice fields. These are supplied with sacrificial goods on a daily basis.

White, Red and Black

Bali's rice terraces, which run along the centre of the island on enormous, steep slopes, are evidence of the popularity of different rice varieties that are grown here. In addition to of white rice of various qualities, Bali also grows red rice and a black variety that is used mainly to make rice pudding. The flour of the white sticky rice on the other hand is used to make small flat cakes that are fried and eaten.

White rice, the variety eaten on a daily basis, is called nasi putih. A traditional rice dish that is known all around the world and that comes from Java is Nasi Goreng – rice fried in a wok along with chicken, shrimps, grated cabbage, green beans and bean sprouts, flavoured with fresh coriander and served with a fried egg.

»Indonesian Rijsttafel«

Rice comes in a large variety of colours, flavours and prices and naturally the ways in which it is cooked and prepared in Bali are equally diverse. The grains are thrown into cold, warm or boiling water, served in bowls, plates or banana leaves and eaten with the fingers or with a fork. Every Balinese person will know dozens of rice dishes, first and foremost Nasi Kuming, yellow rice served with meat, vegetables and seafood, and Ketupa, rice steamed in woven baskets, as well as Lontong, rice steamed in banana leaves.

The »Indonesian Rijsttafel« is famous around the world. A 'rice table', which was once reserved for big celebrations, is made up of

The rice fields climb up the mountains in southern Bali like natural artworks

steamed rice along with small bowls filled with different dishes such as fish, meat, vegetables and eggs along with hot and sweet-and-sour chutneys, fruit, nuts, kroepoek (deep fried crackers) and grated coconut.

The mighty **banyan tree** (Sanskrit: nyagrodha), a species of fig tree typical of Southeast Asia, is considered to be sacred. The Ficus bengalensis in Bali reaches a height of up to 30m/98ft. It possesses a broad crown whose branches are supported by numerous aerial roots. Banyan trees seldom grow alone and because they suppress other species of trees they can form whole forests. The banyan tree is considered to be **worthy of veneration** because Siddharta Gautama achieved a state of enlightenment in southern India under such a tree and is said to have later entered Nirvana as the first Buddha . Almost every village in Bali has one or more banyan trees.

Commercial plants

Bali's lush flora serves first and foremost to provide the population with food. Pineapples, bananas, vegetables, coffee, coconuts and betel nuts thrive on plantations. The betel nut, especially popular with the older generation, is enjoyed for its intoxicating effects. For consumption, small pieces of the not fully ripened **betel nut** are wrapped in a betel pepper plant leaf brushed with slaked lime and then chewed. The attraction of this narcotic is that although it has a euphoric effect, it does not diminish the ability to work. However, with continuous use, it stains the teeth, saliva and lips red; furthermore, tannins in the betel nut can induce chronic inflammation of the oral cavity. Although Balinese **coffee** is an important export commodity, the cultivation of tobacco, tea and spices has only secondary significance and because of the small amounts produced these crops are destined only for the local market. Great importance is attached to coconut palm and fast-growing bamboo, both being popularly used as building materials. There are fewer orchids here than in other Southeast Asian countries; **lotus blossoms**, on the other hand, are plentiful.

FAUNA

Land fauna

Balinese land fauna is equally diverse. Although many years ago the Bengal tiger was common in Bali, it is now thought to be extinct – at least none have been seen for a long time. Still calling the place home are some smaller varieties of crocodile, monitor lizards, iguanas and turtles. There are also snakes in the regions grown over with jungles, including venomous varieties. There are great numbers of **monkeys living in the wilds** of the Balinese forests as well as many species of **tropical bird**. Along with quite a few varieties of parrot and finch, Bali is the last refuge of some 200 remaining specimens of the **Bali mynah** or Rothschild's mynah, a bird about 25cm/10in in size, white except for blue markings around the eyes and black-tipped wings and tail, which is threatened with extinction and is therefore rigorously protected (▶ill. p.17). Bats and flying foxes are held to be sacred and are venerated.

Water buffaloes are not just agricultural animals, they are »athletes«
too: at the annual buffalo race in Negara

The gecko (in Bali: tokeh), a harmless Southeast Asian descendant of
the lizard family, is an endearing little animal seen primarily in the
evening and night time hours that has proved its usefulness in exter-
minating insects. Geckos like to gather in numbers around lamps and
lanterns, call attention to themselves with quacking noises, but then
disappear at the slightest attempt to approach them.

Among the domestic animals, the apparently slow and ponderous
water buffalo is used as a beast of burden as well as to work on the
rice fields, where hundreds of small ducks dive and feed on the bot-
tom. Other domestic species often encountered include the **pot-bel-
lied pig** and the **banteng**, a species related to the wild ox, as well as
geese and chickens. Pig husbandry is of some significance in Bali but
because the rest of Indonesia is Islamic, sucking pigs and pork are
exported to such far-flung places as Hong Kong.

The ocean surrounding Bali is **rich in fish**. The catch consists prima-   Marine fauna
rily of tuna and perch. Fishing is not very intensely pursued because,

according to Balinese belief, the ocean is the abode of many evil spirits and demons. One denizen of the deep, however, is revered as sacred, namely the black and white banded sea snake.

NATURE AND ENVIRONMENTAL PROTECTION

Rubbish Environmental protection has only recently been assigned **greater status** in Bali. Problems with the environment, brought on not least by the flood of tourists, have become all too apparent. Just by walking through Denpasar, for example, a certain discrepancy becomes apparent. On the one hand, the Balinese are (like Asians in general) very particular about cleanliness and hygiene in their own private spheres, but on the other hand, they allow the piles of rubbish to grow ever higher and broken glass to accumulate on the beaches, posing a potential hazard for people going barefoot. In the absence of organized refuse disposal, trash is still fly dumped and ignited; waste water is simply piped into the ocean. Governmental campaigns have had little effect. The number of waste bins, at least, is being increased at the sites frequented by tourists.

Traffic The increasing amount of motor traffic on the island is associated with big problems. At times, in Denpasar, thick exhaust fumes make a walk something of a strain. One of the causes of this particular problem is the distinctly bad habit of leaving the motor running while waiting. The high (and greatly increasing) number of motorbikes, an important form of transport for the Balinese, poses a marked environmental problem. Awareness of the need to develop a sensible way interacting with the natural environment is often sadly lacking. Many think nothing of changing their motor oil without bothering to collect the used oil. However, slowly but surely, a process of readjustment in Balinese thinking on these matters is taking place; in fact, methods are being considered for proper waste disposal and how to avoid generating so much.

Population growth A less obvious problem is that caused by the growing population on the island. Large families with a dozen children or more are the rule rather than the exception in Bali. In order to feed them all, more and more primeval forests are being cleared for agricultural purposes.

Soil erosion One of the unpleasant results of this, not often taken into consideration, is an increase in soil erosion. The forest loses part of its function as an important factor in a balanced climate. Fortunately, there have been to date no devastating floods or other natural catastrophes – apart from erupting volcanoes.

The greatly increased sea traffic between Bali and Lombok and the Gili Islands, and the cleaning of the ships' motors that goes along with it, present no small danger for the coastlines. In addition, anchors often damage parts of the beautiful coral reefs.

Future prospects

Population · Politics · Economy

Indonesia is a multi-national state, which can be seen alone in the number of languages and dialects – more than 250 of them. The majority of the population, however, belongs to the Malayan-Polynesian (Austronesian) family, often called Protomalayan or Old Malaysian.

POPULATION

Originally, Bali was inhabited by nomadic peoples – as were some other Indonesian islands, too. A strong growth in population started around 3000 BC when peoples who had up to that point been living in southern China left their hereditary homeland and spread out over large parts of today's Southeast Asia. During the course of this migration, the extent of which can only be guessed at today, those groups familiar with the open seas reached, among other places, the Indonesian archipelago. These people had a close association to nature, and venerated their ancestors along with spirits and demons – indeed, elements of this religious belief are still retained today in the basic Balinese view of the world. A second major migration began shortly before the start of the Christian era. The Protomalayan (Old Malayan) people were joined by the Deuteromalayan people, who gradually merged completely with the original inhabitants of the island. Other peoples who settled in Bali and on its neighbouring islands (e.g. Chinese), however, have remained minorities to the present day.

Origins

At present around 4 million people live on the island of Bali. The annual rate of population growth has been successfully limited to about 1.8% thanks to a **birth control** programme propagated by the Indonesian government (slogan: »Dua Anak Cukup« = »two children are enough«). A problem is the fact that a male successor is still considered indispensable in Balinese society, above all to assume the father's religious responsibilities. The result is that the island population still continues to grow considerably and it seems there will be a time in the foreseeable future when Bali is overpopulated and the products

Population

Location:
Westernmost of the Lesser Sunda Islands
8° 30' south latitude, 115° east longitude

Pacific Ocean

Borneo

Sulawesi

Sumatra

Ne
Guine

Jakarta ■

INDONESIA

Java

Indian Ocean

Bali

Area:
**5,632 sq km/
2,175 sq mi**

Population:
3.89 mil.

Population density:
**691 people per sq k
1,782 per sq mi**

▶ Administration

Bali is divided into **eight administrative districts** (Kabupaten). The smallest administrative units are **quarters** (Banjar), which are collected into city districts or villages (Desa). Each of these is headed by a **mayor** (Walikota).

Capital: **Denpasar**

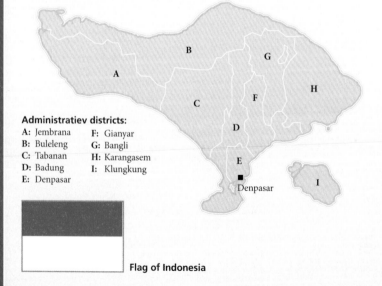

Administratiev districts:

A: Jembrana   F: Gianyar
B: Buleleng   G: Bangli
C: Tabanan   H: Karangasem
D: Badung   I: Klungkung
E: Denpasar

Denpasar

Flag of Indonesia

Economy

Tourism is the major economic factor. About 22% of the working population is employed in this industry. Most tourists come from Australia, China and Japan.

65% of the island is used for agricultural purposes (rice, vegetables); major exports are coffee, coconuts, spices and pork.

▶ Climate in Denpasar

Average temperatures

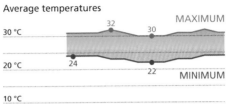

Precipitation

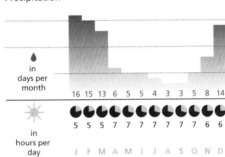

Religion

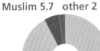

Muslim 5.7   other 2

%

92.3

Hindu

▶ Comparison of four Indonesian islands

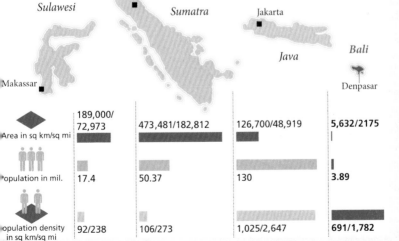

	Sulawesi	Sumatra	Java	Bali
Area in sq km/sq mi	189,000/72,973	473,481/182,812	126,700/48,919	5,632/2175
Population in mil.	17.4	50.37	130	3.89
Population density in sq km/sq mi	92/238	106/273	1,025/2,647	691/1,782

Welcome to Everyday Life

Those who want to get to know Bali away from the beaches and the luxury spas, who want to meet »regular« people, which is all the easier thanks to the friendly open Balinese manner, will welcome these tips from a connoisseur of the island.

VOLUNTEERING

Participating in social projects or helping out in development aid institutions, teaching English to children and adults, or supporting teachers in orphanages: for a fee the organization »Students Go Abroad« will find a placement and accommodation on the island as long as you have at least four weeks available.

www.studentsgoabroad.com

TEMPLE FESTIVALS

It is an unforgettable experience to witness a temple festival. Sit on the floor and enjoy the sacrificial goods prepared especially for the festival – delicacies that are not served at any other time. The gods are invited to visit the temple via meditation, prayers, mantras and special rituals. Gamelan music creates a magical atmosphere. Most tourist information offices keep a list of current temple festivals.

VISITING A
»TRADITIONAL VILLAGE«

Although somewhat touristy, it is nonetheless an authentic experience to hire a guide and visit the small village of Penglipuran 5km/3mi north of Bangli, where it is possible to visit the houses of the inhabitants and be informed about the way of life of a tribe that still lives in a very traditional manner. The people in the village live off of producing crafts and woven goods, which they try to sell to tourists. It is a good opportunity to visit traditional Balinese farmsteads and engage in conversation with those who live there.

BATHING WITH HINDUS

The former moated palace of »Tirthagangga« near Amlapura, which has largely been restored and transformed into a public bath after a volcanic eruption – is a popular location for the devout Balinese population to enjoy a princely bath. Some of the women hop around in the water wrapped in cloths, and the children have fun too. Those who keep their eyes open will be able to experience how the people make sacrifices to the gods at the small altars to be found everywhere; even young girls sprinkle water over wide open lotus blossoms with graceful hand gestures.

PASAR BADUNG

Pineapples in all sizes and price categories, oranges and lemons built into pyramids, vegetables that resemble leeks and have an unpronounceable name, baskets and bags made of straw, accessories for temples and home altars: the largest market in the capital Denpasar is not aimed at tourists but at the local population, which is why it is not decorative, but purposeful and full of life.
Daily 5am–midnight

Advertisement for the small family

of the island's agriculture alone are no longer sufficient to feed the Balinese people.

Another problem in Bali is a certain amount of rural to urban migration that has brought more and more people to the south of the island, in particular to the densely populated city of Denpasar, which is dominated by tourism. Here, people assume, the chances of earning a living are better.

Since 1984 there has been **general compulsory education** for the length of six years in Indonesia and thus also in Bali, followed by, when aptitude merits, a high school education (three years of junior and three years of senior high school). Children start school between the ages of six and eight. Education at a state school is free. Denpasar has a university and two polytechnic colleges. Members of the Balinese upper class attend at least one of the colleges in the Indonesian capital of Jakarta or an institute of higher learning abroad. A **reduction in the rate of illiteracy**, which in the early 1970s was still around 40% in rural areas, has been achieved through stricter control of school attendance.

Health care   The health care system in Bali is only modestly developed. Although in recent years there has been an increase in the number of doctors' practices, the only hospitals are in Denpasar. However they are extremely poorly equipped and suited at best for primary care. Outside Denpasar there are heath centres (puskemas) maintained by the state in the cities, as well as medical out-patient clinics that are capable of handling the usual illnesses and minor injuries. The costs for medical treatment are borne by the Indonesian state, but medicine must be paid for by the individual. The treatment of severe diseases and serious injury due to accidents, on the other hand, is well-nigh impossible in Bali; such patients are usually transported to Jakarta. There are a couple of good Australian clinics in Denpasar that tourists can consider using. There is no well-developed ambulance system approaching Western standards; particularly in the island's interior, it can take a long time for one to arrive.

POLITICS

Ever since the severe economic crisis that began in Thailand in 1997 and spread out over all of Southeast Asia, Indonesian's state and society (242 million inhabitants) has found itself in a phase of fundamental upheaval. In Indonesia in particular this has resulted at times in violent unrest, and though the island of Bali has by and large been spared a similar fate, it has been indirectly affected by the events in the region. Ibrahim Suharto, the head of state who enjoyed absolute rule since 1967, was removed from office after bloody violence broke out in Jakarta. However his successor was also unable to solve Bali's economic problems and thus relieve the tension between people and government. With the economic crisis that began in 1997 and the overthrow of Suharto in 1998, a **process of democratization** could be observed. This led to Indonesia's first free and democratic elections in 2004. 24 parties were up for election; the strongest party, at 22%, was Golkar, a union of convenience formed from representatives of various sections of society. The first directly elected president of Indonesia is the former general Susilo Bambang Yudhoyono, who first entered office in October 2004 and was confirmed again at the presidential election of July 2009. The Democratic Party (PD) he established obtained the most parliamentary seats at the elections in April 2009, with 20.8% of the vote.

Indonesia's current situation

Within Java's political sphere of influence from a very early date, Bali gained independence as far back as the 16th century. In the period when Java was being Islamized (up into the 16th century), Bali became a **refuge for Hindus**. In the 17th century, Bali also ruled over the island of Lombok and the eastern tip of Java. In 1839 Bali fell under Dutch suzerainty, and from 1908 was administered by the Kingdom of the Netherlands. From 1942 to 1945 the island was occupied by the Japanese, and in 1946 acquired the status of an autonomous territory. As one of the sites of the struggle for independence, it was only incorporated into the Republic of Indonesia in 1949. In 1950, the historical principalities that had only been reintroduced in 1938 were abolished again and replaced by government districts (▶p.26).

Bali's special historical role

Growing rice is the cornerstone of Balinese agriculture

ECONOMY

Indonesia: a threshold state

Indonesia is a newly industrializing, so-called »threshold country« that for a long period participated in the economic upswing in the whole Southeast Asian region, until the onset of the severe financial and economic crisis. Since 1997, when economic turbulence emanating from Thailand severely affected the whole region, Indonesia's economic future has become more uncertain than ever before, even though the Indonesian economy was previously enjoying almost unfettered economic growth: annual growth rates of up to 8% were the rule. The fall in the price of exported oil alone cast a shadow on the steadily upward trend of development (as a member of the Organization of Petroleum Exporting Countries, OPEC, Indonesia suffered especially badly). The World Bank linked their offer of aid to the condition that the banking industry – whose policy of unrestricted credit was seen to be one of the causes of the problem – would be subject to fundamental reform. The president at the time, Jusuf Habibie, however, not only considered himself forced to accept the reforms but also to decree an emergency that resulted in a drastic reduction of state expenditure (with particular effect on food subsidies). In turn, distrust grew in the population. Habibie was accused of opposing reform, not least because of his good relationship with Suharto, the ex-head of state, and was eventually voted out of office. Because of developments in the rest of Indonesia, Bali's economy also suffered, even though the agriculture that dominated the island's economy was not affected to the same extent. The decline in Bali's tourist numbers was also only temporary; the advantageous exchange rate soon drew an increased number of visitors.

Rice cultivation continues to play a central role in Balinese agriculture. The development of the cleverly devised irrigation system for the **predominantly terraced rice fields** dates back to the 6th century. Bali, one of the nation's smallest provinces, provides an impressive 5% of Indonesia's total rice harvest. This is mainly wet rice, i.e. rice grown on fields first artificially flooded with water. The water is drained away only after the hand-planted seedlings achieve a certain maturity. When the leaves of the stalks start to turn yellow, the rice is harvested – again by hand – and then threshed, after which it is ready for milling (▶MARCO POLO Insight, p.20 and p.228).

Rice cultivation in Bali

Further agricultural products are vegetables, natural rubber, tea and coffee (more than 10% of all of Indonesia's coffee is harvested on Bali). The cultivation of **vanilla** also produces good yields; Indonesia is the second-most important supplier of this spice after Madagascar. There is a small wine growing region in the northeast of the country, however, the results are still of mediocre quality.

Further agricultural products

Fishing plays an if anything subordinate role. The profits are so small that many fishing families live below the poverty line and require state support. For that reason fish is largely imported from Java. One reason more intensive fishing has not developed here is that according to the Balinese faith, the ocean is home to demons.

Fishing cultivation in Bali

A special feature of Bali's agriculture is the union of farmers of one or more village districts (banjar) in **cooperative organizations** called »sekaha«. These in turn are divided into groups, the »sekaha menanam« responsible for planting the fields, the »sekaha panen« for the harvest, and the »sekaha me jukut« for weeding. A fourth

Sekaha and subak (cooperatives)

group, the »sekaha bajak«, is responsible for ploughing. Revenues earned through the sale of the agrarian products are equally divided among the members, with a portion put aside as a reserve.

In wet cultivation, the cooperatives are called »subak«. In southern Bali, they were presumably formed in the 10th/11th century at the suggestion of the ruling princes of the time. The farmers in the north did it on their own initiative: at that time, not all farmers in a given banjar had their own irrigation canals, so the others declared themselves willing to share their water. It is then the obligation of each member of the subak to not only contribute services to the association (e.g. dam building, monitoring and maintenance of the irrigation system), but also to pay a water tax. The subak principle was therefore created out of **village solidarity**; even today customary law is still observed over Indonesian laws. A subak should not be considered just as a division of labour for rice planting; it is also a social group in which the Hindu religious concepts of its members play an important role. Accordingly, the assembly of all subak members, for example, determines the scheduling of religious festivals and ceremonies honouring the rice goddess Dewi Sri and the water deity Vishnu (in South Bali, instead of Vishnu, the sea god Baruna is honoured; he has the task of keeping all vermin away from the rice). Every subak has its own temple (pura bedugul) standing among or on the edge of the rice fields. The farmers' major festival during the course of the year is the harvest festival (ngu saba), for which all subak members contribute offerings. Those who shirk the duties and obligations set forth by the association are subject to a fine payable in kind (in many subaks, the fine is 1kg/2.2lb of rice to be delivered to the association). The head of a subak is a »Klian« chosen by the general assemblage. He distributes the available water to the members, mediates disputes and leads the meetings. A comprehensive reorganization is supposed to have taken place during the Dutch colonial period, but while the Dutch introduced more efficient irrigation technique, the organization of the subak remained untouched. Since the early 1980s, a cooperative organized on the model of the sekaha has distributed loans to the farmers guaranteed by the Indonesian state bank.

Tourism The island of Bali is undoubtedly Indonesia's best developed region for tourism . Since the mid-1970s, reserved tourist enclaves with hotel facilities reaching international standards have been built, primarily in the south of Bali (Nusa Dua, Kuta, Legian, Sanur, Seminyak, Jimbaran). From year to year, the revenues from tourism play an increasingly important role in the total national economy. A stopover in Bali on flights between Europe and Australia is popular. Several million tourists visit Indonesia each year; an exact number cannot be determined because the number of people from neighbouring Asian

A wide sandy beach and good surfing conditions: Kuta is one of Bali's most popular holiday destinations

countries visiting their relatives is included. Between 2.5 and 3 million of these tourists come to the island of Bali, for the most part from Australia, China, Japan, the USA, Germany and the Netherlands. About 60,000 British visitors arrive on Bali's shores annually.

Religion

Approximately 93% of all Balinese are Hindus; other religions such as Buddhism, Islam and Christianity play only a minor role in Bali.

This means the province has an **exceptional position within Indonesia** because, taking the country as a whole, about 87% of the population are Sunni Muslims. In the course of time, however, Buddhist elements have found their way into the Hindu-Balinese religion (Agama Hindu Dharma). Hinduism came to Bali from India by way of Java in the 8th/9th centuries. There are only marginal differences between the Balinese version and its Indian original, though a **much less strict caste system** is practised in Bali.

Religious denominations

Hindus praying

HINDUISM

Balinese version of the world religion

Hinduism is one of the world's five great religions. A total of about 900 million people profess this belief. In contrast to the monotheistic belief in one god, Hinduism, like Buddhism, Confucianism and Taoism, is a monistic religion orientated toward a de-personified principle. For some decades now however, a denomination has been gaining strength in Bali that noticeably approaches monotheism, recognizing one god with whom everything had its beginning: the **Sangyang Widi**, the »all-encompassing god« . The fundamentals of Hinduism developed over the course of millennia, but it represents no firmly structured religious principle. One of the original elements, which remains an essential part of Hinduism to this day, is Brahmanism, and this in turn took its basic concept from Vedism, an ancient Indian religion.

So what does a Hindu believe? Having become a human being, he has earned a place on the middle rung of the symbolic ladder. Initially, he is caught in the eternal cycle of birth, death and rebirth of the soul (Samsara), which no living being escapes unless, after many non-quantifiable lives, he achieves entrance into Nirvana. Into which mortal frame the soul of the Hindu is reborn is not predictable; a further existence as a human is possible, but that of an animal, plant or a celestial or hellish creature equally so. It is possible to influence the cycle, however: good or bad deeds (karma) are rewarded or punished in the next life with a better or worse existence. The goal of every Hindu, however, is to no longer need to be reborn, to enter Nirvana and thus break the cycle of birth–death–rebirth forever. To achieve this goal, it is important to observe the »**Three Paths of Salvation**« (Tiga Marga). The first prescribes offerings to the gods and demons and their manifestations; the second consists of the striving for knowledge and insight, along with respect for other people, especially priests and the elderly; the third provides for escaping the embrace of the five elements through the path of turning inwards (meditation), which is the only possible way to a union with the divine principle.

Eternal cycle of birth, death and rebirth

The Hindu also has a relatively solidly structured image of the cosmos which is based on mythological and philosophical concepts as well as simple observation of natural processes. The world, formed from the basic matter of the universe (prakriti), is in a constant cycle of development and destruction. These phases are separated from each other by a pause phase, a state of rest. Man sees himself as a small world (buwana alit) in a larger world (buwana acjung); he is therefore himself a part of the macrocosm.

Cosmology

The lotus (lotus, nelumbo; ▶MARCO POLO Insight, p.38) is the symbol of the concepts of Balinese Hinduism; it is regarded as a likeness of the world. In Bali, the **eight-leafed lotus (padma)** is portrayed more often than the four-leafed lotus (panca dewata). The eight direction gods – Vishnu, Sambu, Ishvara, Maheshvara, Brahma, Rudra, Mahadevi and San(g)kar – are arranged clockwise around the god Shiva in the centre. The deities are attributed with colour, personality and body organs, along with many other auspicious qualities and meanings; four of them stand for the four points of the compass: Vishnu for the north (kaja), Brahma for the south (kelod), Mahadevi for the west (kauh) and Ishvara for the east (kangin). The lotus blossom can be found in Bali in a variety of forms, e.g. carved in stone or as one of the most sacred elements of traditional batik art.

Lotus cultivation in Bali

From birth on, every individual belongs to a caste (Indian: »varna«). The transition from one caste to another is, on principle, only possi-

Castes

»Island of the Gods«

Bali could just as well be called »Island of Temples and Ceremonies«. There are countless sacred places – more than 20,000 temples alone. They mystical atmosphere of the gods and demons can be felt in the smallest villages. Pura Besakih at the foothills of the holy mountain Gunung Agung is the most important temple and centre of religious life.

▶ **Religion is everyday**
The Balinese are accompanied by religious festivals and customs from birth to death. The clear majority of the Balinese are Hindus of the Hindu Dharma faith

■ Hinduism 92.3 %　　■ Islam 5.7 %　　■ Christian 1.4 %　　■ Buddhism 0.6 %

▶ **Layout of a balinesie temple complex**
Balinese temples belong to a village, a family, an occupational group or a caste. A village usually has three temples – the original temple (Pura Puseh), the temple of the great council assemblies (Pura Desa) and the temple of death (Pura Dalem). Most temples face mountainwards (Kaja) towards the mountain of the gods. The entrance faces the ocean (Kelod -- oceanwards).

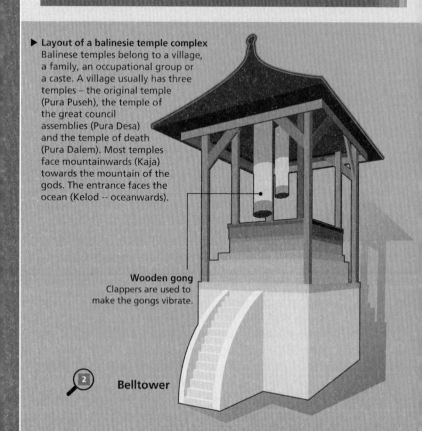

Wooden gong
Clappers are used to make the gongs vibrate.

2

Belltower

▶ **Hindi world view**

On Bali Hinduism is symbolized by a lotus flower. The eight leaves of the lotus, also called Padma, shows the god Shiva in the centre. Around him the eight directional deities are arranged, of which four stand for the four cardinal directions. The deities are also associated with colours, characteristics and bodily organs.

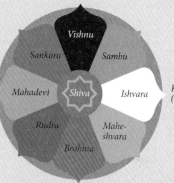

(north or towards the mountains)
KAJA

Vishnu

Sankara — Sambu

KAUH *(westwards)* — Mahadevi — Shiva — Ishvara — KANGIN *(eastwards)*

Rudra — Maheshvara

Brahma

KELOD
(south or towards the ocean)

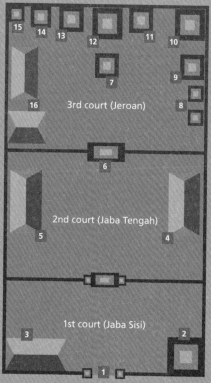

15 — 14 — 13 — 12 — 11 — 10

7 — 9

16 — 3rd court (Jeroan) — 8

6

2nd court (Jaba Tengah)

5 — 4

1st court (Jaba Sisi)

3 — 2

1

16 Place for offerings

15 Taksu (shrine for the mediators between humans and gods)

14 Maospait (shrine for the settlers from Majapahit)

13 Shrine for the deified Gunung Batur

12 Meru (shrine of Sang Hyang Widhi)

11 Shrine for the deified Gunung Agung

10 Padmasana (throne of the sun god)

9 Gedong pesimpangan (place for the visit of the souls of the village founders)

8 Ngrurah (shrine of a helping deity)

7 Paruman (resting place for gods and souls of the ancestors with offering platform)

6 Kori Agung (closed gate, entrance to the god's grounds)

5 Balé (roofed area for pilgrims)

4 Balé Gong (place for music and dancing)

3 Paon (kitchen)

2 Kul Kul (belltower)

1 Candi Bentar (divided gate)

ble through the process of rebirth, that is, in the next life. Although the origins and purpose of the caste system remains a mystery to this day, it is assumed that the members of the first castes sought to preserve their ethnic, cultural and social traditions within a firmly structured unit (clan, village), unadulterated by influences from outside. Originally there were only four castes: Brahmins (priests), Kshatriya (warriors), Vaishya (farmers and craftsmen) and Shudra (labourers). Over the course of the centuries, however, a complicated system developed out of these four castes through mixed marriages and the admittance of persons alien to the castes; this new system gradually superseded the traditional division. Those who did not belong to a caste were largely ostracized by society and considered in India as »pariahs«, »untouchables«. This is a classification not adopted in Bali, however, where only four castes are known. Although marriage into another caste is possible, there are problems attached to it. What has remained is the traditional high standing enjoyed by the Brahmins. That is mostly because princes, intellectuals and officials belong to this caste.

Sacred animals Unlike India, Bali has no sacred animals. The pious Balinese Hindus (with the exception of the Brahmins) are allowed to eat beef.

Hindu pantheon In the Hindu concept, all forms of life (plants, animals, humans) have a place on the ladder. The highest rung belongs to the gods and deities that inhabit the pantheon on **»Mount Meru«**; beneath them are saints, kings and, at the lowest level, spirits and demons. There is a multitude of gods and deities. The »divine« trinity **(Trimurti) are** considered the most important: Brahma , Vishnu and Shiva . **Brahma**, the creator of the world, was once the highest god in Hinduism. Today he has about the same status as Shiva and Vishnu. **Vishnu** is the upholder of the world, who took on human form as Krishna. **Shiva** is considered the destroyer and undoer of the world. In Bali, one of his many manifestations is called **Sangyang Guru**. Shiva is often portrayed as a lingam (phallic symbol). The wives of Brahma, Vishnu and Shiva are named Sarasvati, Lakshmi and Shakti; they symbolically stand for knowledge, happiness and sacred power. There is an important difference between the traditional Indian Hinduism that has monotheistic characteristics and that followed by most of the believers in Bali. They believe in **Sangyang Widi**, a god who holds the all-encompassing divine principle within him. He is the supreme deity in Balinese Hinduism and corresponds to the incarnation of all three main gods. The rice goddess **Dewi Sri** is one of the most important goddesses. Her name has Sanskrit origins and means something like »goddess of brilliance«. At the time of the year's first rice harvest, she assumes the form of grains of rice (nini), which in turn are venerated as the personification of Shiva. **Dewi Danu** is also veryimportant; first and foremost within her sphere of influence is Lake Batur, and she is also venerated as the ruler of other lakes on the island. Two of Vishnu's numerous manifestations are the god **Dewa Sedana** and his wife **Dewi**. They are considered to be the god and goddess of prosperity and wealth and are therefore especially eagerly worshipped at temple festivals. Further down in the hierarchy are gods whose responsibilities include natural phenomena and the forces of nature: Indra (rain), Surya (sun), Soma (moon), Vayu (wind), Agni (fire), Varuan (masses of water), Yama (death), Kama (love), Kubera (riches), Skanda (war) and Ganesha (elimination of obstacles). There are some gods among the lower orders that to a greater or a lesser extent intervene in the course of the world, playing either a good or an evil role.

Depiction of the rice goddess Dewi Sri at the edge of a field

The lowest rung on the ladder of Hindu belief is occupied by spirits and demons, most of which are to be found far below the level of the gods. Although spirits and demons are loathed manifestations, some of them have the extremely important task of keeping even worse spirits away from temple grounds.

Spirits and demons

RELIGIOUS TRADITIONS

There are lots of different religious customs on Bali, but they all have one thing in common; they are always a welcome excuse for a festival, celebrated either within the family circle or, as is usually the case, together with the other villagers. The rituals, which are mostly Hindu and are held before or after a transition to a different stage in life, are especially important in the lives of the Balinese. Strictly speaking, the **transition from one phase in life to the next** corresponds to a »small death«; the beginning of a new phase in life, on the other hand, to a »small rebirth«. The people in Bali call these transitional points »manusia yadnya«.

Life in Bali is marked by many festivals

Built-in Belief

The small boy stood in the gateway, made a beckoning gesture and said, »Come in, Mister! Please. Come in!« He took a step to the side of the narrow wall opening to clear the way leading into his parent's family compound (kampong).

The entrance to a Balinese family kampong is as narrow as possible and just behind it stands yet another shoulder-high wall, making a real obstacle course. Narrow openings and protective walls are an essential part of the family compound. **Because lurking outside are evil spirits, demons and other scary characters.**

Belief Articulated in Stone

If unwelcome guests of that ilk cannot be eradicated completely, then they should kindly stay outside. Religious belief is the bedrock of Balinese architecture and is perhaps the most fitting explanation of why traditional family compounds are built in this manner in Bali. The family kampong consists of houses called »bales« and is surrounded by a solidly-built outside wall. It not only serves to ward off undesired, invisible guests, but is also the visible symbol of the cohesion of the Balinese extended family.

Uniformity

Visitors to the island may feel alienated by seeing exactly the same universal arrangement of buildings everywhere. Kampongs are lined up one after the other in a Balinese village with all of the door openings facing the same side. Inside the rectangular enclosing wall, the indispensable family temple invariably stands on the same spot and the arrangement of the individual buildings is almost a stereotypical repetition; at least no essential differences can be seen at first glance. Rich or poor, the family temple, living and sleeping buildings, kitchen, rice granary, shelter for domestic animals and the bale

Residential and sleeping quarters of a traditional Balinese farmstead

for a variety of ritual occasions are arranged with dependable uniformity on every rural holding. Only one feature distinguishes a family's higher rank in the social hierarchy. More affluent Balinese have one additional bale in which the ceremonies prescribed by Hinduism are held. The number of houses for living and sleeping is determined by the size of the family living in the compound. The most prestigious, always situated directly next to the family shrine, is that of the grandparents, who enjoy the greatest esteem in the family. Occasionally unmarried girls and young women also live in the grandparents' bale. Without exception, the children of each sex sleep separately. It is the rule and not the exception in Bali, at least in the rural areas, that the whole extended family sleep under one roof, so to speak. More often than not, three or even four generations live in a single-family compound. After a wedding, the newlyweds move into the kampong of the groom's family.

Pregnancy and birth The purpose of the various ceremonies carried out during the first months of pregnancy is to keep evil spirits away from the embryonic life and allow the good ones to enter the body of the future addition to the human race. Sacrifices in the temple play here a major role, which can only be offered by relatives and close friends because the mother is consider unclean during pregnancy and cannot enter a temple or set foot on a rice field. When the child is born, ritual prescribes the placing of the kanda mpat, his »four mythical brothers and sisters« (uterine water, placenta, umbilical cord und blood) in a painted coconut shell next to the bedroom door. The god Rare Kumara, for whom a separate place of offering is prepared, watches over the child from above the bed. Bands and bracelets and anklets are put on the baby's wrists and ankles that are meant to keep evil spirits at bay. On the 12th and 42nd day after birth, the mother and child must undergo a further cleansing ceremony of Brahmanic origin. Before the 210th day (the first birthday according to the Balinese calendar), the child is carried everywhere; its feet are not allowed to touch the ground. A great festival is held on this day and the child is set on the ground for the first time, officially crossing over the boundary between divine transcendence and mortal existence. The child and its »four brothers and sisters« are given new names to confuse the spirits. .

> **?**
> MARCO POLO INSIGHT
>
> *Sacrifices for demons*
>
> It is customary on Bali to make sacrifices three times a day. Small sacrificial bowls made of palm or banana leaves and filled with rice, flowers or salt, such as can be seen on the threshold to a shop or on the pavement, are to placate invisible yet existing demons. That the people of Bali do this more out of pity for the demonic creatures than out of fear is indicated by the fact that the locations they choose for the sacrificial gifts are not highly valued. Gifts for gods on the other hand are handed over in temples.

Puberty Normally after entering puberty, both boys and girls are subjected to the **ritual of tooth filing** (matatah). This involves a Brahman priest filing the four upper incisors as well as both canine teeth (which belong to the gods) into an even line; the lower teeth remain unfiled because they belong to the demons. This eliminates the six evils (greed, jealousy, stupidity, lust, anger and lack of self-control) that are tolerated in the child but not in the adult.

The procedure of tooth filing is very painful; nevertheless, this ritual of initiation is considered to be an extremely important step in the life of a (Hindu) Balinese that must be taken. Moreover, young people are only then considered marriageable. However, in many regions in Bali today, tooth filing is only done symbolically.

The ceremony of **circumcision** is only performed on boys whose parents profess Islam (particularly on the neighbouring island of Lom-

During ceremonial tooth filing all the teeth are made the same length

bok). A few ethnologists are of the opinion that tooth filing, as a ritual of initiation, has a similar function.

Strictly speaking, marriage is only possible between members of the same caste. There is the possibility of getting around this: the groom must abduct the woman – with her consent – and hide out for seven days. After this period of time, the caste constraint is lifted. With marriage, the Balinese man gains the right and responsibility of performing in future all of the rituals his parents had performed up to this point in time. As a sign that he is now a fully-fledged member of society, he assumes responsibility for the well-being of the gods honoured in the family's house temple. The family gathers several times during the year for this purpose, with all family members travelling to their native village for the occasion.

Death is the most important rite of passage for the Hindus. It is the passage from the material and sensory world. The body, originally provided with divine breath by Brahma, is only seen as a **shell for the soul** and disintegrates after death, reverting back to its five com-

Marriage

Death

ponents, the elements earth, air, fire, water and ether. These re-enter the world of the gods and demons. Visitors will search in vain for cemeteries along Western lines in Bali, because the dead are cremated according to Hindu ritual, although the body of the deceased is first buried for a period of at least 42 days; Brahman priests are embalmed according to strict regulations and lie in state until a date determined by an astrologist using complicated calculations. After the minimum period of 42 days, which often extends to several months or even years, the mortal remains are disinterred and prepared for cremation. If little remains, a sandalwood doll is used symbolically in place of the corpse. Whether the time that the soul must remain in the body is short or long is determined by the relatives' financial situation, because cremation of the dead is an expensive matter. To facilitate the soul's escape from the body, a bamboo cane is placed in the tomb.

CREMATION

Celebration The cremation of the dead is probably the most extravagant celebration in Bali, serving as it does to make possible the smooth passage of the deceased to another, better world. The preparations can take weeks, even months.

Preparations and procession After the body has been exhumed three days before cremation, it is cleansed and wrapped in clothes and laid in a transport coffin, richly adorned with flowers and a number of ritual accessories, that is used to carry the corpse in an incredibly **colourful procession** from the home of the deceased to the cremation grounds. But the event in no way resembles a silent and solemn funeral procession; rather it is a joyful event. Even though the death of a close relative causes sadness and pain, the Balinese live in the hope that the deceased will be born into a better existence in his next life. Often the body is transported in a cremation tower (bade), a pagoda-like structure up to eleven storeys high. The relatives of the deceased are not the only ones to follow the coffin; almost all of the villagers join the procession. A gamelan orchestra provides the funeral music, which transports the crowd to a state close to ecstasy. On the way to the cremation grounds, the bearers of the cremation tower will suddenly turn in circles or abruptly strike out in another direction; this is meant to confuse the spirits. Often the deceased's first-born sits on one of the lower floors of the cremation tower, which, because of its flimsy construction, is not particularly safe.

Coffin forms of the different castes Upon reaching the cremation grounds, the body is removed from the transport coffin or bade and placed in the cremation coffin. To which caste the deceased belonged can easily be seen from this coffin. Brahmins (e.g. priests) have them in the form of a black-and-white spotted bull. If it looks like a lion or a stag, then the deceased belonged to the Jaba or Vaishya caste. Members of the Kshatryia caste have cremation coffins in the form a black bull for men and white bull for women with a colourful snake or dragon figure carried ahead of it. The cremation coffins of the members of the Pasek caste are an exception; while the coffins of the aforementioned castes are capable, as it were, of rising into the skies (the Hindus envision the lion with wings and the bull is considered to be the mount of the god Shiva), these people are cremated in a coffin based on Gajah Mina, the elephant-headed fish.

Finally, the coffin is set on fire and while the soul rises into the air through the **cleansing fire**, the mood of the crowd rises to the verge of rapture. Then the transport shrine is also set on fire. After everything has burned, the relatives gather the ashes and lightly singed pieces of bone and lay them in a small litter that is then carried in a procession to the sea (or a nearby river) and committed to the water. The elaborate ritual is not nearly over with the cremation, however. On precisely prescribed days after the cremation follow yet more elaborate ceremonies meant to help cleanse the soul of the dead from all wickedness and evil.

Cremation

TEMPLE FESTIVAL

Every temple in Bali annually celebrates its anniversary or birthday, i.e. the anniversary of its original consecration. The whole village takes part in these odalan festivals, as they are known. As a rule, the preparations take weeks or even months. The exact time at which particular preparations may begin – for example making the offerings – is decided by highly elaborate calculations that a Brahmin carries out according to the Javanese-Balinese calendar. The **gods are symbolically invited** to the temple festivals, coming down from the Pantheon and taking a seat in the precinct of the holy temple (Bale Paruman) that has been prepared and specially cleansed for them. From there, they can monitor how precisely the prescribed rites are followed.

Odalan festivals on temple anniversaries

The temple anniversary festival **lasts three days**, each day serving to fulfil a particular task. On the first and most important festival day, the gods are received in the temple, which has been cleansed and decorated with colourful cloths, and provided with offerings. So that the gods won't be annoyed by the odd demon wandering around, the villagers butcher a pig on the morning of the first festival day and its meat is placed at a suitable spot ready for the demons. Then the Brah-

Three days of festivals

Artistically arranged sacrificial goods for a temple anniversary

man priests remove small figures of sandalwood from the gedong – a small, closed building in the inner courtyard of the temple – and take them ceremonially to a small pavilion where they are cleansed with holy water (tirtha), and then dressed and displayed. When the time approaches for the gods to arrive, the priests light a pot of incense. The rising smoke is meant to serve the gods as a symbolic stairway from heaven. Accompanied by the booming of an ever louder clanging gong, the gods begin their descent. The crowd of people, who arrived earlier in the temple precinct with elaborately stacked layers of offerings, fall silent. The gods are now ready to be honoured. For this, they use the help of the priests. The crowd is sprinkled with consecrated water; lotus blossoms are taken between the fingers tips, raised three times above the brow and finally let fall. Symbolic washings of the face and torso follow. Women bear offerings in the form of skilfully stacked fruit and food into the temple where they are accepted by the priests and symbolically presented to the gods. These offerings are usually picked up again in the evening, the gods having taken the spiritual essence of the fruit by then.

The gods then have the opportunity to observe the three days of festivities that now begin with great exuberance. They are entertained as much as the villagers by the cock fights, shadow theatre performances (p.72 and ►MARCO POLO Insight, p.74) and musical background provided by the gamelan orchestra. On the second festival day, the village is cleansed of all the wickedness and evil left over from the previous year. On the third day, the evil spirits are driven out with the help of the gods, and the temple and village are prepared for the waiting new year. Late in the evening, the gods are bid farewell. The clothing is taken off the sandalwood figures and they are then taken back to the gedong. The festival ends with the closing of the inner gates of the temple; the inner precinct will only be opened to the public again on the next temple anniversary.

History

From Hindu Empire to a Republic

Now an incredibly popular holiday destination, Bali, a province of Indonesia shaped by Hinduism, frequently had to defend itself against foreign masters and colonial rulers throughout its eventful history.

PREHISTORY AND EARLY HISTORY

500,000 years ago	Oldest evidence of humans on Java (Homo erectus)
200–100 BC	Peoples from southern Asia settle on Indonesian islands

The oldest evidence of human life in Indonesia was uncovered on the island of Java in the form of remains of early hominds (**Java man**; lived c. 500,000 years ago), which have been classified as Homo erectus. Several fossil skulls of so-called Solo man were found in the 1930s; they resemble Neanderthal man. Traces of Palaeolithic cultures on Sumatera (Sumatra), Kalimantan (Borneo) and Sulawesi (Celebes) show a similarity to those of the Southeast Asian subcontinent, which was connected by land to a greater part of Indonesia during the Ice Age. Several waves of people emigrated from the southern Asian mainland during the second and first centuries BC.

Java man

INFLUENCES FROM INDIA

6th–7th century	The Hindu Empire of Srivijaya has control over a large part of what is now Indonesia.
9th–10th century	The Hindu religion increasingly gains in importance in Bali.
from 1037	Javanese versions of both of the Hindu epic dramas of creation, the Ramayana and Mahabharata, take shape during the reign of Raja Erlangga.

The Hindu Kingdom of Srivijaya existed in the seventh century in southeastern Sumatra. Its centre was near the present-day city of Palembang and it controlled the flow of trade in the Malacca and Sunda

Hindu Kingdom of Srivijaya

The Puputan Memorial in Klungkung commemorates the mass suicide of 1906 during the fight against colonial rule in Bali

straits. Indian culture and religion influenced the leading classes of society on the main island of Indonesia. An **ingenious irrigation system** was developed in Bali. Alongside the language already existing on Bali, the use of Sanskrit spread.

Mataram and Singharasi dynasties

The Javan princess Mahendratta of the Mataram Dynasty married the Balinese prince Udaya around 1000. **Bali and Java were united** under the rulership of their son Erlangga (1016–1042) and experienced a cultural heyday at that time. In 1284, Kertanagara, the last of the East Javan rulers of the Singharasi Dynasty, conquered Bali; however he soon lost it again. The seat of the government of the Hindu empire was moved from Mataram (central Java) to East Java. **Hindu thought** emanating from here increasingly gained in importance in Bali.

Majapahit Empire

The Majapahit Empire, the last great Javanese empire, spread out over large parts of Indonesia between the 13th and the 16th century. The initial basis for a system of administration was created in Bali. In the 15th century, merchants from the Middle East began spreading **Islam**. The decline of the Majapahit Empire began in the first half of the 16th century. The son of the last prince fled with his followers to Bali where he founded the **Gelgel Dynasty**. Sultanates were founded in Bantam in West Java and in Demak in East Java.

COLONIZATION

1487	With the discovery of a sea route to India, Europeans advance for the first time into South Asia.
1602	The Dutch East India Company begins colonizing the Indonesian archipelago.
1839	Bali is placed under Dutch suzerainty.
c1900	The Dutch gain sovereignty over all of Indonesia.

European influence

After the discovery of the sea route to India (1487), the Europeans pushed into South Asia. The Portuguese began building fortresses in the early 16th century in the east of the Indonesian archipelago, not least to challenge merchants from the Middle East in the lucrative spice trade . About one hundred years later, the Dutch also gained a foothold there, initially establishing bases on Java. The **founding of the Dutch East India Company** followed in 1602, which greatly expanded its sphere of influence under Governor-General Jan Pieterzoon Coen, the founder of the city of Batavia (1619; today's Jakarta). Following the fall of the Gelgel Dynasty in Bali, the island disintegrated into a dozen independent principalities. There were continual armed conflicts between the individual rulers. The regency of Klung-

Balinese prince with entourage (around 1888)

kung was established in 1686. The independent Balinese rajas recognized the Dewa Agung of Klunkung as having the highest ceremonial rank. The Dutch East Indies fell to Great Britain during the Napoleonic Wars in Europe. From 1811 to 1816, Stamford Raffles, the founder of Singapore, held power in Java. In 1816, the East Indies were returned to the Netherlands. The colonial power then became involved in bitter struggles with insurgents.

In the 1830s, the colonial administration started building up a well-devised plantation economy with payment in natural produce replacing the forced labour practised until then. It was also dictated to the farmers in Bali what their main crops were to be, namely **rubber, coffee and tea**. The traditional cultivation of rice, on the other hand, was neglected, which subsequently led to famine. After Bali became subject to Dutch rule in 1839, a Dutch expeditionary force landed in 1846 and placed part of the Island under its administration. From 1870, Indonesia was opened up to European capital and enterprise. In 1882, Singaraja became the official seat of the Dutch colonial administration. On 26 August 1883, the volcano **Krakatoa** (part of an island group between Sumatra and Java) erupted. Tens of thousands of people fell victim to this tremendous natural catastrophe. The **discovery of oil** on Sumatra (1885) led to the formation of »Royal Dutch Shell«, now one of the world's largest oil companies. The

Effects of the plantation economy

The Indonesian president Sukarno (right) and General Suharto (left) surrounded by the country's civilian and military leaders (1966)

Dutch gained control of all of Indonesia around 1900. The plundering of a Chinese merchant sailing ship provided the Dutch with a welcome excuse to expand their power over Bali. A blockade was imposed on the southern part of the island, which was also placed under colonial administration, and war was declared on the Prince of Badung. In September 1906, Dutch soldiers undertook a further punitive expedition against Bali, during the course of which they also attacked the civilian population. The Balinese royal family, together with members of the upper class, committed ritual mass suicide (called a puputan). Two years later, all of Bali was declared a **Dutch colony**.

Independence movements

In the early 20th century, several independence movements, influenced by Islam, began a struggle against the Dutch colonial power, among them the »Budi Utomo« (»Pure Endeavour«) and the »Sarekat Islam« (»Union of Islam«). The Indonesian Communist party was established around 1920, and in the subsequent period, freedom fighters joined together in the »Partai Nasional Indonesia« (PNI), formed in 1927 by **Raden Ahmed Sukarno** (▶Famous People).

In the first half of the 20th century, Chinese immigrants were able to gain key positions in commerce and business. This led to clashes with the Malay population. In 1938, the historic principalities were re-established in Bali, but they were not to achieve their former importance. Japanese troops occupied the Dutch East Indies during the Second World War, and European supremacy in Bali was ended.

Asian influence

INDEPENDENT STATE

1945	Declaration of the Republic of Indonesia
1946	Bali is the scene of a bitter resistance struggle by Indonesians against the Dutch.
1950	Dissolution of the historic principalities, and establishment of governmental districts. Sukarno becomes president of the new Republic of Indonesia.
1959	Denpasar made capital of Bali.
1966	General Suharto takes over power.

The Indonesian Nationalists established a state administration and declared Indonesia's independence on 17 August 1945. **Sukarno became the first president** of the new republic. Initially, the capital was Yogyakarta, later Jakarta. The Dutch attempted in 1947 and 1948 to regain their sovereignty by force. Under pressure from the UN and the USA, however, they were forced to recognize Indonesia's independence (first of all as the »Republic of the United States of Indonesia«) at the Hague Round Table Conference of 1949. Indonesia, however, remained linked to the Dutch crown until 1954.

Indonesian indepen- dence

Sukarno installed his system of a »Guided Democracy« in 1959. He endeavoured to achieve a balance between the various domestic powers (religious groups, parties, military). The state also guided the economy, paying especially close attention to limiting the influence of foreign companies. Despite this, the country was shaken by internal conflict, which reached its height in the **Darul Islam rebellion**. Dutch New Guinea came under Indonesian control in 1963. A little later, Sukarno became involved in a confrontation with the neighbouring state of Malaysia (temporary resignation from the UN, 1965–1966), and increasingly worked together with the communists as well as seeking support from the People's Republic of China. A communist-initiated revolt took place in the autumn of 1965, which General Suharto was able to crush; for several months, communists and Chinese were the victims of bloody persecution.

»Guided Democracy«

In March 1966 the military government led by Suharto seized power and ousted Sukarno. The new leaders put an end to the policy of con-

Suharto seizes power

frontation and attempted to end social and economic injustices with aid from Western countries. Relations with the People's Republic of China were suspended in 1967. Indonesia took part in the founding of the »Association of South Asian Nations« (ASEAN), and, in 1968, Suharto had himself elected **president**. The Indonesian government propagated a national family-planning programme for the whole country; its motto, »Dua Anak Cukup« (»two children are enough«, ▶p.25) was intended to contribute to the lowering of the birth rate. In 1969, the controversial incorporation of West New Guinea took place, today West Papua region. The general elections of 1971, 1977, 1982 and 1993 brought victory to the »Sekber Golkar«, a coalition of civil servants, technocrats and military men loyal to the government. Disregarding international protests, Indonesia annexed what had hitherto been Portuguese East Timor in 1976. A resumption of diplomatic relations was agreed upon with China in July 1990.

Economic crisis
At the beginning of 1997, the whole of Southeast Asia was gripped by an economic crisis originating in Thailand. The Indonesian rupiah lost close to two-thirds of its original value. The old resentments against Indonesians of Chinese descent erupted in the population once again; further fuelled by the dramatic rise in the price of basic foodstuffs, severe unrest broke out in the capital of Jakarta and soon engulfed the whole island nation.

Bali was affected only slightly by these events. Although there were some demonstrations in Denpasar, they remained of little consequence. One focus of public criticism though was Suharto's well-established system that refused at first to carry out the state and social reforms demanded by the World Bank. Only after clashes between students and the military, some of which were bloody, did Suharto feel compelled to resign on 21 May 1998. **Bacharuddin Jusuf Habibie**, Suharto's close friend, took his place, declaring he was prepared to carry out the reforms needed to help get the ailing economy back on its feet.

Although the opposition assured their support, they made no secret of the fact that they considered Habibie to be no more than a transitional president. Renewed unrest flared up in November 1998 when the reforms were slow in delivering the desired results. Once again, Jakarta was the centre of the turmoil. Surprisingly, Habibie did not put forward his candidature in the elections of October 1999 and was replaced by Abdurrahman Wahid.

Abdurrahman Wahid's Presidency
The Islamic scholar Wahid (also called Gus Dur), quickly named **Megawati Sukarnoputri**, the daughter of the nation's founder, Sukarno, as vice-president and promised a radical new beginning. One of the signs that lent credibility to these intentions was the granting of independence to the long-disputed territory of East Timor . The favo-

Megawati Sukarnoputri at an election rally (1999)

urable exchange rate in 1999 brought Bali an **increase in visitors** of about four percent. Meanwhile, there were fierce clashes on the neighbouring island of Lombok between religious and ethnic minorities, leading to street fighting and looting. Tourists still remaining on the island were evacuated to Bali. In 1999, the Gunung Batukau volcano on Bali erupted. The eruptions were less severe than expected and there were happily no casualties.

THE PRESENT

2002	Bomb attack claims 202 lives in Bali.
2004	First free and secret elections
2004	A tsunami devastates Southeast Asia.
2005	Renewed attack in Bali (22 deaths)
2006	An earthquake and another tsunami claim several thousand lives on Java.
2007	UN Climate Change Conference takes place in Bali.
2008	Suharto dies on 27 January at the age of 86.

The 21st century was greeted in Bali with the hope for domestic stability in Indonesia as well as further growth of the revenue-bringing tourism industry. The news that East Timor was to be granted independence in 2002 and that the island would from then on form its own nation, the independent »República Democrática de Timor-Leste«, was greeted positively by the international media.

East Timor Independence

Terrorist attack in Kuta

A devastating Islamic terrorist attack caused a huge shock internationally. On 12 October 2002, a bomb exploded in a bar in Kuta, followed seconds later by a second bomb detonated in the popular Sari Club, a disco frequented mainly by Australians. 202 people were killed and over 200 seriously injured. Most of the victims were tourists. Members of the **Jemaah Islamiyah terrorist organization** were found guilty in 2003 and executed in November 2008.

Another bombing by Islamic terrorists on 1 October 2005 claimed the lives of 22 people when three bombs went off in Jimbaran and Kuta. Some of the extremists identified as being behind the bombings still have not been captured. According to the opinion of the German foreign office, it is likely such attacks will occur again in the future. The locations preferred by foreign visitors are believed to be the most at-risk areas.

Natural disasters

At Christmas 2004, Indonesia suffered probably the **greatest natural disaster in its history.** On 26 December a seaquake unleashed a 15m (50ft) tidal wave or **tsunami**. Amongst the places hit were the coastlines of the Indonesian provinces of North Sumatra and Aceh, bringing death and destruction. Around 238,000 people died in the

Floral tribute to the victims of the tsunami of December 2004

floodwaters. Villages and the infrastructure were razed to the ground.

In 2006 an earthquake struck near Yogyakarta on the neighbouring island of Java, resulting in the deaths of almost 6000 people and leaving hundreds of thousands without shelter. In November 2010 the Merapi volcano erupted on Java, the most severe eruption for this volcano in more than a century. It claimed the lives of more than 100 people. 100,000 people were evacuated. The ash cloud rose several kilometres into the sky and the World Heritage Site of Borobudur 30km/18mi away was covered in a layer of acid ash 3cm/1.2in thick.

The following year, in October 2011, an earthquake measuring 6.8 on the Richter scale hit southern Bali. The epicentre was located approx. 100km/60mi from the island's southwest coast. Fortunately the only damage was material. People did not come to any harm, apart from a few who were injured.

In April 2012 people feared a further tsunami when a seaquake measuring 8.6 occurred 500km/300mi to the northwest of Sumatra's coast. However, the wave never came.

In this extremely dangerous time, observers are especially grateful for positive political developments. Since 2004, the Indonesian president has been elected by the people – Indonesia is now officially recognized as a democratic state. The first directly elected president was the retired general, **Susilo Bambang Yudhoyono**, who took over from Megawati Sukarnoputri, the daughter of the founder of the nation, Sukarno. She had been in office since 2001. During the presidential elections in July 2009 Susilo Bambang Yudhoyono was re-elected, having not just run a clever election campaign, but also being able to point to successful domestic and economic policies.

Recognition of Indonesia as a democratic state

In 2007, the UN Climate Change Conference, hosted by the Government of Indonesia, took place at the Bali International Convention Centre. Its 10,000 participants included representatives from over 180 countries. The conference culminated in the adoption of the Bali Roadmap, which consists of a number of forward-looking decisions that represent the various tracks essential to tackling climate change. Part of the Roadmap, the Bali Action Plan, charts the course for a new negotiating process to be completed in 2009.

Bali Roadmap

On 27 January 2008, at the age of 86, Indonesia's second president General Suharto, died of multiple organ failure. He had ruled the republic for 32 years until being compelled to announce his resignation on 21 May 1998. He left office in the face of mass protests over corruption and abuses of human rights, but did not stand trial on health grounds.

Suharto's death

Art and Culture

Cultural Independence

The Balinese play a special role in the Indonesian republic. The primary reason for this is that, despite quite a number of challenges from outside, Bali has managed to maintain its religious traditions and with them its cultural independence. This does not mean, however, that over the course of the centuries Bali has remained an island totally beyond the influence of foreign cultures.

Hinduism has always remained the most influential force, even if the form practised today in Bali is moving towards the veneration of a single godhead more indicative of a monotheistic faith. Given this background, there have of course also been changes in the cultural life, which have eventually had an influence on artistic depictions. Compared with the diversity of representational means that, for example, were used on neighbouring Java before Islamization, Balinese art, especially that of earlier centuries, may seem folkloric, even simplistic. On the other hand, Balinese temples are impressive precisely because of their simple design and decoration. Here, the flat or sculpted representation of motif and meaning are always a means to an end, having only the task of making religion and religious views tangible.

Temple Architecture

Compared with the colourful splendour of Thai temples, the religious sites on Bali are rather plain, functional buildings. But when a festival is held, Balinese temples are decorated, dressed up to the nines with flowers, colourful ribbons and cloths. A temple that has no upcoming festival or where one had just been celebrated stands there silent and abandoned.

The island of Bali is often regarded as one huge temple: the western tip of the island with the port of Gilimanuk represents the entrance gate, and the mountains in the east (Gunung Agung and Gunung Batur) are symbols for the mountain of the gods, Meru. Most of the temples in Bali are aligned toward these mountains (kaja = mountainward), while their entrances face the sea (kelod = seaward). The-

Bali, island of temples

An elaborate process of make-up and dressing is necessary for the Legong dancers to look like princesses

re are more than 20,000 temples (pura in the local vernacular, ►MARCO POLO Insight, p.38) in Bali. This figure does not include the family temples (sanggah) in every pekarangan or kampong (family compound). The highest ranking temples are the **six »state temples«**, the Pura Besakih being the most important. Other honoured temples are the sea temple, Pura Tanah Lot, and the mountain temple, Pura Batukau. Some natural shrines dedicated to the gods of the mountains, the seas, and the rivers and springs are also highly revered. Temples equipped with places to bathe, not only for the gods but also for mere mortals, have a special role (e.g. Pura Tirtha Empul (Holy Water) near Ubud).

Three Temples
As a rule, a village community owns three temples. The **Pura Puseh** is the main temple, dedicated to Brahma (the god of creation) and always built on the side of the village facing the holy mountain of Gunung Agung. The village community gathers in the **Pura Desa** (occasionally also called Pura Bale Agung, and dedicated to Vishnu, the maintainer of world order) to hold the general religious ceremonies, while the **Pura Dalem**, which is usually outside the village near to the place of cremation, is dedicated to the goddess Durga (one of the incarnations of Shiva, the god of death and destruction) and hosts the ceremonies accompanying cremations. The Pura Dalem temple always faces the sea.

The temple facilities in Bali do not serve all of the inhabitants of the province; rather they belong to either a family, a whole village community, an occupational group or a caste. An exception is the state temples or royal temples mentioned above. These are used in common by all the islanders.

Temple grounds
A temple in Bali usually corresponds to the layout of a typical kampong or family compound; it always faces the mountain and consists of three courtyards. They are not only considered to be a symbol for the three worlds (upper, middle and underworld), but also indicate the continuing cycle of birth, death and rebirth. The Jaba Tengah (middle courtyard), in which believers gather during a temple festival to prepare and become attuned for the arrival of the gods, is entered through the first courtyard (Jaba Sisi), where primarily non-religious structures can be found. The jeroan, the holiest area of the temple, is almost exclusively reserved for the gods and their earthly representatives, the priests. Normal mortals may only enter to bring offerings.

STRUCTURE OF BALINESE TEMPLES

Candi bentar
Candi korung
The first courtyard of a temple compound is almost always entered through an elaborately decorated, so-called **split gate** (candi bentar),

A typical Balinese village temple

whose passageway is relatively narrow. Its form goes back to a legend. When Mount Mahameru, seat of all Hindu gods, was transported to the island of Bali, it fell apart and split into two pieces, creating the mountains of Gunung Agung and Gunung Batur. The candi bentar now symbolizes these two halves of Mount Meru. The artistic and richly decorated **covered gate** (candi korung or kori agung) in the second courtyard leads into the third part of the temple, the innermost of the temple's courtyards, which symbolizes Mount Meru and, with it, the highest of all worlds in Hindu cosmology.

A **wall protecting against demons**, an aling-aling, is always erected behind the gate. Evil spirits are supposed to bounce off it because they can only move straight ahead – if they even make it that far be-

Aling-aling

cause in front of the gate are a number of ferocious-looking demons (raksasa), whose sole task is to scare their own kind to such an extent that they do not even dare to enter the temple grounds.

Bale   A bale, of which there are often several within a temple compound, is a **pavilion** open on all sides. If the bale is in a pura desa (one of the three village temples), it is called a bale agung and serves the village elders as a place to congregate. At larger temple sites there are several bales in which the offerings for a temple festival are prepared.

Gedong   A gedong is either a small, closed structure (gedong penimpanan) or a large building (gedong agung). All that is required to provide shelter for the gods during their visit on earth is stored in a gedong penimpanan. This can consist of a small statue, as well as an elaborately carved mask or even a kris (dagger). A gedong agung, on the other hand, is where the ancestors are venerated.

Padmasana   The seating arrangement for the gods varies. While the richly decorated stone throne in southern Bali stands in the northeast corner, in northern Bali it is in a central spot. This is because of the fact that the backrest must always face the holy mountain of Gunung Agun. The **throne of god** also has three parts: the lowest level symbolizes the underworld, the middle level the middle world and the top level the sacred Mount Meru, which represents the centre of the universe. The highest throne in a jeroan belongs to the god Shiva, who is called Sangyang Widi in Bali and visits earth in this manifestation. If more seats are available, they belong to various gods of different ranking. The seats for the gods or deities, by the way, are not symbolic of the respective god or deity, but are their property.

Meru   A **tiered pagoda** in the innermost temple area is called a meru and serves as a symbol for the world mountain of the same name, the home of all Hindu deities. Its several tiers (tumpang) are covered with either palm tree fronds, rice straw or sometimes even corrugated iron.

Pelinggih   Just once a year, namely on the occasion of an odalan festival (▶p.47), the god who lives permanently in the temple leaves the pelinggih, a **holy shrine** with one or two roofs. Up to eleven tiers (tumpang) stand above it, also symbolic of Mount Meru. Additional pavilions, shrines , sacrificial altars and pagodas in varying numbers complete the facilities.

Kulkul   As a rule, the **bell tower** is in the first courtyard. From there, the faithful are called to assemblies and festivals in the shrine by two men, or occasionally young boys, who rhythmically strike a long, hollow log (or, rarely, a gong or metallophone) with beaters.

Sculpture · Painting

Whether there existed any sculptural art in Bali in pre-Hindu times is not clear. Researchers have until now been of the opinion that ancient Balinese cult sites tended to be rather plain. Recent finds, however, prove that the inhabitants of the island were quite capable of depicting venerable figures – initially of the Buddhist, and later of the Hindu religions – in sculpted form, primarily as reliefs.

Hindus persecuted on the neighbouring island of Java, among them priests and artists, sought refuge in Bali in the 15th and 16th centuries. The subsequent influence of Hinduism on Balinese art expanded its variety of creative means and the use of Javanese elements increased. Since that time, the focus has been on the portrayal of the deities. In Bali's sculptural art this meant a highly artistic addition to low and high reliefs through statuary in the round on the Indian model. In the subsequent further development of relief carvings, the Balinese love for opulently rampant ornamentation became obvious. It is the repetition of details that allows Javanese-Hindu sculpture to be clearly classified as Balinese relief. While the tuff walls around a temple, for example, were kept fairly plain up to the period of conversion to Hinduism, they are now decorated on the front surfaces and corners with elaborately worked, detailed embellishments. These consist first and foremost of the hideous faces of demons and witches, whose job it is to frighten away their own kind and keep them from the holy area. In other places, there are scenes depicted from the Ramayana or Mahabharata epics, as well as scenes from the daily lives of the Balinese people. Modern sculpture is modelled heavily on the works of earlier centuries. Further artistic development barely takes place these days, simply because of the constant demand to replace statuary destroyed by the ravages of time with new ones of a similar type.

Enlivened by Hinduism

Painting in Bali is plain and still exhibits vernacular characteristics. There is little evidence of the work of previous eras, because the Balinese characteristically paint on less substantial materials such as textiles. The subject matter consisted of scenes that are also familiar in Balinese **shadow theatre** (▶MARCO POLO Insight, p.74). The paints used (warm tones likes red, orange, ochre, yellow and a clear white) were purely of organic origin. One of the most beautiful examples can be found in the Kerta Gosa courtroom in Klungkung.

Old Balinese Art of Painting

European
influences
With the arrival in Bali of large numbers of European-influenced artists around 1930, a change in style, expression and subject matter became unmistakable. One of the most important innovations that painters like **Walter Spies** (►Famous People), Le Mayeur (►MARCO POLO Insight, p.124), Rudolf Bonnet and W. O. J. Nieuwenkamp inspired was the introduction of central perspective. Balinese painters, who had until then been limited to two dimensions, were introduced to a third. At about the same time, a change in subject matter is noticeable. Up until that point, it had been difficult to differentiate between foreground and background, but now the main person or figure became the focus. The European artists founded painting schools where they taught young Balinese how to use European painting equipment while at the same time only cautiously influencing expression and style. This explains why Balinese painting assimilated European influence while losing hardly any of the strength of its natural expression and originality.

Crafts

Even though many wooden objects, e.g. vessels and bowls, primarily had a practical purpose in everyday life, the art of woodcarving in Bali also has a religious and cultural background.

Woodcarving
The extremely **skilfully carved wooden masks** have become known all over the world. They can be divided into two groups; those that have great religious value and as such are rarely if ever offered for sale, and those that are expressly produced for the tourist trade. The layman, however, would notice no difference – the same terms (e.g. rangda mask) are used for both. In addition, there are a great number of different dance masks used in the performance of Balinese dances. A number of requirements are attached to the production of a rangda mask employed for religious purposes, particularly those used in the dances. For example, they must be made exclusively from the wood of a pohon pule tree; a priest determines by calculation when the tree can be taken from the forest. When the mask is finished and painted (only with organic paints), it is said that holy water (tirtha) flows from it every 32 days. But a lot of other beautiful things are made from wood. Whole families of woodcarvers live from the production of timeless wooden figures. Since the 1920s, many figures have taken on an overtly slender form. High-quality woodcarving comes at a price, by the way, because the Balinese mentality demands only time-consuming production by hand.

Attractive textiles are for sale almost everywhere in Bali

Even if the origins of **batik production** are most probably to be found on Java, where the highest-quality examples of batik artistry are still produced today, the Balinese have developed an extraordinary skill at it. Today there are even schools in the tourist centres in Bali offering special courses in the production of batik. But there is a special process in Bali that, although based on batik, has little in common with it. Cotton threads are used that are dyed only after weaving. To achieve a distinctive, subtle colouring, the batch that is not to be dyed is tied up. The name **ikat** came from this very complex technique and literally means »tied« or »knotted«. A distinction is drawn between warp-ikats and weft-ikats. The difference has to do with whether the warp thread (tied securely to the warp pegs of the loom) or the weft thread (which is threaded through the warp threads with a shuttle) is dyed. A more complicated ikat process called **double ikat** is used on the neighbouring island of Lombok; in Bali, this process is used only in the village of Tenganan. Here, both warp and weft threads are dyed. The production of a piece of double ikat takes months, if not years. The islanders attribute magical powers to double ikat cloth (▶MARCO POLO Insight, p.108).

Textiles

Dance · Music

Balinese dances are an extremely important part of life, both religious and secular. The various kinds of dance usually presented in the form of expressive dance could be termed »lived religion«.

No temple festival takes place without a dance performance. Today, there are also Balinese dances especially adapted for tourists and their cameras. Whether these still have anything to do with tradition is a matter for speculation. In fact, it is increasingly difficult for tourists to find a dance performance that is uninfluenced by commercial considerations: such dances are more likely to be performed in a private setting in the evening or at night. Travellers who stray far off the main tourist routes, for instance, may make contact with locals (usually without difficulty) in a village and have a chance of experiencing unadulterated Balinese dance. Indeed, it is not unusual to be invited to a festival that just happens to be taking place.

Barong dance
The barong dance is undoubtedly the most famous of the Balinese dances and the one presented most frequently. There are several versions of it; these vary, though only in nuances. Actually, the Barong dance can be seen to be more of a drama in several acts because of the complete story it tells. Accompanied by a gamelan orchestra , several main characters – disguised in animal masks – take to the stage. In the beginning, a solo **legong dance** is presented (p.69). The main characters are the **witch Rangda**, who appears wearing a hand-carved mask with the most frightening face imaginable, and **Barong**, a figure in the shape of a lion animated by two dancers. While Rangda stands for evil, Barong symbolizes the opposite – which of the two ends up winning the battle remains to be seen.

Baris dance
The baris dance is performed exclusively by men wearing various weapons. Originally featuring no single main role, over the course of time a form of the dance has developed that stresses the solo abilities of an individual dancer. The focus of the dance are the various feelings and emotions of a warrior, such as courage and fear, compassion and callousness toward the enemy, elation over the victory and grief over defeat, and so on. The gamelan music accompanying the baris dance follows the movements of the dancers – not the other way around.

Kebyar Dance
Perhaps the most symbolic of Bali's solo dances is the kebya dance. The form seen today developed around 1915. Although danced by a

grown man, it portrays the temptations and moods of a pubescent youth. The costume is of little significance (a cloth draped about the hips with a long train suffices); the focus is on the facial expressions and gestures of the dancer, who sits cross-legged on the floor and »dances« only with his upper torso and arms and hands.

The kecak dance, performed only by men, is certainly one of the most impressive ritual dances that a visitor to Bali can experience. At any rate, it is the noisiest. In addition, it is considered to be the youngest of the Balinese dances: its present form first developed in the 1930s. At this time, elements of the Ramayana epic were built into the action. The inspiration for this was given by the German painter and musician Walter Spies (▶Famous People), who acted as artistic advisor on the set of »Island of Demons«, a documentary about Bali (1932; directed by: Friedrich Dahlsheim and Victor von Plessen). Originally, the kecak dance was performed to drive away evil spirits and demons with between 70 and 100 bare-chested men sitting in a spiral-shaped circle. They symbolize the followers of the monkey Hanuman. The kecak got its name from the sound, a percussive »cak-cak«, chanted by the men, accompanied by conjuring movements of the arms and upper torso.

Kecak dance

If the kebyar dance is about the moods of a pubertal boy, then the legong dance can be seen as its female counterpart; although physical maturity only plays a role insofar as the girl is no longer qualified to perform as a legong dancer with the onset of menstruation. A perfect body is required for a girl to be allowed to learn the legong dance, at about the age of five. A trained dancer functions as teacher. As with many Asian dances, the **»language of the hands and fingers«** play an important role in legong. Every movement of the body, every position of the hands and every motion of the fingers have their meaning. Legong is danced by three girls with one of them appearing as a soloist. It tells the story of the son of a prince, Raja Lasern, who seeks the favour of the girl Rangkesari, ultimately in vain, and in the end meets his death in battle. Although the girls change roles during the performance, they do not change costumes. For this reason, most non-Balinese spectators find the legong dance hard to understand.

Legong dance

The most important prop in the kris dance is the kris (dagger) itself. Inhabited by a guardian spirit, it possesses magical powers and is therefore the **»holy« weapon of the Indonesians**. Always made by hand and usually elaborately and imaginatively decorated, the kris is the pride of every man, especially in Bali, and is a symbol of full membership in the village community. Craftsmen specializing in its production are among the most respected occupational groups in

Kris dance

Bali. The correct method of making a kris is passed on orally from generation to generation. But even then, the most respected smith cannot start work without first asking a Brahmin to name the most propitious time to begin working the raw metal.

GAMELAN

Typical Indonesian style of music There is no village in Bali that does not have its own gamelan orchestra; many even have several. The term gamelan (►MARCO POLO Insight, p.204), though, is used for a variety of musical groupings. For example, the term gamelan can refer either to an ensemble of just a few musicians (gamelan legong) or an orchestra sometimes composed of **up to 30 or 40 players** (gamelan gong). The gamelan is used for all celebrations in Bali, as well as with dance, drama and shadow theatres. The word »gamelan« comes from old Javanese and means »to touch«. The roots of Balinese music can also be found on the neighbouring island of Java, although differing combinations, forms and terms for the instruments used have developed in Bali over the course of the centuries. The first instruments were created during the Bronze Age (2nd/1st millennium BC).

Musical basics In contrast to the music based on octaves subdivided into twelve semitones customary in the West, music practised in Bali in most cases uses a pentatonic scale (Javanese: slendro). There are three scales each with five whole tones. The gaps between these five tones are approximately the same, so there are no semitones. In addition, gamelan uses scales with seven, six and four tones, as dictated by the occasion for which the gamelan orchestra is performing. The scale used at funerals contains four tones, for example. Balinese metre is also different from its Western counterpart. As a rule, the rhythm is even and only the tempo varies.

Ensembles and instruments It is common to all forms of gamelan that the musicians play several instruments equally well so that, in the case of the gamelan gong, 30 to 40 musicians play **up to 80 instruments**. The range of instruments is very extensive. Among the melody instruments are the gender panembung (bronze sheets hung over tuned tube resonators), gongs tuned high, middle and low, bonangs (small gongs called kettles or pots hung in a wooden frame), bamboo flutes and the rebab (a stringed instrument with a curved sound-box). The rhythm is set by drums (gendang) of different sizes and tuning. The variation of the sequence of notes established by the melody instruments is the task of the gender barung (similar to the gender panembung, but with more octaves) and the tilempang, a type of zither.

However this list does not exhaust the range of instruments available. Various instruments are added according to the size of the gamelan, but all are based on the materials of the aforementioned instruments. The instruments are always produced by hand and here, too, a myriad of rules prescribed by tradition have to be followed. Old instruments are particularly respected and can even be considered sacred. For this reason they are allowed to be played only by a few select musicians and then exclusively on high holidays and major festivals.

The melodies have been passed from one generation to the next for centuries. Even today – of course based on formal rules –free improvisation and playing from memory are still practised. Although in earlier times some core melodies were written down on palm leaves, it is thanks to the German painter and musician Walter Spies (▶Famous People) and the American Colin McPhee, both of whom studied Balinese music intensively in the 1920s and 1930s, that quite a few pieces of music for gamelan orchestras were recorded in a form of musical notation especially developed for the purpose. This has since made them available to an interested Western audience.

Current situation

The instruments of a gamelan orchestra largely consist of gongs, kendhang and metallophones

Shadow Theatre

Even though shadow theatre (wayang kulit) is spread across almost the entire Asian continent, a relatively independent form has developed in Bali.

Shadow theatret wayang kulit

The central role in the performance of the wayang kulit plays, which are sometimes several hours long, is taken by the puppeteer, the dhalang, who performs behind a white screen illuminated by the flickering glow of a petroleum lamp. It is his job to bring the flat figures, usually **cut out of tanned buffalo leather** to life. The dhalang develops great skills and can manipulate up to ten puppets at a time. The action in the wayang kulit is based on themes from the Indian Ramayana and Mahabharata epics (▶p.73). It is a permanent feature of temple festivals, but is also sometimes performed during the celebrations accompanying rights of passage. Audiences of all ages, enthralled by the story, sit transfixed in front of the screen, at time breathless with excitement, following the action and dialogue, which is often in the form of a soliloquy. A gamelan ensemble usually provides the sparse musical accompaniment.

The spirits of ancestors, mythological heroes, gods and demons all feature in traditional Balinese shadow theatre

In the wayang topeng masked theatre (topeng means mask), it is the masks and not the people wearing them that are the important part of the storyline. When the dancer takes the mask out of the cloth in which it is kept and puts it on, he assumes the role the mask represents. The moment of donning the mask is therefore preceded by a certain pause to turn inward and meditate, during which the wearer of the mask works himself perfectly into the role. Although topeng masks are available in souvenir shops, such masks would never be considered appropriate for the performance of a wayang topeng. The real masks are believed to possess a spirit and are sacred; for this reason, their production is tied to strictly prescribed rituals. The plot of a wayang topeng consists of stories from the times when Bali was still ruled by princes.

Masked theatre wayang topeng

Literature

Balinese literature had its origins in Indian works of literature. As in many other Asian countries, Hindu missionaries ensured that stories, fairy tales and legends from India also came to Bali, whose native population then altered them according to their own understanding. The source of each individual work, however, is usually still recognizable.

Origins in India

The Ramayana is the **most important story of Indian origin**. It is a kind of chivalric poem. Its central theme is the story of the eternal struggle between the gods and demons. The first part was possibly written down in the third century BC. Altogether, the work of that time was composed of 24,000 verses. Unknown chroniclers later added two additional books in which the hero of the story is made into an incarnation of the god Vishnu. There is no single version of the Ramayana as there are regional religious variations and a great number of differing interpretations, in which often only a part of the original core of the story can be recognized. The following is the customary version of the story in Bali. Vishnu comes to earth for the seventh time in the person of Rama and is born as one of the three sons of Rajah Desarata, the king of Ayodhya (a city on the river Sarayu in northern India). Rama falls in love with Sita (also called Sinta), the daughter of a king, and gains the favour of her father because he is the only one capable of stringing his bow. However it now emerges that years ago Rajah Desarata had promised to fulfil two wishes of his first wife. Although he would love to see his favourite son made his successor, he must keep his promise and instead declare his second son, Betara, to be his successor. The second demand of his first

Ramayana

Wayang kulit

The shadow puppets probably come from pre-Hindu times when it was believed that the ancestors' spirits could be contacted through shadows. Later stories took up themes from the Indian epics Ramayana and Mahabharata before a backdrop of old Balinese performances.

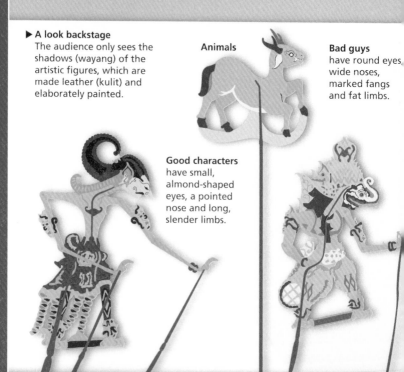

▶ **A look backstage**
The audience only sees the shadows (wayang) of the artistic figures, which are made leather (kulit) and elaborately painted.

Animals

Bad guys
have round eyes, wide noses, marked fangs and fat limbs.

Good characters
have small, almond-shaped eyes, a pointed nose and long, slender limbs.

▶ **A theatre full of symbolism**
Along with the various characters of the figures the parts of the theatre are also symbolic.

Dhalang: embodies the acts of God

banana tree trunk: symbolizes the earth

Theatre screen: is heaven

Lamp: a symbol for the light of life

Puppet chest: symbolizes the human world

Puppet chest for new puppets

Expansion of shadow dramas

The shadow dramas came to Asia Minor during the European Middle Ages. Today it is still found in the traditional Karagöz theatre of Ramadan. In Europe shadow theatre replaced classic theatre in rural regions as the theatre of the lower classes. It experienced its high point in the 18th and 19th centuries in France as »ombres chinoises«.

Comedians

entertain the audience and translate the Kawi texts into Balinese. They contribute comedy to the presentation through their fat stomachs and whimsical limbs.

Theatre screen

Kayonan

is a kind of stylized world tree. Every performance begins and ends with its appearance on stage. It also comes out before scene changes and important appearances before being thrust firmly into the banana tree trunk.

banana tree trunk

The puppet master »Dhalang«

traditionally plays a very important role. He has the puppets appear according to a strictly defined ceremonial order; they wander from one chest to the other and in this way he transmits his message. He is accompanied by a gamelan orchestra.

Puppet chest for old puppets

wife hits him even harder: namely that he must send Rama into exile for a period of 15 years. When Desarata dies and Betara ascends to the throne, Rama and Sita more or less voluntarily leave their homeland, although Betara wants to give up the office and title in favour of his stepbrother. The beautiful Sita, however, is abducted by the demon king Rawana, who wants to force her to live with him. Rama now recalls the mission in life bestowed upon him by Brahma: to destroy the demon king. Brahma had, however, once assured Rawana that no god could defeat him. The way around this was a deception: to have Vishnu come to earth, born again as a man. Rama succeeds in defeating Rawana after several successful adventures with the aid of the monkey king Sugriva and the monkey Hanuman. Although Hanuman is at first able to sneak into Sita's prison and bring her the message that Rama is on the way to rescue her, he is taken prisoner by Rawana. Hanuman is able to escape, however, and set fire to the palace with his burning tail. With the support of the sea god, Waruna, one of the monkeys builds a bridge from the Indian mainland to the island of Ceylon (Sri Lanka) to which Rama is able to flee with Sita and his followers. However, Rawana pursues him and embroils him a bloodbath that lasts for six days and six nights, at the end of which, naturally, Rama emerges as the shining winner. Rama and Sita return

Balinese dancers performing the Rama epic at the »International Ramayana Festival« in Denpasar

to their homeland where Rama's stepbrother Betara again offers him the office of ruler. But the people are against this as long as Sita has not proven that Rawana had not influenced her with his evil thoughts during the battle. She passes the test; as a sign of her innocence, she emerges unscathed from a pyre of burning wood.

The Indian story known as the Mahabharata is even longer than the Ramayana. It is composed of 110,000 couplets and **presumably has a historical nucleus**, the battle of the Pandava (five sons of King Pandu, ruler over the area around what is now Delhi). Of course, the actual story is also intertwined here by a large number of other stories, mythologies of the gods, heroic legends, love stories and religious and philosophical treatments that are only loosely still related to the core of the story. The Mahabharata was written sometime between the fourth century BC and the fourth century AD. Of the entire work, the section relating the events before the decisive battle between the Pandava and the Kaurava plays the most important role in Hinduism.

Mahabharata

VICKI BAUM (1888–1960)

The Vienna-born writer and harpist Vicki (also Vicky) Baum came to Bali in 1935, during the period of the Dutch colonial rule. Fascinated by the Balinese people, who, unimpressed by their foreign masters, maintained their own culture, she was inspired to write a book, Tale of Bali, during her nine-month stay on the island, which was published in 1937. She not only succeeded in burrowing deep into the history of the island and its people, she also **understood the mentality of the Balinese**. Using the example of a Balinese village, she describes what influence the Dutch tried to exert on the traditional village life of the people; their success, however, was only very superficial. Vicki Baum died on 29 August 1960 in Hollywood.

Austrian writer and musician

ANTONIO MARIA BLANCO (1926–1999)

The Spaniard Antonio Maria Blanco is one of the most significant painters who chose to work in Bali. After attending school in the Philippine capital of Manila, he studied at the Art Academy in New York and then lived in Florida, California, Honolulu, Oahu, Hawaii and Japan. Blanco came to Bali for the first time in 1952, where his much awarded artistic work that mixes **comical impressionistic elements with erotic elements** greatly impressed the son of the Prince of Ubud, who let him have a former summer residence in the midst of a spacious garden as home and studio. Blanco left Bali in the early 1950s only to return permanently a few years later. The painter, who was a perfect master of the art of showmanship, was married to a Balinese woman and before his death in 1999 had even converted a large part of his residence in Ubud into a museum.

Spanish Painter

WALTER SPIES (1895–1942)

Born in Moscow, the son of a wealthy and respected merchant family, Walter Spies was one of the painters whose works were greatly influenced by a stay on the island of Bali. Spies lived up to the age of 15 in the Russian capital and then moved with his family to Germany, where he attended high school. Spies came into contact with painters in Berlin such as the Expressionist Oskar Kokoschka and Otto Dix, one of the most famous representatives of the New Objectivity, as well as the composer Ernst Krenek. Leaving Germany in 1923 he travelled on a freighter to Java, where he earned a living in the first

Russian-born German painter and musician

Vicki Baum opened up a view of the island's exotic culture and history with her novel »Love and Death in Bali«

weeks after his arrival as a pianist in a bar. On 1 January 1924, the Sultan of Yogyakarta named him the conductor of his court orchestra that was formed along western lines. However very soon Spies was making a name for himself by researching music. He not only learned to play all the instruments customarily in a gamelan orchestra, but also eagerly collected Old Javanese, later also Balinese, compositions to save them for posterity. In addition, he made them also accessible to the Western world on instruments tuned to the European key. Spies first came to Bali in 1925, where he settled permanently two years later. Fascinated by the landscape and the people, he lived there in the palace of the princes of Ubud, who were appreciative of the arts. Later he built his own house, called it »Campuan« and made it into a **meeting-place of numerous artists** who were living permanently or temporarily in Bali; among others, Austrian writer Vicki Baum lived in »Campuan« and wrote her novel Tale of Bali there. Spies influenced local artists, but also learned from them, particularly with regard to their mental attitude toward art. When German troops marched into the European Netherlands in 1940, the German nationals in the Dutch East Indies were interned, Spies among them. While they were to being transferred to British India in January 1942, only a few days before the Japanese invasion, a Japanese bomber sank the ship. There were only a few survivors: Spies was one of those lost. Walter Spies is honoured to this day in Bali. Some of his most beautiful works can be seen in the Neka Museum in Ubud.

RADEN AHMED SUKARNO (1901–1970)

Indonesian Politician

The founder of the sovereign state of Indonesia, Raden Ahmed Sukarno , was born on 6 June 1901 in Blitar on Java, the son of a Javanese father and a Balinese mother. After attending school in Surabaya and then studying engineering, the young Sukarno, gravitating toward politics advocating independence , founded the »Partai Nasional Indonesia« (PNI) in 1927 and placed himself at its head. Sukarno was imprisoned from 1929 to 1932 and was exiled by the Dutch colonial government to the island of Flores in 1933 and to Sumatra in 1938. Freed by the Japanese in 1942, he worked together with them for Bali's independence. Sukarno's declared goal was to **shake off the yoke of colonial rule**. The greatest difficulty was convincing all the provincial princes that it was necessary to take action together to form a unified state, which came into being on 17 August 1945, when together with Mohammed Hatta, a comrade-in-arms from the underground movement fighting against Dutch, he proclaimed the State of Indonesia. The Dutch eventually recognized Indonesia's independence in 1949. While Sukarno sought to realize the principle of a »Guided Democracy« with a powerful figure at its head, Hatta preferred a democracy in the Western mould.

Sukarno always strove to create and maintain a certain balance between Indonesia's political and social groupings. The basis for this was the Five Principles (**Panca Sila**), in which he attempted to create a link between Hindu-Javanese, Islamic and socialist values (belief, nationalism, democracy, humanity, and a just and affluent society). This basis of a dynamic society that should continually discuss its principles, redefining them, can be seen on innumerable memorials, walls and posters throughout the entire country and is meant to remind all Indonesians of their common nation.

Sukarno at a lecture at Berlin's Technical University (1956)

During Sukarno's years in power, the influence of the Communist Party increased in many Asian countries. At the close of the 1950s, Sukarno moved closer to the People's Republic of China and around 1963 distanced himself from Western-oriented Malaysia. His role in a viciously crushed attempted coup staged by the communists in 1965 remained unclear, which was one of the reasons for his overthrow two years later. Initially, his rights as president were curtailed and in 1967 General Suharto finally removed him from office and placed him under house arrest for life. Raden Ahmed Sukarno died in Jakarta on 21 June 1970.

ENJOY BALI

What culinary delights are there to be enjoyed on Bali? What is an Oggo Oggo? Where best to find a nice hotel? What are the best experiences on Bali? The following pages provide answers, along with tips for active holidaymakers and souvenir hunters.

Accommodation

Living in a Tropical Garden

The hotels on Bali are among the most beautiful in the world. There are virtually no high-rise hotels or massive developments of the sort known from other countries.

The complexes, which tend to be only two or three storeys high, are harmoniously embedded in the tropical landscape. They are often furnished with Indonesian arts and crafts, teak furniture made by local craftsmen as well as impressive antiques from the colonial era (►MARCO POLO Insight, p.113). Gods hewn into stone and statues of guards with fierce expressions adorn the park-like gardens that are accessed via the foyer. Foyers on Bali are often a massive, open wood-and-bamboo construction. Naturally circulating air and fans keep the climate pleasant. In addition, gamelan musicians create the musical backdrop so typical of Bali.

The biggest collection of four and five-star hotels is to be found in **Nusa Dua**, on the Bukit Badung peninsula: dozens of architecturally interesting resorts have been integrated in a tropical landscape park here.

Since Bali's more affordable low season is during the rainy season from October to March, it is possible to enjoy luxury hotels here for moderate prices as long as the severe, albeit mostly very brief, downpours are not a deal-breaker.

Renting a villa is an increasingly popular option, particularly with families and groups. They are available at a wide range of prices, depending on size, interior spec and location. They tend to include an outside pool, a TV as well as an internet connection, along with staff such as maids and night porters. It is furthermore possible to take advantage of the services of a chef who will also do the shopping on request.

Fortunately it is not necessary to spend a lot of money on Bali or Lombok to live well. For a small to medium-size budget, expect a well-kept establishment and friendly customer service in the many small hotels and guesthouses. **Homestays** and **Losmens** are even less expensive. They are privately run guesthouses, which can be found in almost every town.

While hotels tend to be cheaper when booked through a travel agent, and small hotels and guesthouses can be reserved via the relevant websites (there is often a marked price reduction when booking online), it is best to seek out private accommodation in situ to ensure

Get the jungle feeling in the Laguna Resort & Spa Nusa Dua on the Bukit Badung peninsula

Five-star luxury on Lombok: the »Oberoi«

the place is clean and the quality as required; this will also allow price negotiations. Visitors wishing to stay for several days or even weeks will usually get a discount from the owner(s).

Lombok The choice of accommodation is less plentiful on Bali's neighbouring island of Lombok. Here the hotels (including five-star complexes such as the »Oberoi«) and guesthouses are largely grouped around Senggigi Beach to the north of the capital Mataram.

HOTEL PRICES
Price Categories
The hotels recommended in this travel guide in the chapter »Destinations from A to Z« are divided into the following price categories (one night in a double room incl. breakfast):

££££ = more than £120
£££ = £80–120
££ = £40–80
£ = up to £40

HOTEL GUIDE
Bali Tropical Villas
www.bali-tropical-villas.com
One of the oldest and most renowned agencies with more than 500 villas to choose from; they will also find longer-term accommodation.

BaliOn
www.Balion.com
The BaliOn agency has more than 50 villas in every price category.

Hotels in the Bali Style

Be woken in the mornings by the croaking of frogs and the song of tropical birds, while the swathes of mist gradually disappear from the jungle valley. Enter the open bathroom on thick, shiny teak floors and enjoy a shower outside. The COMO Shambhala Estate somewhat outside of Ubud, surely one of the most beautiful hotels in the whole of Asia, demonstrates that the much-described Bali Style is much more than just tropical design.

It is not luxury and design that impress; it is rather the way in which the residences are perfectly integrated into nature and the rooms are furnished using ancient principles of symmetry and order.

The hotel's history sounds like a fairy tale: Bradley and Debbie Gardner, a couple of British entrepreneurs, are said to have fallen in love with the incredibly beautiful jungle valley before acquiring eight hectares (20 acres) and planting 3000 trees.

A lot of work and the help of architect **Cheong Yew Kuan** resulted in the creation of five residences among the hills, built over eight years. They incorporate the environment and are dedicated to the five elements. Each of these unique residences possesses four to five suites.

Residence of the Wind

The »**Bayugita**« was named after the loud breezes that circulate over the terraces there. The »Residence of the Wind« possesses a large open living room on the top floor that is accessed steps that go across a lily pond. The style is characterized by thick teak 150-year-old floorboards from Java, oversized Batavia colonial sofas, rugs from Mongolia and China, a huge Venetian four-poster bed in the master suite and a porcelain WC from the Dutch era, with a floral decoration.

Archaic Indonesian art in turn dominates the »fire« residence »**Teja Suara**«, which was built using 1200 tons of stones from the island of Sumba. The »**Tirta Ening**« residence has been designed as a water palace, in which water gardens and 200-year-old teak walls from Java, hand-carved doors and bathtubs chiselled out of stone create a unique atmosphere.

Natural Living

In the 1990s the term »Bali Style« became synonymous with a very particular tropical, relaxed interior design and living style that found imitators around the world. Designers primarily sourced their ideas from their love of a simple life in the midst of nature, which is given special significance in architecture and interior design. Natural materials typical of the country, such as teak and rattan, are used, as are batik, developed on Java in the 15th century, and statuary with cultic and religious motifs. Balinese people are excellent artisans. When furnishing a house, there is a lot of choice from among furniture and decorative objects of outstandingly high-quality workmanship.

Colonial and contemporary, traditional and ultra-modern, simple and luxurious, lavish and purist all at once: the Bali Style manages to combine otherwise irreconcilable contrasts; it lives off their tension and their synthesis. Living in the Bali Style stimulates all the senses: Instead of being in a »smooth« environment based on artificial materials, this style uses materials that exhibit different surface textures, stone, granite and oiled timber underfoot, grass and bamboo up above – materials that address deeper levels of perception when they are touched.

Light & Air

Further elements of the Bali Style include light, air and a lavish use of space. **Open pavilions** invite visitors to enjoy life outside and feel the tropical breeze on the skin. Clear lines and a focus on just a few carefully selected items, including some modern objects, emphasize the lightness and the playful nature of this interior style. The surroundings are always incorporated. Fans and freely circulating air create a pleasant climate – there are no closed off, air-conditioned rooms.

Water & Earth

The bathrooms generally possess an outside shower, which introduces the experience of nature first thing. In Bali, a country of paddy fields, running water is part of life. This is why the living space also contains all kinds of ponds, small and large ones, some with rectangular masonry walls and some with natural outlines, fed by spring water. Stepping stones that lead across the ponds connect the element of water with the house and the element of earth.

Alila Villas

However, the Bali Style also features new, contemporary developments. Pioneers here are the Alila Villas, designed by the multi-award-winning, Singapore-based architecture and design company WOHA, which has particularly made a name for itself with sensational construction projects in the Asian world. In early 2012 the German Architecture Museum in Frankfurt held an exhibition about the WOHA construction philosophy entitled »Breathing Architecture«.

Visitors to the Alila Villas in **Uluwatu** will not find Balinese folklore; instead they will encounter an interior that is purist, young and refreshingly different. Furthermore it meets the most stringent ecological standards. In addition to recycled wood (the island's old telegraph poles), igneous and volcanic rock was used, formed by eruptions of Mount Merapi on Java. That was clearly a good luck charm because in 2011 the villas in Uluwatu received the »**International Award**« of the Royal Institute of Builders and Architects (RIBA) in London for their outstanding, sustainable architecture.

Villas Soori

The Villas Soori, set between paddy fields and near the Tanah Lot temple on the water, are no less

The »Four Seasons at Sayan« pool has views of a lavish jungle landscape

impressive. The purity and simplicity of the surroundings create a special experience of space that even the materialistically minded will experience as a liberating, uplifting atmosphere. It starts with the views of the always busy bright green paddy fields, and of the mountains rising up in the distance. Bali Style is embodied here by a near spiritual experience, a meditative atmosphere where less is more and every item inside the villas, every accessory, is chosen with care. It is not the undoubtedly exquisite, modern and purist architecture and the classy minimalist interior that are the main protagonists here; instead it is Bali's magical surroundings, the exceptional and truly blessed setting that liberates visitors from their everyday lives and lets them breathe more freely. The Bali Style, highly praised all over the world and often imitated, is much more than just a marketing trick or a particular interior design. And the actual magic of the Alila Villas is not primarily their luxury but their harmony with the natural environment.

Exotic Holidays

Bali is a paradise for children. They are welcomed everywhere. Besides the beaches, a suitable place for the whole family to visit on a day trip is naturally the zoo. Elephant rides are among the highlights for the little ones.

Quacking ducks that waddle through the bright green paddy fields, monkeys that climb from branch to branch in the trees of the hotel gardens, stealing tropical fruits from the buffet at lightning speed, little girls practising magical dances in the dress of Hindu goddesses – Bali is a paradise for children. The tropical island has an exciting number of new and unfamiliar experiences to offer. In addition to organized excursions to secret temples, water palaces, bat caves and volcanic craters, even simple walks through the peaceful villages are an experience, where children learn that the people in Bali lead very different lives from those at home. In Ubud, for example, walks through the town inspire further exploration of the surrounding paddy fields. It is best to get the map »Ubud Surroundings« from one of the local bookshops, before heading off with the right head covering and sufficient water. Along the way children always enjoy stopping at a street stall for freshly pressed juices or an exotic soft drink along with a package of peanuts.

Holiday in Paradise

Among the other attractions are the beaches and hotel pools, where little ones meet children from all around the world, making new friendships and learning how to communicate in English to others to whom it is a foreign language, or without many words.

Older children will definitely enjoy the English-language children's books available in Bali. »Gecko's Complaint« is beautifully illustrated for example. It is a Balinese folk fairy-tale that deals with the complaints of a young gecko that is prevented from sleeping by the many glow-worms.

However, before travelling it is best to consider the vaccinations, the long flight, the time difference and also sufficient sun protection, among other things.

And if for once a longer tour of a temple complex or a simple excursion without the children is planned, some of the larger hotels offer very good supervised children's programmes, full of variety, that are also open to non-residents (for a small charge).

The different water slides make the Waterbom Park in Kuta an exciting day out

Attractions for children

INFOS & TIPS
www.travelforkids.com
An extensive selection (in English) for families travelling to Bali with children: arts and crafts courses, visits to zoos, riding on elephants and a lot more.

ACROBATICS
Bali High Flyers
Bali Dynasty Resort
Kuta South Beach, Kuta
Tue–Sun, 9.30am–10.45am
7–12-year-olds, 11am–12.15pm
and 2pm–3.15pm for teenagers
Cost: 325,000 rupees
4 courses 1,000,000 rupees
Tel. 03 61 7 84 29 27
www.highflyersbali.com
Trapeze artists in the making get their chance here. Children and teenagers from Australia, Asia and Europe can learn here how much fun it can be to control their bodies and how exciting it is to perform the tricks they learned to an audience.

WATER PARK
Waterbom Park
Jl. Kartika Plaza
Tuban, Kuta
Daily 9am–6pm
Entry: 31/19 US$ (adults/children up to age 12)
www.waterbom-bali.com
Children will have something to do all day in the most popular water and leisure park in Bali. They have a dozen flumes to choose from. In addition there is an extensive selection of sports to choose from as well as a spa for relaxation.

CREATIVITY
Bali Center for Artistic
Creativity (BCAC)
Nyoman Art Gallery
Jl. Raya Petulu, Ubud
Cost: 2.5-hour course for children 350,000 rupees, 3 x 2.5 hours 970,000 rupees
www.baliartclasses.com
Being creative in an inspiring environment: on the northeastern beach of Ubud children and teenagers can devote themselves to the joy of painting and creating in a course lasting several hours at the renowned Nyoman Art Gallery.

House of Alaia
(House of Happiness)
Jl. Batu Bolong
Canggu
Tel. 8 21 47 34 87 46
www.houseofalaia.com
Courses: 3-day course (always 9am–noon) in metal working for 7–18-year-olds: 450,000 rupees (silver), 350,000 rupees (brass)
2-day course (always 2pm–4pm) in making friendship bracelets with small pearls, for 6–18-year-olds: 250,000 rupees.
Designing friendship bracelets, for children aged 6 and up (9am–noon or 2pm–5pm): 150,000 rupees.
Located on Bali's southwest coast, 11km/7mi west of Denasar, this school offers a lot of courses in the creative sector, such as designing jewellery, e.g. necklaces, pendants, earrings and friendship bracelets, for children and teenagers.

Pondok Pekak Library and Learning Centre

Monkey Forest Road, Ubud
Daily 9am–9pm
Tel. 03 61 97 61 94
The cultural centre does not just offer courses for adults. There are also lots of courses (dance, gamelan) for children as well as a well-structured children's library.

HORSERIDING *Insider Tip*

Bali Horse Adventure

Kuda Bahigia
Jl. Pura Dalem Lingsir
Banjar Pengembungan, Pererenan
Tel. 03 61 3 65 55 97
www.balihorseadventure.com
Fancy a hack across paddy fields or along the beach? Or riding a pony on a training pitch? The Kuda Bahagia stable near Canggu, 12km/7.5mi west of Denpasar and a five-minute walk from the beach offers more than just hacks (1 hour: 350,000 rupees, 2 hours: 600,000 rupees, 3 hours: 900,000 rupees). It also offers children's riding experiences on ponies (for children up to age 5, 80,000 rupees), a children's camp (Sat or Sun 9am–noon, 400,000 rupees) as well as a five-day children's horse camp (daily 8.30am–12.30pm, 1,800,000 rupees).

ZOOS

Bali Bird Park

Jl. Serma Cok Ngurah Gambir
(2km/1.2miles north of Batubulan)
Daily 9am–5.30pm
Entry: approx. 26/13 US$ (adults/children up to age 12)
www.bali-bird-park.com
There are all kinds of strange birds to be discovered in the middle of an exotic landscape. Living right next door are snakes, crocodiles, turtles and some komodo dragons.

Bali Safari & Marine Park

Jl. Bypass Ida Bagus Mantra
Km 19.8 (road to Klungkung, 10km/6mi east of Gianyar)
Daily 9am–5pm
Entry: starting at 49 US$
Tel: 03 61 95 00 00
www.balisafarimarinepark.com
Lavish vegetation and many wild animals that are approached in a safari bus. Visitors can ride elephants and have their picture taken with orang-utans. There are also cultural events and animal shows. Watch the elephants take a bath, be there when young gorillas are fed and get to know some of the animals a bit better in the petting zoo. There is also a large restaurant, souvenir stalls and a shuttle service from many of the hotels in Kuta and the surrounding area.

Elephant Safari Park

Taro
(approx. 20km/12mi north of Ubud)
Daily 8am–6pm
Entry: starting at 65/44 US$
(adults/children)
Tel. 03 61 72 14 80
www.baliadventuretours.com
Here it is not only possible to pet and feed the creatures, but also to explore the surroundings from the back of an elephant. In addition, the animals can be observed painting and there is an elephant museum to visit.

Every Day a Festival

When the Balinese call on their gods in the temple, they do this in part with the intention of blessing every living thing – a truly magical atmosphere, which open-minded visitors can experience at the numerous temple festivals. Somewhere on the island, one of these festivals is celebrated almost every day.

Odalan festivals, temple anniversaries, are easy to recognize as not only the temple but also the village streets are elaborately decorated with bamboo garlands, prayer flags, flowers and other ceremonial ornaments.

According to an unofficial count, there are well over a thousand festivals and celebrations in Bali throughout the year. temples or by the fair held there prior to the festival. Celebrations of a religious nature are held all year round in Bali. As the festivals in Bali and Lombok are held according to three customary but differing calendars, causing the dates to shift from year to year, it is practically impossible to name a fixed date in advance.

The tourist information offices in Denpasar and in Senggigi (Lombok) provide annually published brochures (in English) with the current festival dates. Questions relating to this can also be answered at the hotel receptions. In addition, the »Bali Echo«, a tourist magazine (in English), is published regularly with a current events calendar.

Every day a holiday

CALENDAR SYSTEM

Apart from the everyday Gregorian calendar, there are three other calendar systems in Bali: the uku calendar and the saka calendar play an important role in determining the dates for religious festivals. Their structure and use are so complicated, however, that only Brahmins and special astrologers are capable of interpreting them. They can in any case hardly be measured against Western systematics and logic. Added to these is the Islamic calendar, which is less important in Bali.

Almost everything that is of importance to the Balinese is calculated according to the Javanese-Balinese **uku** calendar, above all the many »birthdays«. Birthdays are not only celebrated for people, but also for farming equipment, weapons, cars and machines. Even the individual occupational groups celebrate their birthdays – rice farmers as well

Four calendar systems

Some of the kites flown at the annual Kite Festival in July are quite unusual

Oggo-Poggo on Nyepi

In Western countries, the turn of the year is celebrated with colourful rockets, exploding firecrackers, and bubbly, and the old year is seen off in a boisterous, jovial way. Not so in Bali.

And there is undoubtedly no other place on the face of the earth that celebrates the transition from one year to the next as it is marked on the island of gods, spirits and demons. The Balinese observe their **New Year's festival (Nyepi) in spring**, at the time of the equinox, to be precise. But they begin with the preparations weeks ahead. The major preparations actually take the form of a competition among the Balinese boys to conjure up a uglier and more fearsome **oggo-oggo, an oversized monster** made of a bamboo frame, papier mâché, paste and paint, than the youths in the neighbouring village. Spirits are used to frightening things, so the demon made by human hand naturally has to look wilder and more shockingly scary than even the very worst of the spirits.

Traditions Surrounding the New Year

Three days before the festival celebrating the beginning of a new year, on **saka day**, thousands of festively dressed Balinese march to the island's coasts and lay down offerings to gain the favour for the coming year of the spirits and demons dwelling in the sea. This festival is especially beautiful to watch on the beach at Sanur. It is appropriate to wear a sarong for the occasion. On the **day of penge-rupuk**, the last day of the year, the islanders make offerings in their temples to thoroughly cleanse the

New Year's celebrations in Ubud

A terrifying Oggo-Oggo is carried through the streets at New Year

island. Bamboo poles decorated with yellow and white ribbons, set up along the roadsides days beforehand, are intended to show the gods that they are welcome. Above all, it is the designers of the monster figures that most feverishly look forward to the parades planned all over the island for the night of New Year's Eve. The parades in Kuta and Denpasar, where masses of people line the roads, are the largest and most colourful. Those in the villages in the interior of the island are no less worth seeing though, and perhaps even a little more primal. The Nyepi festival reaches its climax during the **night on the eve of the New Year**. After nightfall, in a manner somewhat similar to the carnival processions elsewhere in the world, the rickety oggo-oggo figures are paraded about, carried by their makers and preceded by musicians creating deafening sounds on their instruments. Any evil spirit not awakened, frightened and inspired to make a hasty exit to parts unknown would have to be as tough as old boots! Yet it cannot be ruled out that the odd, particularly stubborn spirit ignores this exorcism. So, the next day, the Balinese, an extremely mistrustful people, pretend that Bali is **completely uninhabited**. This is the reason that no fire can be lit or light turned on anywhere on the whole island, any visible human movement must be stopped, and all work is held in abeyance. By the way, not even tourists are allowed to leave the hotel on »Nyepi«!

? MARCO POLO INSIGHT

Did you know...

...that the Balinese year only has 210 days? The year is based on the Javanese-Balinese calendar and consists of six months of 35 days, divided into 30 weeks of seven days each. The weeks are called Wuku and every week of the year has its own name. Bookshops sell attractive calendars – an exotic and inexpensive souvenir.

as artists, craftsmen and intellectuals. These events are moved to dates promising blessings, which are still of fundamental importance for the traditional farming population; essential dates such as the day on which the rice harvest can begin and the day on which it must be finished. Naturally, the most auspicious days for the temple anniversary or »birthday« festivals are calculated. The great festival for the state temple is the most important.

The birthdays can only be determined by lengthy calculations and observations, which may then be on a completely different day the following year.

Hindu-Balinese calendar
The Hindu-Balinese calendar – **saka** – is more similar to the Gregorian calendar than the others, but is oriented to the lunar cycle; the year (caka) has twelve months, each with 29 or 30 days. As this method of calculating the year diverges from the astronomical year, a »leap« month is added every 30 months. The Hindu faith knows no numbering for the years because, to the Hindu, everything that happens is continuous and bound in an eternally repeating cycle. So there is no »year zero«.

Islamic calendar
The Islamic calendar also has a part to play, though it only has a secondary role on Bali (it is more important on Lombok). It is also lunar oriented.
The Islamic calendar has 354 days arranged into twelve months, each with 29 or 30 days. Again, the variance to the astronomical year is evened out with the inclusion of a leap month. The Islamic calendar begins with the year of the Prophet Mohammed's flight from Mecca (»Hejra« or »Hijra«; AD 622 = year 1).

Western calendar
The Western calendar, along with central Indonesian time, is quite customary in Indonesian public life – this applies equally to Bali and Lombok.

Calendar of Events

FIXED HOLIDAY DATES
1 January
New Year's Day (as in the West, also on Lombok)

21 April
Kartini Day (comparable to Mothers' Day)

17 August
Indonesian national holiday
(Proklamasi Kemerdekaan = decla-
ration of independence of the Republic of Indonesia in 1945).

1 October
Panca Sila Day (Day of the Five
Principles). Commemoration of
the address delivered by state
founder Sukarno (►Famous People), which forms the preamble to
the Indonesian constitution.

5 October
Indonesian Armed Forces Day
(military parades, etc.).

25/26 December
Christmas (as in the West, also on
Lombok)

EVENTS
January / February
Chinese New Year (first day of the
first Chinese lunar-month).

March
Nyepi (►MARCO POLO Insight,
p.98)

March / April
Major temple anniversary (odalan
festival) in the Pura Besakih and
the Pura Batu in Kintamani

July
Kite Festival: kite-flying competition in Padang Galak near Denpasar

September / October
Odalan festival in the Pura Kehen
in Bangli

October / November
Odalan festival in the Pura Jagat
Natha in Denpasar

HOLIDAYS IN LOMBOK
Once a year, the island inhabitants
(Sasak) meet in Kuta on the south
coast of Lombok for a festival to
fetch the legendary Byale worm
from the sea. But in contrast to
Bali, the number of festivals on
the neighbouring island of Lombok is pretty small. This is because
the Islamic faith prevalent here offers less occasion for exuberant
celebrations than Hinduism does
in Bali.

Islamic festivals
New Year (Hijra), the Prophet Mohammed's birthday (Mawlid al-
Nabi), the two-day festival of
breaking the fact at the end of
Ramadan (Id-ul Fitri), and the
three-day sacrificial festival (Id-ul
Adha) for the Haj, the pilgrimage
to Mecca. The dates of the festivals are based on the Islamic lunar
calendar of 354 days; each festival
is held eleven days earlier than the
year before.

Food and Drink

Fresh and Fruity

Graceful women dressed in tie-dye sarongs and blouses balance baskets on their heads that are filled with freshly picked fruit and vegetables – a widespread view in Bali. The women shop on the market every day before preparing fresh meals.

Influenced by the Chinese, Indian, Portuguese, Dutch and British cuisine, Indonesian cuisine sometimes suffers from the prejudice (not entirely unjustified) that it is less diverse, sophisticated and interesting than other national cuisines of Asia. However, it makes up for it all when it comes to the typical accompaniments that are served alongside the rice and meat dishes: sambals are spicy and sometimes sweet and sour seasoning pastes.

Indeed, the name **sambal** denotes that a lot of fresh chillis were used. A thick sauce is made from them as well as lemongrass, turmeric, garlic, dried shrimp paste, vinegar, brown sugar, lime juice and many other ingredients, which is then fried in hot oil. Other popular accompaniments besides sambals are spicy chutneys made of vinegar, exotic fruits, chillis, lemon juice, garlic and ginger. Every household has its own seasoning pastes known as **rempah**.

The **cookshops** so typical of many Asian countries are known as **warungs** on Bali and traditionally act as a mix between a snack stall, a kiosk, a bar and a café. There are warungs of varying quality and price on Bali: there are those where guests simply sit on wooden benches and where food is prepared at a cooking facility visible to diners, and then there are those luxurious warungs that are fitted with antiques and feature an extensive menu. It is definitely worth eating here at least once, not least because warungs sell classic Balinese dishes.

Ubud has a particularly large number of warungs; most of them have their tables set up along the streets and serve sucking pig from a spit-roast, the famous babi guling; some are also found hidden among tropical greenery.

International cuisine arrived in tourist locations and hotels years ago. Food choices here include Italian, Mexican and American classics such as pizza, pasta, tacos, burgers and steaks. The larger hotels regularly host evening music events during which visitors can also enjoy lavish buffets of Indonesian delicacies.

Have dinner in a beach restaurant in Jimbaran on Bukit Badung peninsula and be treated to a magnificent sunset for dessert

Sambal and Rempah

The tasty satay kebabs tend to be served with a spicy peanut sauce

FOODS

Soups   **Baso** is a soup consisting of a spicy broth with rice noodles, vegetables and pieces of meat added. **Bubur ayam** is a thick rice soup with chicken; **bakmi kuah** is a simple (usually spicy) broth with vegetables and noodles. **Soto babad** is a soup with beef and vegetables. When the temperature is high, often just a portion of **capcay kuah** (cabbage soup) is sufficient.

Kebabs   The meats (beef, lamb and pork, occasionally also offal) on a wooden skewer known as **satay** (sate) are grilled over a charcoal fire and enjoyed as a small snack as well as an essential part of the Indonesian rice table. When the meat is cooked, it is dipped for a moment in a sauce to which ground peanuts have been added.

Main dishes   The preparation of the good, nourishing main dish called **nasi goreng** is simpler than its exotic name might suggest. Cooked rice is fried with vegetables, onions sautéed in oil and strips of beef or pork. It is seasoned with finely chopped peppers and chillis. A version of nasi goreng goes by the name of bami goreng in Java; there, noodles are used instead of rice. Fried chicken (**ayam goreng**), pork (**kolo bak**) and sucking-pig meat (**babi kecap**) in a sweet and sour sauce is popular. **Babi guling**, a Balinese speciality, is very tasty: it consists of sucking pig grilled over an open fire with rice added as a side dish. **Bebek betutu** (duck meat cooked in banana leaves) and **bebek panggang** (grilled duck meat) are quite delicious. **Cap cai**, inspired by Chinese cooking, is actually a version of the world famous chop suey: meat and vegetables cut into bite-size pieces are fried in a pan and served with rice.

Martabak is a kind of crepe filled with lamb, onions and spices, folded together and fried briefly on each side. Krupuk is a speciality of Indonesian cooking: crisp crackers made from tapioca flour and dried shrimp or fish are cooked in oil.

Crepes and prawn crackers

Bananas deep-fried in batter (pisang goreng) and rice pudding are popularly served for dessert. Acar is a savoury dessert of gherkins, small onions, sweet and sour pickled ginger and roasted peanuts.

Desserts

FRUIT

The **art of fruit and vegetable carving** is widespread in Bali. There are specialized employees in the kitchens of the large hotels who are true masters in creating designs from fruit and vegetables. **Pineapples** (nanas) are fresh from April to July. Some varieties are customarily consumed locally in a fermented state, which can have a laxative effect. **Bananas** (pisang), available all year round, are soaked in coconut milk and grilled. Tip: the smaller the bananas, the sweeter they taste. Even if Europeans find it takes some getting used to, the somewhat mealy flesh of the **durian fruit** – also called stinky fruit because of its overpowering smell – is considered a delicacy by Asians (ripe from April to June). On the other hand, **jackfruit** (nangka), a roundish fruit weighing several kilos, is sweet and aromatic. It is cut into slices and served on ice cream (August and September). The yellow-green to dark blue oval **passion fruit** (up to 20cm/8in long) is also widespread. Its juicy, jelly-like flesh is scooped out with a spoon and has a sweet-sour taste. The flesh of the hard-husked **coconut** (kelapa) is extracted with a narrow spoon after the coconut milk has been poured out (see drinks: fruit juices). **Limes** are the local alternative to lemons and available all year round. The larger, yellow lemons have to be imported and are therefore quite expensive. **Lychees** are cultivated more in other parts of Indonesia than in Bali. When ripe, the

Artistic presentation

Typical Balinese Dishes

The quality and taste of the traditional dishes vary depending on how they are prepared and on the vegetables used. The best food tends to come from the small restaurants and cookshops typical of this country. Since they are generally speaking hygienic, it is safe to sit down there and enjoy a small culinary adventure.

Gado Gado: Every restaurant on Bali serves this inexpensive and tasty vegetable dish. Gado Gado, which is served with a peanut sauce, is made of sliced potatoes, fresh soy sprouts, green beans, carrots, cabbage, fresh cucumbers and a hard-boiled egg.

Soto Ayam: A nutritious chicken soup seasoned with fresh ginger, coriander seeds, cumin and lemongrass; the main ingredients are carrots, chicken, soy sprouts and a lot of fresh coriander leaves. To serve, soy sprouts are put in the soup bowls before pouring the hot broth on top. The whole thing is garnished with cooked, chopped eggs as well as finely chopped spring onions.

Tahu Goreng kacang: Deep-fried diced tofu served in a sauce of crushed peanuts, garlic, sambal olek, shallots and soy sauce that is gradually bulked up with coconut milk and seasoned with chilli paste and fresh lemon juice. The dish is served with freshly grated cucumbers and carrots, which are placed on a plate as a base; then the peanut sauce is added, topped off with fresh soy sprouts. The version served without peanuts is also popular.

Ikan Goreng: Ikan is the Indonesian word for fish, which is prepared in countless ways on Bali. Ikan Pang-gang is fish grilled in banana lea-ves, Gulai Ikan refers to the prepa-ration with coconut milk and spices, Ikan Kecap are fish steaks fried with a lot of spices and seasoned with soy sauce; Ikan Bali are fish steaks fried to a golden brown colour in peanut oil and ser-ved in a sauce made of garlic, gin-ger, lemon rind, palm sugar and soy sauce.

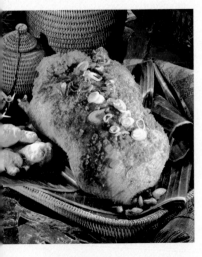

Bebek betuta: A classic of Balinese cuisine is braised duck prepared in banana leaves – a popular dish for family celebrations, but one now commonly found on the menus of many restaurants. The taste varies depending on the seasoning paste that was rubbed on the meat; crus-hed chillis, garlic and peanuts are always included, however. The duck is stuffed with a mix of seaso-ning paste and fresh spinach, so-metimes also with a type of cabba-ge grown on Bali, before it is cooked in an oven. The result smells and tastes irresistible.

Babi Guling: The favourite dish of many Balinese people: sucking pig cooked over charcoal, stuffed with a mix of shallots, chopped garlic, fresh ginger, a lot of chopped chil-lis, crushed peppercorns and lime leaves. Served with rice, different chilli sauces as well as traditionally Jukut Nangka Mekuah, the flesh of the jackfruit cooked in coconut milk.

»Journey to Gastronomy«

The fruit and vegetable market of Jimbaran starts in the middle of the night, as does the nearby fish market. When it is still dark, at around half past three, the vendors have already set up their stalls: mangos, mangosteen, bananas, papayas and dozens of other tropical fruits await buyers here; in addition there are onions, garlic, ginger and much more besides, and all in varying quality and size.

An old woman dressed in a sarong, a Balinese lace blouse and a sash, the typical cotton belt, sits gracefully on a piece of hessian on the floor. Spread out in front of her are hundreds of sacrificial gifts – small baskets made out of folded betel leaves and held together by tooth picks are filled with a bit of cooked rice, small sweets or yellow and pink petals.

The majority of these sacrificial goods intended for the countless temples the locals have in their homes are already sold by the time the visitors who have booked the »Journey to Gastronomy« in the nearby hotel »Alina Villas Uluwatu« arrive.

Culinary Journey

Set out from there in the morning after breakfast to arrive at the famous market of Jimbaran before 8am, accompanied by one of the hotel's chefs. His knowledge of the local products and the explanations received while looking at the unfamiliar fruits and vegetables mean that participants will look at the stalls with renewed interest and sometimes get into conversation with the vendors.

Located in a hidden corner of the covered market, we are led to a stall that still sells the old, traditional kitchen utensils that are rarely used these days: pots made out of

First the ingredients for the different dishes are purchased from the market in Jimbaran

clay, in which the food was cooked over an open fire. The black mortars made of natural stone are also used in the hotel kitchen: they weigh several kilograms and mean that herbs and spices can be processed into powders and pastes with very little effort.

The lavish, colourful market sometimes surprises visitors with its pungent, almost unbearable smells, such as the smell of the durian fruit, whose stench is legendary. Indeed, once opened it has such an unpleasant smell that hotels have a durian ban.

Beach Picnic

Walk along the beach, past white and sometimes pink outrigger boats to get to the fish market. The choice of different fish and seafood is enormous here. Stored in countless plastic boxes and kept cool with a thick layer of ice, the fish sold here are what the fishermen caught during the night. After a price has been negotiated, the fish are cleaned, gutted and filleted.

With these impressions in mind, leave the market and head to Balangan Beach, an insider tip for surfers, particularly from Australia. The beach is lined by adventurous-looking shacks on stilts: restaurants and cafés that feed the surfers for little money.

Guests of the »Journey to Gastronomy« are served a picnic on the beach as the hygiene of the restaurants is not always a hundred percent. This picnic features stylish cushions on a bamboo rug. A snack consisting of open coconuts and other sweet treats is laid out on a low table.

»Base be Pasih«

Back in the hotel, enjoy a cup of tea before sampling Soto Ayam, a spicy chicken soup, as a pick-me-up for the upcoming cooking adventure. Then the participants get to work in an open-plan kitchen that adjoins the restaurant.

The menu will feature Balinese cuisine, consisting of a starter, several mains and a dessert. The initial step involves creating a seasoning paste, the »base be pasih«. Consisting of spices and vegetables, such as chillis, garlic, shallots, tomatoes, ginger, fresh turmeric, dried shrimp paste and coconut oil, a blender is used to create a spicy paste that is then cooked in a casserole on medium heat for ten minutes.

The paste is used to marinate the main dishes, such as »tambusan be pasih«, grilled fish in banana leaves, a satay of chopped chicken on bamboo kebabs as well as a green papaya salad with shrimps. The dessert is »sumping waluh«, coconut pumpkin cake in a banana leaf.

After a bit of time you will be told »lunch is ready«, whereupon it is time to enjoy the food you just prepared, which tastes all the more delicious for that.

A half-day course »Journey to Gastronomy« costs 1,200,000 rupees, a day course is 2,100,000 rupees.

Alila Villas Uluwatu
Jl. Belimbing Sari
Banyar Tambiyak, Desa Pecatu
Bukit Badung
Tel. 03 61 8 48 21 66
www.alilahotels.com/uluwatu

Exotic fruit basket with »hairy« rambutan fruits

light-coloured flesh of the fruit with the reddish skin tastes sweet and fresh (May to August). **Mangos** (mangga), along with pineapples, are probably the tourists' favourite. This fruit is sweet, juicy and aromatic only when it is fully ripe (yellow skin; does not keep well). Mangos are cut in half and the flesh is either spooned out or sucked out (March to June). **Oranges** have a thin, green skin in Indonesia; those with a yellow colouring are particularly sweet. **Grapefruit**, usually with the pleasant-tasting pink flesh, are fresh all year round and are popularly eaten with a pinch of salt. **Papaya**, native to the American tropics, is the cheapest of all Asian fruits and available at any time of year at every market stand. In hotel breakfasts, it is served in halves with a lemon. But beware: enjoyed in larger amounts, papaya is a sure laxative. The small, red, hairy-skinned **rambutan fruit** that grows on a variety of the soapberry tree tastes similar to a grape. The **malabar plum** has the form of a pear with a rust-coloured, waxy skin and a porous, light-coloured flesh; both skin and flesh are edible. As the fruit has a somewhat sour taste, it is preferably eaten with sugar and a pinch of salt (January to March).

DRINKS

Get enough fluid

Given the high temperatures in Bali, it is best to drink **at least two to three litres (three to five pints) of liquids daily**. In which form the moisture lost through perspiration is replaced in the body is left up to the individual, but absolutely the wrong way to go about it is to stick with alcoholic beverages, as the tropical heat increases the unpleasant side-effects of alcohol. Good thirst-quenchers are mineral water, tea or fruit juices.

The national drink of Indonesia is tea. It is served hot at meals (teh panas) and ice cold (teh es) as a refresher. Some caution is necessary: tea is sometimes chilled with ice cubes and if there are doubts about hygiene, it would be better to go without. Coffee (kopi) is prepared Turkish-style and served complete with the grounds. Tea and coffee

Beer (bir) is brewed in Indonesia under license to foreign companies: these include German, Dutch and Danish beers bearing their internationally known brand names. A large beer in a bar is called »bir besar«, a small one »bir kecil«; beer is sold in large and small bottles in the supermarkets. Compared to prices at home, beer and other alcoholic drinks are relatively expensive. Beer

Arak, high-proof brandy typical of Indonesia, is more suited as part of a mixed drink, for example mixed with rice wine or lime juice and honey in long drinks. All the usual international spirits are available in hotels, but are often very pricey. Spirits

The rural population of Bali drink rice wine (brem) or the slightly tart palm wine (tuak) made from fermented palm fruits. Rine and palm wine

Shopping

Jewellery, Batiks and Carvings

Shopping paradise Bali – instead of air-conditioned shopping malls, the island features small shops, boutiques and the chance to buy straight from workshops and studios.

The Balinese are talented artists and craftspeople. Their imagination and ability to copy from designers mean that shops are constantly filled with new objects and creations. The heart of artisan production is in Ubud and its surroundings, where the people create huge works of **stonemasonry, filigree silver works, woodcarvings** and **batiks**. There are also lots of painters in Ubud who work in every artistic style imaginable and exhibit their works in galleries and shops.

Artistic souvenirs

It is also possible to buy **items for the home** and **fabrics** in every price category. It is particularly inexpensive to buy directly from manufacturers as well as on markets, as long as you haggle properly. The first guideline is to take around 50% off the first offer in order to get to a realistic price. The shops in towns visited by tourists, such as in Nusa Dua, Sanur, Seminyak and Ubud, tend to have fixed, slightly elevated prices.

One of the most popular places for shopping trips is **Kuta**. Many of the boutiques there, however, are owned by young designers and entrepreneurs from Australia, the United States and Europe. The road between Kuta and Seminyak is one long shopping mall. In addition to shops selling clothes, jewellery, wood carvings and pottery for little money, there are also plenty of upmarket shops in Jalan Raya Seminyak.

Legian meanwhile has a good reputation for sewing. The small workshops will reproduce visitors' favourite items from back home for little money and usually in outstanding quality; it is also possible to commission copies from fashion magazines. Some souvenir ships can also be found in all the larger hotels, but the price and quality vary significantly. This is also true for the 'market days' organized by the resorts, generally once a week; local artisans will offer their products at small stands in the hotel grounds.

A BRIEF SHOPPING GUIDE

Real antiques have their price on Bali too – however, compared to Europe it is quite low. Even taking the transport costs and taxes into account that come into play when shipping furniture and larger items for the home, the effort is still worthwhile.

Antiques

Colourful batik fabrics are sold right on the beach

There are several large furniture shops outside of Kuta and Ubud – real treasure troves for interior designers when it comes to decorating a home in the typical Balinese style. They sell large, wonderful antique sofas and carvings from the neighbouring islands.

Generally speaking the reproductions of antique furniture, carefully made by established artisans, are inexpensive. It is best to buy from professional establishments that have their furniture and sculptures shipped; they usually require a minimum of one cubic metre in freight space.

Wood carvings
The small artisan town of Mas near Ubud is the centre of Balinese woodcarving art. The wood carvers tend to work together with other family members in open workshops, creating dancing masks, Buddha figures and objects for the home.

Baskets and pots
The selection of baskets, bags and containers made of bamboo, rattan and palm leaves are among the most inexpensive souvenirs and because of the items' light weight, they are among the easiest to transport. The goods often come from the neighbouring island of Lombok, as do the items of pottery, very beautiful pots and bowls that are often adorned with braiding and shells.

Art
Ubud, the island's artistic centre, is home to countless painters' studios. Before buying anything it is a good idea to visit several exhibitions and get information about prices. The »Agung Rai Museum of Art« (▶p. 206) in Peliatan, somewhat to the south of Ubud, will provide a good overview of the variety of traditional and contemporary Balinese art.

Shadow theatre figures
Shadow theatre figures have been associated with Indonesian culture for 2000 years and are now a typical and popular souvenir (Wayang kulit, ▶MARCO POLO Insight, p. 74). They are used to tell the stories from the Indian epics »Mahabharata« and »Ramayana« and in which the gods and demons are the main actors. Wayang kulit are mostly made of buffalo leather. The filigree punched-out patterns are typical, as are the rods, which are show considerable signs of wear in older specimens.

Beware when high prices are justified with the alleged age of the figures. These items are often not antique. Instead they have undergone an artificial aging process. This does not lessen their exotic appeal, but it does not justify their high price. Wooden hand-rod puppets, wayang golek, which are also for sale, often come from western Java.

Jewellery
There are outstanding silver and goldsmiths working on Bali. The village of Celuk near Ubud is known for them. It is increasingly becoming the destination of tourist buses. Bali uses sterling silver

Shadow play characters are cut from buffalo leather and then painted

(92.5% fine), which is processed in the traditional silver workshops, almost exclusively into one-off items. The sought-after champagne-coloured farmed pearls come from Lombok, while gems mostly come from Kalimantan (Borneo).

Anyone searching for quality should not buy from beach vendors; only buy from select jewellers. Old Bali hands have jewellery produced according to their own specifications. Working from a sketch or a photo, silversmiths create made-to-measure objects. There is just one drawback: it usually takes about 1–2 weeks to complete an order.

The small village of Batubulan to the south of Ubud is the centre of **Sculptures** outstanding stonemasonry. Standing imposingly along the road are temple gates several metres high, fabled creatures, reliefs and Buddha statues made of volcanic tuff. There are also pretty lanterns and storm lamps along with small stone statues that will easily fit into a suitcase.

There's one craft sector on Bali that is steadily growing and has **Textiles** tailored itself to the wishes and tastes of the island's visitors. Sports and leisure clothing, women's fashion in bright colours, skirts and dresses made of tie-dye fabrics, cotton and silk scarves and T-shirts with motifs typical of Bali can be found in Kuta as well as in all the other tourist towns.

Batik and Ikat Fabrics

Indonesian textiles fascinate people around the world. The country has an immense wealth of traditional fabrics and production methods to offer. This diversity comes in part from Indonesia's ethnic and linguistic heterogeneity, since the country is home to more than 300 different ethnic groups.

Originally the island nation's fabrics, some of which look back on a history going back thousands of years, did not just depict profane motifs for clothes; instead they also symbolized the status of their wearer and were occasionally understood as ritual connections to the transcendent world.

In a culture in which such outstanding importance was attributed to woven fabrics, even the manufacture of the starting material was given ritual significance. Spinning and dyeing resembled a meditative practice, while the loom was only prepared on days considered favourable by astrologers and at the time of the full moon.

Fabrics as an Investment

Although it is nigh on impossible to count the sheer number of different fabrics, the batiks from Java and the woven ikat fabrics of Bali and Lombok are among the most famous representatives of their genre.

Indeed, the term »ikat« means nothing other than »knotting« in some Indonesian languages – a clue to the production process of the fabrics, which are distinguished by the fact that the warp thread used is dyed prior to the actual weaving process.

The patterns were produced in the weaving process by knotting or binding the warp thread with fibres that prevent dyeing – an unusually elaborate and complicated technique that requires the utmost of experience, concentration and patience.

It is therefore not surprising to learn that the making of a fine woven fabric could take up to five years in times gone by. Such precious cloths acted as an investment comparable to real estate today.

Geringsing

Geringsing fabrics, which are woven by in the village of Tenganan, inhabited by the tradition-conscious Bali Aga tribe, are legendary and have become collector's items (older specimens in particular).

Geringsing means »warding off disease«; the double ikat fabrics, believed to be provided with magical ritual patterns, are said to create an atmosphere around their wearers that protects them from demonic influences.

It is a very laborious process to manufacture these fabrics. Elaborate calculations and complex binding and dyeing techniques are necessary for the manufacture of the two-sided fabrics.

The number of artisans who are capable of weaving the precious and beautiful Geringsing fabrics is shrinking year on year; at the same time the traditional significance of the fabrics is disappearing.

A weaver in Tanganan uses an elaborate knotting and weaving technique to produce double ikat fabrics

Batik

A simpler method of textile production is the batik technique, formerly part of religious and cultural ceremonies in Bali, but now largely a component of the souvenir industry.

Batik fabrics require talented draughtsmen who sketch an initial pattern on raw cotton or silk fabrics with a pen. The most popular motifs traditionally include depictions of flowers and abstract animals as well as lavish geometric patterns. Connoisseurs can tell from a batik where it has come from and how old it is. The sections of the design that are not to be dyed are covered in liquid wax prior to the individual dye courses. The wax subsequently has to be removed again, either with a sharp knife or with hot water, after which further dye courses take place.

The batiks dyed with gentle plant-based dyes are particularly lovely. In this case the dyeing process can take several days. The hallmark of high-quality batiks is that the pattern is equally strong on both sides of the fabric.

Sport and Outdoors

Active Ways of Exploring the Island

Surfing, playing golf, trekking – Bali is also an enticing destination for active holidays. However, the main focus is on dis-
covering the island on foot.

Behind every corner and every hill there is a new, unusual view, particularly in the interior. Pass quacking ducks, meet farmers on their
way to their paddy fields, be greeted by laughing school children before looking up and seeing the entrance to a splendidly decorated
temple complex full of Buddhas, gods and demons.

Bali is also a great destination to explore by bike, but stay away from
the busy main roads. Many hotels now keep bicycles for their guests.
The bicycle tours organized by many hotels are very popular. They
last one to two hours, during which you will learn with amazement
that Balinese village life in all its facets is taking place right next door.
Tourist centres such as Sanur, Kuta and Legian now have lots of bike
rental facilities. It should go without saying that it is important to
check how roadworthy a bicycle is before hiring it.

Guided bike tours with mountain bikes, e.g. on the »Batur Trail« are
organized by the long-established company »Sobek« in Kuta.

Bali is not altogether a paradise for a seaside holiday. Visitors will
look in vain for beaches with bright white coral sand, because the
sand on the island is mixed with volcanic ash. Those who can live
with this will be happy at the seaside resorts of Kuta, Legian and Nusa
Dua (South Bali), Candi Dasa (East Bali) and Lovina Beach (North
Bali). There are very beautiful beaches in Lombok and on the islands
just off Bali: Gili Air, Gili Meno and Gili Trawangan. Be sure to use a
sun cream with a high sunscreen factor when swimming and snorkelling. Since the beaches are often dirty, it is best to use bathing
shoes. Beaches suitable for bathing are marked.

It can be extremely dangerous to swim at other spots because waves
can occasionally tower up several metres high and dangerous underwater **rip tides**, not obvious at first glance, can pose a serious threat
to even the most practised swimmer.

The colourfully landscaped, famous 18-hole **Bali Handara Golf
Course** in the highlands of Bedugul is uniquely situated in the midd-

Discover Bali

Seaside holiday

Golf

**The rafting adventure on the Ayung, Bali's longest river, is also a
remarkable jungle trip**

le of the crater of an extinct volcano. The 6km/3.5mi course lies at an elevation of 1142m/3747ft, resulting in pleasant and constant temperatures ranging from 16°C/61°F to 20°C/68°F (green fee: US$ 150). Along with a clubhouse, there is a gym and a restaurant. Located among the hotel complexes of Nusa Dua, right on the Indian Ocean, is the **Bali Golf & Country Club's** 18-hole course, easy to reach by bicycle for holidaymakers living in one of the nearby up-market resorts. The green fee for this 6263m/6849yd course is US$165. From November to March, it is advisable to reserve tee-off times in the cooler morning and evening hours. At other times of the year, cooling ocean breezes also make playing pleasant around noon.

The 18-hole course in Lombok, Lombok Golf Kosaido, has been exquisitely designed in harmony with the surrounding landscape (green fee US$ 60). Just 40 minutes away by car from Senggigi, the course offers a view of the Gili Islands and Mount Rinjani.

Rafting The river Ayung is a great spot for white-water rafting on Bali. Trips set off from the small town of Kedewatan near Bedugul; it is around 11km/6.5mi to the destination just above Ubud. The boats used are fit-for-purpose inflatables operated by employees familiar with the terrain. However, it is not an entirely inexpensive adventure.

Flights Seeing the island of Bali from above is an exciting, albeit expensive bit of fun offered by Bali Avia.

Sailing There are very appealing sailing areas all around Bali. The number of charter boat providers is limited, however. It is standard that you will have to hire a crew familiar with the waters as well.

Surfing Surfing the waves off the Balinese coast can be enticing, especially if you are a skilled surfer. Beginners do well to stay between Kuta and Seminyak . More demanding surf can be found south of the airport and in Canggu, 20min northwest of Legian. Expert surfers, though, are drawn to the high waves off the coast of Bukit Badung near Pura Luhur Ulu Watu, on Nusa Lembongan or on Padang Padang.

Diving Bali is not a particularly favoured destination for divers, but it nevertheless unquestionably has a couple of beautiful spots for both beginners and advanced divers. Several hotels in Nusa Dua, Sanur and Kuta as well as at Senggigi Beach in Lombok have diving centres offering the necessary equipment for hire. While staying in Bali, it is also possible to qualify for »PADI certification«, a type of basic training for divers recognized worldwide. There are beautiful places to dive at Sanur, Nusa Dua, Padang Bai, Tulamben, Gili Tepekong (▶MARCO POLO Insight, p. 194), Amed, Singaraja-Lovina and around the islands of Menjangan and Penida.

Activities Information

GOLF

Bali Handara Golf Course
Desa Pancasari
Tel. 03 62 3 42 26 46
www.balihandarakosaido.com

Bali Golf & Country Club
Kawasan Wisata, Nusa Dua
Tel. 03 61 77 17 91
www.baligolfandcountryclub.com

Lombok Golf Kosaido
Jl. Raya Tanjung Sire Bay, Lombok
Reservations: tel: 03 61 8 52 85 21
www.sirebeachgolfclub.com

CYCLE TOURS

Sobek
Jl. Bypass Ngurah Rai
Simpang Siur, Kuta
Tel. 03 61 76 80 50
www.balisobek.com
Also offers rafting trips

RAFTING

P.T. Bali Adventure Tours
Jl. Bypass Ngurah Rai
Pesanggaran
Tel. 03 61 72 14 80
www.baliadventuretours.com

HORSERIDING

Umalas Equestrian Resort
Jl. Lestari 9
Banjar Umalas Kauh, Kuta
Tel. 03 61 73 14 02
www.balionhorse.de

Accompanied hacks to and along the beach, as well as through paddy fields and villages; ponies available to children.

Stable Kuda Bahagia
Jl. Pura Dalem Lingsir
Banjar Pengembungan
Pererenan
Tel. 03 61 3 65 55 97
www.balihorseadventure.com
A ten-minute ride through a village and paddy fields to get to the beach and on to Kuta.

SIGHTSEEING FLIGHTS

Bali Avia
Jl. Bypass 04, Tuban 8036, Kuta
Tel. 03 61 75 12 57
www.indo.com/travel_agents/bali_avia

DIVING

Bali Marine Sports
Jl. Kesumasari 9
Semawang, Sanur
Tel. 03 61 28 93 08
http://balimarinediving.com/

Baruna Water Sports
Puri Bagus, Lovina
Tel. 03 61 75 38 20
www.bagus-discovery.com
Baruna Water Sports maintains bookings offices in some of the larger hotels on Bali and on Senggigi Beach on Lombok.

TOURS

A tropical, exotic world full of lush paddy fields, Hindu temples, glorious beaches and friendly people awaits you on Bali. The island, with its cheerful and relaxed attitude, has much to discover.

Tours Through Bali

Are you interested in temples and culture? Do you want to journey through enchanting landscapes? A little of both? Our suggestions may provide inspiration when planning excursions of your own ....

Tour 1   **In the Centre of Bali**
This is the most beautiful tour Bali has to offer – through fascinating landscapes, past some of the island's major sights.
▸page 126

Tour 2   **The Southeast**
A day trip to the former court of Kerta Gosa with its wonderful wayang paintings, the bat caves of Goa La-wah and on to Amlapura's princely palace.
▸page 127

Tour 3   **The Island Tour**
This tour provides an overall impression of Bali and introduces the charms of its culture and landscape
▸page 129

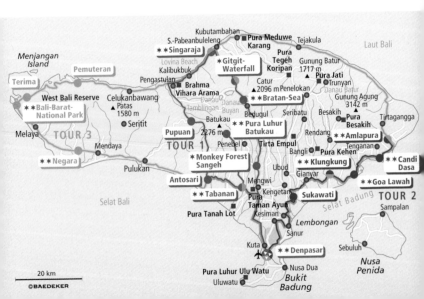

Travelling in Bali

The following tour suggestions are intended to provide ideas for exploring the island of Bali in a rented car without taking away the freedom of planning your own routes. If you plan to use public transport (bus, bemo), count on the tour lasting longer due to the varying quality of the connections. As Bali is a relatively small island, **all of the destinations can be reached on one-day tours** – assuming you start early in the morning and are willing to return late in the evening. Only a round-trip tour of the whole island takes longer: allow two to three days.

Get to know the whole island

The roads on Bali are not systematically numbered, posing a problem; but there are kilometre stones placed along the roads, showing in one direction the distance to the capital Denpasar, and in the other, the distance to the next town or village.

Road system

A break on a tour through the glorious landscape of lakes and mountains in northern Bali

A Cosmic Mandala

The largest Buddhist temple on Earth is located on Bali's neighbouring island of Java. The fertile Kedu Valley, surrounded by volcanoes and lush green paddy fields, saw the development of a unique place of pilgrimage in around AD800.

Covered by vegetation and volcanic ash, the temple, which was built during the Sailendra Dynasty, had fallen into oblivion for centuries and was only rediscovered in 1804 by Thomas Stamford Raffles. Major restoration works began in 1973; in 1991 UNESCO recognized the temple complex as a World Heritage Site.

Meditation Mandala

Even late in the day, when thousands of visitors are at the temple, the complex still exudes a powerful energy. **Borobudur** was created by stonemasons as a **three-dimensional stone meditation mandala** before being blessed by Buddhist priests. 504 life-size Buddha statues and 1460 relief panels were each created from individual pieces of stone. But beforehand square foundations were built measuring 123m/135yd along each side. Atop that stand five square and three round terraces that become ever smaller towards the top; topping off the complex is a stupa with a diameter of 11m/36ft.

Many Layers of Significance

On the one hand it symbolizes Meru, the mythical mountain of Buddhism, on the other the stepped path to enlightenment. Borobudur has four entrances; those who walk through them and around the terraces thereby symbolically walk the path of a practising Buddhist. The foundation depicts scenes from the realm of desire, i.e. human life characterized by hatred and infatuation.

The reliefs on the square terraces are devoted to the life of the historical **Buddha Shakyamuni** as well as his previous lives. Next are the three round terraces, on which 72 open-work stone stupas conceal the same number of Buddha statues. These are Dhyani Buddhas, Buddhas used in meditation, who are to transform the human passions into enlightenment and awareness of the emptiness of all phenomena. Depicted are **Vairocana,** who alters ignorance about the ultimate nature of reality into knowledge of the absolute truth, **Akshobhya,** whose realization transforms anger into its mirror-image, wisdom, **Ratnasambhava,** who transforms pride into the wisdom of equanimity, **Amitabha,** who alters greed into discriminating wisdom, and **Amogasiddhi,** who perfects envy and jealousy into all-achieving wisdom. These statues, also known as Adi Buddhas, can be distinguished by their hand gestures (mudras).

»Borobudur« is presumably an abbreviation of the Sanskrit name Bhumisambharabhudra, which means »mountain of the virtues of the ten levels of the Bodhisattvas«.

A total of 72 stupas each conceal a Buddha statue

This puts the structure of Borobudur into the tradition of Mahayana Buddhism, where **compassion becomes a central category of faith.** Bodhisattvas are those who aspire to enlightenment for the benefit of all sentient beings and who go through the ten steps of spiritual development.

It is traditional to walk around the sacred site in a clockwise direction.

After Borobudur

All travel agencies on Bali offer services such as one-day excursions (with a flight to Yogyakarta in the early morning and a return flight after sunset) or multi-day trips. If at all possible, try to stay several days and enjoy central Java. **Yogyakarta,** 40km/25mi from Borobudur, is a pulsating town of artisans with lots of attractions and stylish accommodation options. In addition, this gives visitors the chance of accessing Borobudur early in the morning when it opens, and to experience the sunrise from here.

Around this sacred site there are a few smaller Buddhist monasteries as well as lots of Hindu temples. The highlight of a visit to Borobudur is spending a night at the **Amanjiwo Resort** (Magelang, tel. 02 93 78 83 33, www.aman-resorts. com). It is not just perfectly nestled into the fascinating volcanic landscape, it also reflects the architectural style of Borobudur with its pale stone columns, lattices and arcades.

The **MesaStila Wellness Retreat** (Magelang, tel. 02 98 59 63 33, www.mesahotelsandresorts.com/ mesastila) is situated not far from Yogyakarta. It was a coffee plantation in the early 19th century and is by far the most attractive accommodation. Guests staying in the plantation villas with their four-poster beds and antiques will have views of the lavish vegetation and enjoy the cultural (music) events in the afternoon as well as the five o'clock tea.

Tour 1 # In the Centre of Bali

Start and Finish: Denpasar   Duration: 1 day
Length: approx. 220km/137mi

This day trip is probably the most beautiful tour that can be taken on Bali. It leads you through fascinating landscapes with lively villages and hospitable inhabitants; moreover, it touches some of the greatest sights on the island. Get an early start!

Enchanting landscape

From ❶**Denpasar,** first take the road to Gilimanuk, turning right after about 40km/25mi at the village of Antosari and heading for Seririt. Leaving ❷**Antosari**, the road runs through a landscape of extraordinary charm. On many places along the way, the winding

mountain road opens up to surprising vistas of artistically arranged rice terraces. The villages in which the rice farmers live are lined up only a few miles apart. ❸**Pupuan**, the next largest town, is known as the centre of vegetable cultivation. Besides its beautiful setting, it has no special tourist sights, so it is best to continue on to the northern edge of the island and Seririt. Turning off here in the direction of ❹**∗∗Singaraja** will bring you – at around noon – to the island's second largest city with the well-known Gedong Kirtya Library. A couple of restaurants in the city centre are to be recommended. About halfway to Lake Bratan, it is possible to take a detour to see the beautiful ❺**∗Gitgit Waterfall. After approx. 15km/9mi the road arrives at** ❻**∗∗Lake Bratan, which** nestles in a gorgeous setting in the midst of an unspoilt tropical landscape. **Pura Ulun Danu** temple, appearing on its western shore, can also be seen by taking a boat around it. If there is still time, **Bedugul** is worth a visit. After taking a look at the wonderfully laid-out botanical garden, head off again, driving south. The rest of the route depends on how much time is left. If you leave Bedugul around 3pm, it is still early enough to choose the route described next before heading back to Denpasar. Or, as an alternative, why not end the trip with a visit to the ❼*monkey forest of Sangeh, which is around 10km/6mi from Mengwi.

The somewhat more time-consuming alternative makes its way via ❽**Tabanan through a lavish jungle landscape to the temple complex of ❾**Pura Luhur Batukau at the foot of the mountain of the same name. Drive south from Bedugul via Pacung to the turning on Road 2 (40km/25mi), then head west towards Tabanan to get to the sprawling temple complex on a good road 28km/17mi further north. Tabanan itself is known for having one of the best gamelan orchestras on Bali. From here, the 23km/14.3mi stretch back to ❶**Denpasar is covered quickly.

MARCO POLO TIP

Don't miss!   Insider Tip

- Banjar: stop at a Buddhist monastery and the hot springs of Air Panas
- Wonderful walks near Lake Tamblingan and Lake Bayan to the south of Gitgit Waterfall
- Picturesque Blayu (south of Sangeh) also has a monkey forest and the small »monkey temple« Pura Alas Kedaton
- Kerambitan: traditional Balinese palaces were transformed into hotels just a few kilometres west of Tabanan

The Southeast

Tour 2

Start: Denpasar
Finish: Amlapura
Length: 140km/90mi

(there and back)
Duration: 1 day

The day trip described below leads into the eastern part of Bali. Along the way are some major sights and places to shop.

Set out from ❶**Denpasar on the road heading east in the direction of Celuk and Sukawati. Enticing gold and silversmith shops line the main road passing through **Celuk**. The town of ❷Sukawati is reached after about 17km/10.5mi. There are numerous shops here offering arts and crafts, but the town itself has little to see. There is an »art market« in the village centre, though, where the prices are mostly lower than in the tourist centres around Denpasar.

The route continues through a varied landscape before coming to **Gianyar** and, after another 13km/8mi, to the city of ❸**Klung-

Shopping and bathing

distances in km (1km = 0,62 mi)

5 km

©BAEDEKER

kung. Here, the courtroom, Kerta Gosa, is certainly worth taking a look at. After Klungkung, the road turns again toward the sea and follows the coastline after Kusamba. The ❹**Goa Lawah** shrine cave is located right next to the road. There are thousands upon thousands of bats at the cave's entrance.

It is only a few kilometres from here to ❺**Candi Dasa**, the tourist centre of the eastern part of the island, which you should reach about lunchtime. The route continues from Candi Dasa through small villages to ❻** Amlapura**. At first, the road runs along the ocean shore, but then it turns inland, in places winding over hills and occasionally offering nice views. There is a major sight in Amlapura, formerly Karangasem, which should not be missed: the princely palace of Puri Agung Kangingan, with beautiful pavilions set in a marvellous park.

Only a few miles outside of Amlapura are the princely baths of **Tirthagangga**, an inviting place to take a refreshing swim. In clear weather the volcano Gunung Agung, Bali's highest mountain at 3142m/ 10,308ft, can be seen in the island's interior.

! **MARCO ⊕ POLO TIP**

Recommended detours   Insider Tip

- Celuk, Batuan and Mas near Sukawati are noted for arts and crafts, in particular the production of jewellery, painting and woodcarving.
- It is only a few miles from Amlapura to the fishing village of Ujung with its impressive, newly-restored water palace set in the middle of a beautiful park. A tour to the east point of the island is wonderful, but beware: before attempting the drive it is advisable to enquire about the current condition of the road.

The Island Tour

Start and Finish: Denpasar   Duration: 2–3 days
Length: approx. 400km/250mi

A tour of the whole of Bali is only recommended for people interested in seeing the less exciting western part of the island. The »only« sight worth seeing in this area is the Bali Barat National Park. However, there are no roads passable for vehicles inside the Park's grounds.

FIRST DAY

Leave ❶****Denpasar** in a northwesterly direction heading for Gilimanuk. About 15km/9mi beyond the two villages of Sempidi and Lukluk, where there are a couple of brightly painted and richly decorated temples to be seen, you will arrive at the town of **Kapal** with the two temples Pura Desa and Pura Puseh. There are some shops along the main road offering sacral figures cast in cement.

It is only 7km/4mi from Kapal to ❷****Tabanan**, the administrative centre of the district of the same name. The route leads through a varied landscape that gradually climbs to the north of the island. The town itself offers no sights to speak of, though there are more to be seen in the surrounding area.

A worthwhile detour is to the small village of ****Kerambitan**, located in the direction of the sea, with the former princely residences of Puri Gede and Puri Anyar. There is an unusually beautiful hotel in Puri Gede that is, however, almost always fully booked because of its limited number of rooms.

The road now leads further westward along the coast to ❸****Negara**, on the way passing the little town of Pulukan, where beautiful beaches are inviting places to take a short bathing break. A few kilometres further lies Negara, which is known less for its sights than for the water-buffalo races that take place here annually in November. If you just happen to visit the village at that time, it is naturally worth staying a little longer.

During the drive, the ocean is almost a constant companion on the left-hand side, while ❹****Bali Barat National Park** stretches out to the right. The main office of the park administration, which issues visiting permits for the park and collects the entrance fees, has been set up just outside of Gilimanuk near Cecik. **Gilimanuk** has next to no sights of note. It is worth a short stop though to observe the bustling activity in the harbour, where the ferries to and from Java arrive and depart. The road between Gilimanuk and ❺**Terima** is the only

Between the ocean and the National Park

passable road through the Bali Barat National Park. It is worth driving slowly along this short stretch, taking time to absorb the extraordinarily beautiful landscape.

Further along the way to Singaraja is the village of oPemuteran, a settlement by the sea that stretches along the road at the foot of blue-grey mountains. There are more than a dozen hotels and guesthouses, from large five-star hotels to individual villas and basic accommodation with just a few rooms right on the crescent-shaped beach with its dark shimmer that comes from the lava. It is predominantly Germans who enjoy the Pondok Sari, a hotel decorated wholly in the Balinese style. Its (German) owners have lived on Bali for decades. Adjoining the well-run hotel and spa is a Werner Lau diving school, a name that fills divers on the island with confidence. A boat will take divers to a number of outstanding dive sites, but it is possible to experience the rich fish stocks and coral gardens just as easily with only a snorkel and some fins. Off the coast of Permuteran lies the island of Menjangan, which is part of Bali Barat National Park and measures around 24sq km/9sq mi; its underwater world is exciting even to experienced divers.

MARCO POLO TIP

! Don't miss… _Insider Tip_

- Makam Jayaprana hill near Terima offers a fantastic view of Java, the Menjangan islands and Gilimanuk.
- Plan to take a break on the way to Singaraja on the tranquil, exquisite sandy beach of Pantai Gondol.
- Some 25km/15mi beyond Singaraja, the coastal road runs past the curious temple of Pura Ponjok Batu. Approx. 3km/2mi further south around 20 temples provide a good reason to visit the mountain village of Sembiran.

The route leads through the well-developed tourist area of **Lovina Beach** just outside Singaraja. There are rows and rows of hotels, restaurants and shops here. ❻**Singaraja** was the seat of the colonial government during the Dutch occupation, and as such the capital of Bali. In order to have enough time to visit the island's second-largest city, it is worthwhile finding accommodation in Singaraja. Alternatively, stay at Lovina Beach and drive into the city from there.

SECOND DAY

Highlights in and around Amlapura

Providing you spent the night in Singaraja or at Lovina Beach, get an early start on the second day. There are two reasons for this: firstly, to watch the island come to life along the road; and secondly to have enough time to see all the sights in and around Amlapura.

The Art Center in Denpasar offers art, theatre, dance and music

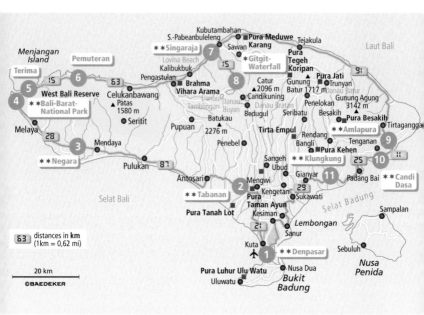

A scenically attractive detour from Singaraja along the Bedugul road leads to ❼*Gitgit Waterfall approx. 30km/18mi further south**. Once back on the coastal road to Amlapura, continue through the agricultural land that includes the largest coffee plantations on Bali. Beyond the fishing village of Tulampen the road leaves the coast and finally reaches ❽**Amlapura**. Amlapura (formerly Karangasem) was badly damaged during the last eruption of Gunung Agung on 17 March 1963. New, modern and functional buildings were constructed on the ruins of the old town. In some places, old soot-blackened walls and houses that have not been rebuilt can be discovered, silent witnesses of the devastating natural disaster. The princely palace of Puri Agung Kanginan survived, however: do not miss a tour of the palace or a visit to **Tirthagangga**, the former princely baths.

Although it is only about 40km/25mi from Amlapura to Klungkung is, it is rather a shame to drive quickly through this part of Bali, as the landscape is particularly worth seeing. The road leads through sometimes hilly country which at some spots opens up to reveal fantastic vistas of ocean and landscape.

Just down the road from ❾**Candi Dasa, a place well-developed for tourism,** is the cave temple of **Goah Lawah**, one of the most important shrines on Bali. The tourist buses that head daily to this temple can be recognized even from a distance. The main attraction is the entrance to the cave itself. Thousands upon thousands of bats cling to the bare rock here.

It is only about 10km/6mi from Goah Lawah to ⑩ ✱✱ **Klungkung**, which is mainly famous for the Kerta Gosa courtroom, which in turn is known for its unique wayang-style paintings. After visiting the busy little town, the tour heads back to Denpasar.

SIGHTS FROM A TO Z

Tropical nature, turquoise water, colourful coral reefs, imposing volcanic craters, artistically laid-out rice terraces, impressive Hindu temples and traditional villages – all these facets of Bali await you!

** Amlapura

✦ Q 6 ✦ Q 6

Administrative seat of the district
of Karangasem:
Region: East Bali
Altitude: 2–90m/6–295ft

Distance:
80km/50mi northeast of Denpasar
Population: 30,000

Amlapura (formerly Karangasem), the administrative seat of the district of Karangasem, is Bali's easternmost town and lies at the foot of the Gunung Agung volcano.

History
Amlapura, known prior to 1964 as Karangasem, the same name as the administrative district, played an important role during the years in which the Dutch were attempting to gain a foothold in Bali. While some rulers of the principalities of central Bali resisted the impending occupation, the rajas of Karangasem agreed terms with the occupying forces, leaving an exposed flank on the eastern part of the island. The Dutch were thus able to sail as far as Sanur on the south coast and attack the defiant princes of Gianyar and Badun near their capitals. Karangasem did not go unrewarded: it became one of the wealthiest towns in Bali and the raja retained his power. Almost all

Amlapura

TOURIST INFORMATION
Government Cultural & Tourism Office
Jl. Diponegoro
Amlapura
Tel. 03 63 2 11 96

GETTING THERE
Leaving Denparar, head to Sakah, then turn right towards Blahbatuh and continue to Klungkung; drive along the coast past Candi Dasa. There are several buses a day that run between Denpasar and Kereneng.

WHERE TO EAT
There are basic but good restaurants around the station and bus terminal.

WHERE TO STAY
Losmen Lahar Mas £
Jl. Gatot Subroto 1
Tel. 03 63 2 13 45
20 inexpensive and basic rooms – some of them have lovely views of paddy fields.

Tirta Ayu £££
Waterpalace, Tirthagangga
(6 km/4mi northwest)
Tel. 03 63 2 25 03
www.hoteltirtagangga.com
Unique situated between rice terraces and lavish gardens, the former water palace has been transformed into a guesthouse with five rooms in the Bali style. The restaurant Tirta Ayu serves international and Balinese cuisine.

The palace complex Puri Agung Kanginan was built in the late 19th century for the princes of Karangasem

of the city's buildings were destroyed during the **eruption of Gunung Agung volcano in 1963**. They, well as the main roads linking the town to the rest of the island, have since been restored.

WHAT TO SEE IN AND AROUND AMLAPURA

Although it was partially destroyed by the earthquake accompanying the eruption of the volcano in 1963, the 19th-century royal palace of Puri Agung Kanginan on the road to Ujung is still well worth seeing. The palace consists of three parts. The traditional festivals were held in the first part, the bencingah; in the second is the garden, while in the third and innermost section are the residential buildings of the princely family. The palace is entered through a gate on a square foundation, guarded by two lions. A second gate to the right of where the entrance fee is paid leads into the garden and then to the actual palace precinct. On the right is an artificial pond with a pavilion (Bale Kambang) and to the left of it is a bale decorated with numerous **scenes from the Ramayana**.

There are some notable buildings in the main palace precinct. The Bale London not only has richly carved doors and well preserved or restored paintings on the outer walls and inside (a leaflet about the

*Puri Agung Kanginan

Why not enjoy a princely dip in the former Tirthagangga water palace?

paintings is available at the ticket office), but it also keeps the instruments of a gamelan orchestra, which are, however, allowed to be played only in the presence of the raja. Standing next to the Bale London is the Bale Pemandesan, in which the ritual tooth-filing was performed on the raja's children. The Puri Madura, the royal audience hall, also known as the **»Maskerdam«**, can accommodate 150 people. It has been closed since the death (in 1966) of the last occupant, Prince A. A. Angurah Ketut Karangasem. It is possible, however, to look in through the windows.

There are several other buildings outside the palace complex and across the main road, which either belong to Puri Agung or were part of two old palaces (Puri Gede and Puri Kertasura). Some of these structures were also destroyed by earthquakes.

ⓘ daily 9am–6pm, entry: 5000 rupiah

About 6km/3.5mi northwest of Amlapura is the former water palace of Tirtha Gangga (Water of the Ganges). It has been converted into an outdoor swimming-pool, which is open to the public. Have a look at the **beautiful water spouts in the ponds** laid out around 1947 by the last raja of Amlapura, as well as the figures and mythical creatures. The water palace was also severely damaged during the volcanic eruption of 1963. Great care was taken in restoring everything to its original form during reconstruction work.

*Tirtha Gangga

⊙ daily 9am–6pm, entry: 20,000 rupiah

The remains of the **Puri Taman Ujung** water palace, largely destroyed by an earthquake, are located near Ujung, about 5km/3mi along the coast south of Amlapura. The original complex was commissioned by the last raja of Amlapura.

Ujung

The road between ▶Candi Dasa and Amlapura leads through extremely attractive tropical hilly countryside. The area surrounding Amlapura is intensely cultivated, with **rice** growing on numerous terraces (▶p. 19 and MARCOPOLO Insight, p.20 and p.228).

**Landscape

** Bali Barat National Park (West Bali NP)

✳ C 2

Region: West Bali	**Entry:** 25,000 rupiah
Administrative district: Buleleng	
Altitude: sea level	**Area:** approx. 77,000ha/300 sq mi

Almost the whole of the western part of the island of Bali was declared the Bali Barat National Park (West Bali National Park or Taman Nasional Bali Barat) in 1983. A more modestly sized national park had previously been established in the same region by the Dutch.

The last tigers in Bali lived in the area that is now the Bali Barat National Park until about a half century ago. Even today, the huge park is still a refuge for quite a few species, including the indigenous **banteng cattle, as well as for red deer, monkeys and civet cats**.
Among the many species of bird is the Bali mynah, which nests mainly in the northern part of the national park. Having become very rare, it is now a protected species. There are only about 200 individuals left, and the species is in grave danger of extinction within the foreseeable future because, despite all appeals, it is still being

Wild Animal Refuge

Bali Barat National Park

GETTING THERE

To get to Bali Barat National Park, head westwards along the coast from Denpasar. There are good bus and bemo connections from Gilimanuk and Singaraia. However, the park is also accessible from the small town of Terima. The headquarters for the park authority are in Cekik (3km/2mi south of Gilimanuk). Further offices can be found in Labuhan Lalang and Teluk Terima; this is where the park fee has to be paid.

WHERE TO EAT/ WHERE TO STAY

Homestays and Losmen are both available in Gilimanuk. There are some modest accommodation choices near the park authority headquarters. More information is available at:
Indonesian Forestry Service (PHPA)
Bali Barat National Park
Jl. Raya Cekik-Gilimanuk
Cekik 82253
Tel. 03 65 6 10 60

Aneka Bagus ££

Pemuteran Beach
Pemuteran
Tel. 03 62 9 47 98
www.anekahotels.com
Friendly, tropical, cosy: a popular beach hotel in a remote location with 60 rooms, suites and sizable villas in the Bali style; a large seaward-facing pool and an open restaurant.

Doubleyou Home Stay £ – ££

Jl. Raya Gilimanuk-Singaraja
Pemuteran
Tel. 08 13 38 42 70 00

http://www.doubleyoupemuteran.com
The family guesthouse is stated on the main road and therefore in the centre of the village. It has four large and quite comfortable rooms with four-poster beds and air-conditioning. There are lots of inexpensive restaurants in the surrounding area.

Naya Gawana Novus Resort & Spa £££

Banyuwedang
Desa Pejarakan
Gerokpak
Tel. 03 62 9 45 98
www.nayaresorts.com
Synonymous with a unique experience of nature: a boutique hotel with 16 two-storey »Lumbung Suites« (living room on the ground floor, bedroom on the first floor) decorated in a luxurious and purist style with a large sun deck to the sea as well as lovely bathrooms, some of them open, with hot spring water, located at the edge of the national park and in Menjangan Bay.

Pondok Sari ££   Insider Tip

Pemuteran
Tel. 03 62 9 47 38
https://www.pondoksari.com
Lovely bungalows by the sea, surrounded by tropical green. The rooms are equipped with Balinese antiques, four-poster beds and open bathrooms. Some rooms possess a cosy veranda with a daybed. The restaurant serves seafood specialities, Indonesian and international cuisine. There are regular music events and Balinese dances. There is also a diving school.

caught and offered for sale at markets. The great variety of other tropical birds, however, will thrill those with an interest in ornithology.

Those who appreciate an almost unspoiled landscape can undertake walking tours along the (few) trails and paths through this unique wilderness. Most of these are in the northwest part of the national park; the southeast has hardly been developed. There is a 25km/15mi hiking trail around the northwestern Prapat Agung peninsula along which lie several refuges that are a welcome place to stop off, particularly during the wet winter months.

Hiking trails

Lying just off the coast in the extreme northwest of Bali Barat National Park is the uninhabited island (pulau) of Menjangan. It can be reached by boat in about half an hour from **Labuhan Lalang** in the bay of Teluk Terima, where plain lodgings are available. Divers will find a fascinating underwater world here, which even those equipped only with a snorkel and a diving mask can explore.

Island of Menjangan

The fishing village of Pemutaran, situated at the northern edge of the national park, is a fast-growing holiday resort with a beautiful beach, coral reefs and tropical fish. There are good spots for diving and snorkelling as well. Visitors to Menganan Island can spend the night here. In addition, there is a nature reserve for turtles.

Pemutaran

** Bangli

N 6

Administrative seat of the district of Bangli	Distance: 41km/25mi north of Denpasar
Region: Central Bali	
Altitude: 392m/1,286ft	**Population:** 40,000

Bangli, the seat of one of a total of nine administrative districts (kabupaten) in Bali, was once an independent principality. The lower slopes of the Gunung Agung volcano begin not far to the north of the city, but Bangli itself lies at the upper end of the well-irrigated central hill country, making possible productive agriculture. Lake Batur, Bali's largest lake, is also in the district.

Bangli is dominated by the **magnificent backdrop** of Mount Batur, especially impressive in the morning hours. Later in the day, the volcano almost always disappears behind a cloud cap. There are a number of temples in the town worth taking a look at, including five

Bangli

TOURIST INFORMATION
Bangli Tourist Office
Jl. Brigjen Ngurah Rai 30
Tel. 03 66 9 15 37

GETTING THERE
Head northeast from Denpasar via Sukawati to Sakah, then turn right towards
Blahbatuh and continue via Gianyar to
Bangli. There are good regular bus connections on the Denpasar – Kereneng
line. Bemos go from Denpasar to Gianyar; to get to Bangli, change there.

WHERE TO EAT
❶ *Pasar Malam* £
A few good warungs (snack stalls, simple restaurants) can be found at the Pasar

Malam (night market) near the bemo
station; there are also some snack stalls
near the market during the day.

WHERE TO STAY
❶ *Artha Sastra Inn* £
Jl. Merdeka 5
Tel. 03 66 9 11 79
14 very different rooms, some of them
in the old royal palace, some in simple
bungalows. The hotel is located right across from the bus station.

❷ *Bangli Inn* £
Jl. Rambutan 1
Tel. 03 66 9 14 19
Basic, clean accommodation with ten
rooms around a courtyard.

dedicated to the powers of the underworld. A large **market**, where
farmers from all over the surrounding area sell their produce, is held
every third day in the centre of Bangli in front of the raja's palace,
Puri Artha Sastra.

History   The first documentary evidence of the city of Bangli, today **one of
Bali's cultural centres**, dates back to 1204, when a huge religious
festival was celebrated here. Later, Bangli became the capital of an
independent principality, whose rulers, however, never exercised any
great political influence. They sought – when the situation demanded
– protection and counsel from neighbouring regions, namely from
the powerful lords of Klungkung.

WHAT TO SEE IN BANGLI

*Puri Artha
Sastra   The former residence of the princes of Bangli, Puri Artha Sastra, was
converted a few years ago into a small hotel; the young prince himself
is the owner. The bales are decorated with traditional Balinese as well
as Chinese paintings. There are a number of statues and figures from
Hindu mythology on the attractive grounds. Take a look at the large
gate leading into the interior of the palace and the ornate reliefs to
the right and left of it.

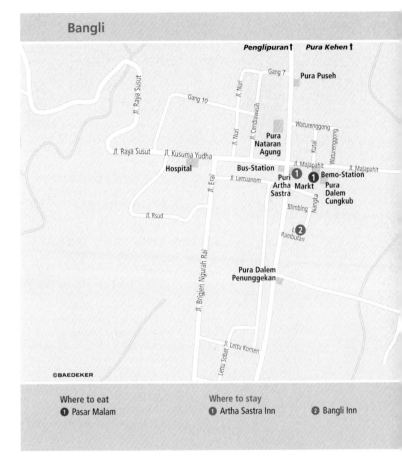

Bangli

Penglipuran ↑   Pura Kehen ↑

Gang 7   Pura Puseh

Jl. Raya Susut

Gang 10

Jl. Nuri

Jl. Cendrawasih

Waturenggong

Jl. Nuri   Pura Nataran Agung

Jl. Raya Susut   Jl. Kusuma Yudha

Kutai   Waturenggong

Hospital   Bus-Station   Jl. Majapahit   Jl. Majapahit

Jl. Erai   Jl. Lettuanom   Puri ❶ ❶ Bemo-Station

Artha Markt   Pura
Sastra   Dalem Cungkub

Blimbing   Nangka

Jl. Rsud

L ❷
Rambutan

Jl. Brigjen Ngurah Rai

Pura Dalem
Penunggekan

Jl. Lettu Konten

Lettu Sobat

©BAEDEKER

Where to eat   **Where to stay**
❶ Pasar Malam   ❶ Artha Sastra Inn   ❷ Bangli Inn

The Pura Kehen (Temple of the Treasury), about 2.5km/1.5mi north of the city centre, is considered to be **one of the most beautiful and is, at the same time, the largest shrine on Bali**. Preserved inside are valuable bronze tablets said to date back to the year 1204 when Bangli was founded. The temple complex itself, built on seven terraces below Bukit Bangli, was founded even earlier, in the 11th century, by the royal priest, Sri Brahma Kemute Ketu. The actual temple is only reached after passing through the first four terraces and a covered gate (candi korung), guarded over by a kala demon, a lion-like mask. To the right is a bale for the musicians of the gamelan orchestra to sit; to the left another bale serves

**Pura Kehen

Pura Kehen

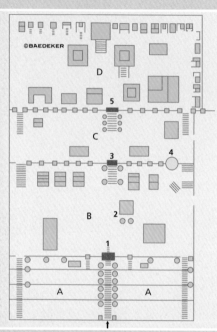

©BAEDEKER

A	four terraces	1	covered gate (candi korung)
B	outer forecourt (jaba sisi)	2	sacred stone (batu kermat)
C	inner forecourt (jaba tengah)	3	split gate (candi bentar)
D	temple interior (jeroan)	4	Waringin tree (kulkul base)
		5	split gate (candi bentar)

as a gathering place for the temple visitors. A sacred stone (batu keramat) can be seen on the way to the second courtyard, which stretches out across yet another terrace. In the two buildings behind the Split Gate (candi bentar) shadow plays are presented during temple festivals (►MARCOPOLO Insight, p.74). In front of the courtyard, the holiest precinct of the temple, pieces of faience of Chinese origin can be seen set in the separating wall. On the front side of the inner courtyard, the side nearest the hill, are a number of merus with varying numbers of tumpangs – the tallest, with eleven tiers, is dedicated to Shiva –, as well as shrines for deities and tugus (stone lanterns which are the abode of gods of lower rank). There is a **splendid view of the whole temple complex** and the mountain scenery from the uppermost terrace of the inner courtyard.

ⓘ daily 8am–5pm, donations requested

The beautiful Pura Nataran temple on Bangli's main street is unfortunately almost always closed. It belongs to the royal family and is their ancestral temple.

Pura Dalem Cungkub On the road running east past Bangli's bemo station is Pura Dalem Cungkub, one of the five underworld temples in Bangli. This temple is also arranged on a number of terraces.

***Pura Dalem Penunggekan** Pura Dalem Penunggekan is on the road in the south of the city leading to Gianyar. It is worth paying it a visit to see its particularly finely worked reliefs. Do not miss the **figures of the witches** on the so-called Flame Gate. The cremation site and a Chinese cemetery are outside the temple.

The Pura Kehen is one of the largest and most important temples on Bali

AROUND BANGLI

The little village of Penglipuran now has a place on many tour orga-
nizers' itineraries. What effect this will have on the fascinating charm
of the village and its 750 or so inhabitants remains to be seen. At any
rate, children and teenagers now stand on the access roads waiting to
guide the tourists through the village once they have paid the obligatory donation and signed the visitors' book. Penglipuran lies a little
way off the road from Bangli to Kintamani in a breathtaking, almost
unspoilt landscape. About 5km/3mi north of Bangli there is a sign
that says **»Traditional Village«** pointing the way. Penglipuran's kampongs, the traditional Balinese family compounds, line the right and
left-hand sides of the road that runs through the village, which is laid

****Penglipu-
ran**

out in a series of terraces. Narrow channels running between the road and the houses serve for waste disposal. The family temples that are a part of each kampong face toward Gunung Agung. At the upper end of the paved road stands the village temple, Pura Desa, an exact copy of a temple in Bayung Gede (near Kintamani, ▶p.209). The older inhabitants of the village in fact claim that their ancestors originally came from Bayung Gede. This suggests that Penglipuran is a more recent settlement.

At the lower end of the road, to the right on the edge of the forest, is another shrine with elaborately worked figures on its base. Letting one of the local children or teenagers act as a guide through Penglipuran usually results in an invitation into one of the family compounds. The villagers are glad to see visitors and give them a friendly greeting everywhere. The inhabitants of Penglipuran live primarily from farming and forestry; some also work as artists.

** Bedugul

L 4

Region: Central Bali	**Distance:**
Administrative district: Tabanan	30km/18.6mi
Population: 2500	south of
Altitude: 1,224m/4,016ft	Singaraja

Lying high in the hills, Bedugul is set in a uniquely stunning and primitive landscape and is the starting point for visiting some special attractions in the surrounding area. Although there is nothing exceptional in Bedugul itself apart from a major vegetable and flower market, a visit to Lake Bratan or an extended stroll through the charmingly arranged botanic gardens are worth the trip.

AROUND BEDUGUL

Lake Bratan Lake Bratan was formed in an extinct volcano and is **surrounded by a superb landscape dominated by the 2020m/6627ft Gunung Bratan. The area and the lake are well developed for tourism; besides swimming, visitors can take out motor boats and go water-skiing.

Pura Ulun Danu A small island is situated near to the village of Candi Kuning on the western shore of Lake Bratan. On it stands the charming Pura Ulun Danu lake temple, which has an unusual feature: to the left of the entrance into the first temple courtyard is a Buddhist **stupa with meditating Buddha figures set in niches in the square base. The

Bedugul

GETTING THERE
The road heads north from Denpasar towards Singaraja (49km/30mi); from there it is another 30km/18mi. There are several good bus connections per day from Denpasar to Ubung and from Singaraja. Bemos are available from Denpasar to Ubung.

GOLF
Bali Handara Country Club
Desa Pancasari-Singaraja
Tel. 03 62 3 42 26 46
www.balihandarakosaido.com
Situated in the crater of an old volcano and surrounded by tropical rainforest, this 18-hole golf course provides unforgettable views of the idyllic Bunyan Lake and the beautiful surroundings. The golf club also has guest bungalows and an outstanding restaurant.

WHERE TO EAT
Strawberry Hill £ £
Jl. Raya Denpasar-Singaraja, Km 48
Tel. 03 68 2 12 65
www.strawberryhillbali.com
The restaurant of the small guesthouse to the south of the town mainly serves classic Balinese dishes: nasi goreng, satay kebabs with peanut sauce and crackers (kroepoek).

Café Teras £ £
Jl. Raya Denpasar-Singaraja, Lempuna (near the golf club)
Tel. 03 62 2 93 12

Japanese, Balinese, Italian: the café in the Japanese style serves pasta specialties on the garden terrace; the chicken curry is also recommended.

Seoul Garden £ £
Jl. Raya Denpasar-Singaraja, Lempuna
Tel. 03 62 2 99 20
Predominantly Korean cuisine (fish specialities, vegetarian dishes) in a glazed conservatory or in the garden: Balinese specialties are also available.

WHERE TO STAY
Green Villa £
Jl. Pancasari-Baturiti (Jl. Bedugul)
Candi Kuning
Tel. 03 61 26 20 22
The small bungalow complex (7 rooms) is located on the hills on the northwest side of the lake, in a small tropical garden. Lake views are available from the balconies and the terrace; the rooms have cooking facilities.

Saranam Eco Resort £ £ £
Jl. Raya Pacung Baturiti
Tel. 03 68 2 10 38
https://www.saranamresort.com
35 rooms Hotel complex beautifully integrated into the landscape (with a pool, library, café and restaurant), between rice fields and woods in a valley that shimmers in every shade of green. Meditation courses are held on a regular basis. There is nearby fishing.

stupa is evidence of the adoption of principles of the Buddhist faith by the Hindus. The Hindu shrine itself, best viewed in the morning when its scenic backdrop is at its most impressive, has a three-tiered meru dedicated to Dewi Danu, the goddess of the sea and of lakes.

The Pura Ulun Danu enjoys a picturesque location on the western shore of Lake Bratan

Another meru with eleven tumpangs is probably dedicated to Dewa Pucak Manu.

❶ daily 7am–5pm, entry 30,000 rupiah

**Botanic gardens

Spread out over an area of some 160ha/400 acres above Lake Bratan are the **Eka Karya Botanic Gardens** (Kebun Raya). Paths and hiking trails through the gardens are especially enticing for visitors with an interest in botany. Growing within the gardens are trees, shrubs and plants from various regions of Asia. There is also a herbarium with some specimens of tropical flowers. Several spots in the park offer excellent views of Lake Bratan and the surrounding hills.

❶ daily 8am–6pm, entry: 20.000 rupiah, www.kebunrayabali.com

*Lake Tamblingan

Leave Bedugul heading north and drive through the little mountain village of Wanagiri. About 11km/7mi past Lake Buyan is a turning to the village of Asah Munduk on the shores of Lake Tamblingan, situated in the midst of a fascinating tropical landscape. The shrine of Pura Gubug Tamblingan on its shores, the ancestral temple of the rajas of Buleleng, should not be missed.

** Bedulu

M 7

Region: Central Bali
Administrative district: Badung
Population: 2500

Altitude:
280m/919ft
Distance:
6km/3.8mi south of Ubud

Bedulu was the centre of the oldest principality on the island of Bali. It lies in the middle of an agricultural area that gradually ascends to the hill country of central Bali. Over the course of time, Bedulu has grown and merged with the neighbouring town of Pejeng.

There are no sights of particular interest in Bedulu itself. There is more to see in the near vicinity and in neighbouring Pejeng (▶p.152). A four-headed figure of a deity can be seen on the main intersection when passing through.

AROUND BEDULU

About 1km/0.6mi south of Bedulu is the spring sanctuary of Yeh Pulu with a 27m/89ft-long and up to 2m/6ft-high rock **relief**, believed to be the oldest in Bali, showing scenes of everyday life; archaeologists, however, are divided as to the purpose and meaning of this relief. Some pictures could possibly represent the god Krishna or relate the legends woven around his many manifestations. The life-size figures stand out well against their background and probably date back to the 14th or 15th century.

**Yeh Pulu

❶ daily 7am–6pm, entry: 3000 rupiah

It is only about 2km/1mi from Bedulu to the famous Goa Gajah Elephant Cave, which has been venerated by Hindus since the first millennium (and possibly by Buddhists even earlier). The cave was discovered in 1923 and the bathing area in front of it was first excavated only in 1954. Actually, it is a **spring shrine** that gained its name from the cave's entrance, which resembles the head of an elephant (there have never been elephants on Bali), although the cave does contain a 1m/3.3ft-high figure with four arms representing the elephant god Ganesha, one of Shiva's sons, which is venerated.

**Goa Gajah (Elephant Cave)

Bedulu

GETTING THERE
Leave Denpasar via Sukawati and Sakah; shortly before Ubud, near Teges, turn right. There are good bus and bemo connections from Denpasar-Kerenang.

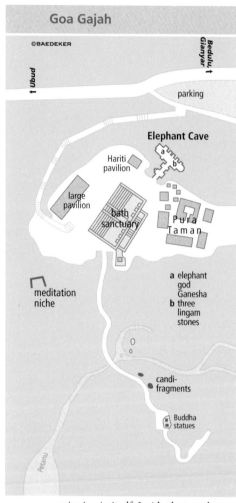

Goa Gajah

©BAEDEKER

↑ Ubud

Bedulu, Gianyar ↑

parking

Elephant Cave

Hariti pavilion

large pavilion

bath sanctuary

Pura Taman

a

b

meditation niche

a elephant god Ganesha
b three lingam stones

candi-fragments

Buddha statues

Petanu

Rising up to the right of it on a stone base are three lingams symbolizing Shiva in three of his manifestations as Brahma, Vishnu and as Shiva himself. Grouped around each lingam are eight smaller phallic symbols representing the eight guardians of the world. One of the bathing basins in front of the cave was for men and the other for women; the purpose of the middle one is unknown – it was possibly intended for use by members of the priestly caste for ritual ablutions. The waterspouts set into the walls are particularly elaborate. Be sure to **take a torch** along when touring the Elephant Cave (they are not available at the site).

❶ daily 9am–4pm, entry: 30,000 rupiah

Just 1km/0.5mi from the elephant cave one of the island's largest temples: **Pura Samuan Tiga**, built in the 10th century, is dedicated to the Hindu trinity, Brahma, Vishnu and Shiva. The impressive main gate is well worth viewing in itself. Inside the temple are several holy shrines holding figures that are highly venerated.

**Archaeological museum

At the eastern end of Bedulu on the road to Pejeng is the well-stocked Gedong Arca Purbakala Archaeological Museum.
A total of **53 tuff sarcophagi** of varying sizes, thought to date from around 300 BC, are kept in the inner courtyard. They were found at 37 different locations in Bali in the early 1970s and gathered to-

When the Goa Gajah was discovered the daemon's grimace at the entrance was thought to be an elephant head

gether here in Bedulu. Some of them show signs of damage, possibly caused by grave robbers or unprofessional excavation. The dead were not laid to rest in the sarcophagi in the traditional Western manner, but in a crouching position. Perhaps this is a symbolic representation of the eternal cycle of birth, death and rebirth, whereby the deceased is then reborn from a fetal position. The sarcophagus found at Taman Bali (near Bangli), fashioned in the **form of two turtles on top of each other**, a symbol of the underworld, is particularly impressive. Amazingly, the head of the lower turtle bears human facial features.

A number of pieces of jewellery, implements and tools dating from both the Stone Age and the Bronze Age are on display. The finds are for the most part not the result of regular excavations, but were found by chance. Do not miss the miniature stupas discovered in the vicinity of Bedulu and Pejeng, thought to date from the Buddhist period in Bali (8th–10th century).

❶ daily 8am–3pm, entry: free (donation requested)

On the left-hand side of the road about 200m/220yds further on down is Pura Kebo Edan, the »Temple of the Crazy Water Buffalo«. In its centre is a **colossal 3.6m/12ft-high figure.** It possibly represents the giant Bhairava and stands on the back of a figure that pro-

*Pura Kebo Edan

bably represents the god of death, Yama. A bull and a giant demon were added to the right and left. On the bales are numerous figures and fragments, some displaying terrifying grimacing faces.

It is possible that the religious rites of the Tantric cult were celebrated here, which culminated in extravagant orgies.

**The Moon of Pejeng in Pura Panataran Sasih

The most significant attraction in the temple of Pura Panataran Sasih, located on the road between Bedulu and Pejeng, is **the biggest kettledrum in the world**, also called the »Moon of Pejeng«. Strictly speaking, it is less a drum and more a gong, because what is struck is a bronze disc. The instrument has a diameter of about 140cm/55in, though it must be admitted that determining the size of this extremely elaborately decorated gong, with its spiralling bands of ornamentation, stylized faces and Hindu symbols, is difficult, because it is hung high up in a bale and is partially hidden from view. While the age of the gong has been established (Dongsong culture, c300 BC), in spite of intensive research it has not yet been possible to determine its place of origin or the meaning of the decoration. The local people are of the opinion, however, that the »Moon of Pejeng« was originally one of thirteen moons in the sky that fell down and landed precisely at the spot where the temple stands today. What's more, the gong is allegedly a threat to life and limb, and the following dreadful story is told in an attempt to substantiate this. The night the moon fell to earth, it landed in the branches of a tree and its bright moonlight disturbed a band of thieves, who were out to steal precious and sacred objects. When one of the thieves climbed up the tree and urinated on it to extinguish its light, the moon exploded, killing the thief. The moon then fell to the ground, in the form of a bronze gong, as the »Moon of Pejeng«.

** Besakih

O 5

Region: Central Bali	**Distance:**
Administrative district:	40km/25mi
Karangasem	northwest of
Altitude: 980–1011m/3215–3317ft	Candi Dasa

The expansive, terraced temple complex, its structures built mostly of dark lava stone, may not seem that impressive – unless it happens to be the time of the annual temple festival when tens of thousands of the faithful flock here from all parts of the island. Bali may have more colourful and more elaborately decorated temple sites, but, for the Hindus, Pura Besakih is the »mother of all temples«.

★★ PURA BESAKIH (THE MOTHER TEMPLE)

Pura Besakih was probably founded as early as the 8th century, **possibly as a Buddhist shrine**, since at the time Bali had not yet been converted to Hinduism. Legend tells of a Shiva priest named Sri Markhadeya who is said to have erected a shrine here. The main parts of today's temple were most likely built by the ruler Kesari Warmadewa in the 10th century. *History*

Cars are banned from the wide road leading uphill to the temple site. Shops selling religious items and souvenirs line either side of the road as far as the first of the **smaller family temples**. It is not only the old royal houses which maintain a temple here; clans and village communities have also set up their shrines and altars here to strengthen their bonds with this sacred site, establishing Besakih as the **symbol of the Hindu-Dharma religion**, which was created out of the fusion of Hinduism with the ancient beliefs of the original inhabitants of Bali The number of shrines will probably increase in the future: when a family achieves a certain importance it erects its own ancestral temple within Pura Besakih. Each of the three main shrines into which the temple complex is divided has smaller satellite temples grouped around it. They stand for the Hindu triad: the creator of the world, Brahma, Vishnu as life-giver and preserver, and Shiva, the destroyer and bringer of death. The spiritual centre is the **Pura Penataran Agung**, in which Sangyang Widi Wasa, an incarnation of Shiva, is venerated. It stands at the end of a 1km/0.5mi processional road. A fairly steep flight of steps guarded by figures from the Indian epic »Mahabharata« (▶p.77) leads to a split gate opening into the interior of the temple complex, through which only Hindus may enter. Inside is the most important shrine of this site, the three-seated lotus throne. It is possible to take a look into the first temple precinct where there are a number of secular buildings in adjoining walled courtyards in which offerings are prepared for the great temple festival. If a temple festival is scheduled to take place in the next few days, it is possible to observe these preparations. Otherwise, **non-Hindus** only have the possibility of viewing the shrine from the outside, which is **quite easy because of the low surrounding wall**. The princely families or *Temple site*

their descendants are responsible for the maintenance of the shrines in the Pura Panataran Agung: the rajas of Bangli for the offertory site for Vishnu, those of Karangasem (Amlapura) for that for Brahma,

> **!** *Temple etiquette* Insider Tip
>
> **MARCO ◉ POLO TIP**
>
> Visiting a temple in a mini skirt or shorts is not desired. Help is at hand in the form of cloths (selendang) that the temple guards give visitors to wrap around their waist. However, it is better to bring your own.

** »*Mother of all Temples*«

Situated on the southwest flanks of the sacred volcano Gunung Agung, which is considered the seat of the gods and the centre of the universe, is the temple complex Pura Besakih, which is venerated in Bali as the »mother of all temples«. It is not, however, just one single temple. Rather, it is a terraced site with more than 30 individual complexes with a total of more than 200 different buildings. Depicted here is the centre of the site of Besakih, the Pura Penataran Agung.

❶ Split Gate

To get to the first of five temple districts, which are separated from each other by walls of differing heights made of lava rock, visitors must take a wide staircase and walk through a »split gate« (candi bentar). To the left and right of the gate is a bell tower (kulkul); it is possible to see the courtyard from here – it is not open to non-Hindus.

❷ Main courtyard

The second temple district, accessed via a »covered gate«, features the honorary seat and several bale where the village elders gather and where gamelan orchestras perform during festivals and sacrificial gifts are prepared. The courtyard is dominated by an eleven and a nine-storey meru.

❸ Honorary seat

The most significant temple of the entire complex of Besakih is a lotus throne (sanggar agung) with three seats, which serves as the honorary seat for Sangyang Widi Wase in his manifestation as the Hindu trinity Brahma – Vishnu – Shiva during the Bhatara Turun Kabeh.

❹ Inner courtyards

There are several bale on the higher terraces that are reserved for priestly rituals as well as several three to eleven-step merus, shrines for gods, ancestors and spirits.

❺ Temple treasure

The temple treasures, such as old wooden inscriptions, are kept in what is known as the Kehen.

Once a year many faithful visit the temple complex for the Bhatara Turun Kabeh, when all Balinese gods gather here.

Merus are towers with pagodas for roofs. They symbolize the mythical Mount Meru, the seat of all Hindu gods.

The views from the Split Gate of the surrounding landscape is attractive and expansive.

©BAEDEKER

Adorned stone figures flank the steep steps at the entrance to the temple.

Besakih

GETTING THERE

Head northeast from Denpasar to Klungkung and from there continue on the road that turns north to Rendang and then on to Besakih (approx. 63km/39mi). Regular bus connections from Denpasar to Kereneng run all the way to Klunung; from there bemos are available. It is not a good idea to take a bemo all the way from Denpasar, however; there is a good connection from Klungkung and Rendang (sometimes only with a chartered bemo).

FESTIVALS

Bhatara Turun Kabeh Festival

According to legend, all Balinese gods come down from the heights of Gunung Agung once a year and live in the temple of Besakih. The people of Bali celebrate this event as the Turun Kabeh festival (March/April)

Eka Dasa Rudra Festival Insider Tip

Apart from the annual temple anniversary (Odalan festival), the Pura Besakih celebrates the Eka Dasa Rudra Festival every hundred years. It is the most important Balinese temple festival. It was celebrated most recently in 1979, therefore outside of the usual rhythm. There was an important reason for that: the volcano Gunung Agung erupted during the preparations for the actual date in 1963. Up until that date the volcano was believed to be extinct. The severe eruptions that went on for several days claimed the lives of more than 2500 people and destroyed many villages of the surrounding area. The festival was then only hosted in 1979.

SIGHTS

Pura Besakih is very touristy and would-be guides veritably besiege visitors. The temple complex is open daily 8am–7pm; the entry fee is 30,000 rupiah per person. Visitors are only allowed to enter the complex in the company of a guide, whose organization demands 20–40 US$ as a donation (20 US$ = approx. 190,000 rupiah); this donation can be negotiated down to 30,000–40,000 rupiah. There is an 800m/880yd avenue lined by souvenir shops leading from the car park to the temple site.

Countless areas of the temple are not normally open to non-believers (especially during festival preparations). However, there is a well-signposted route through the complex, albeit one visitors are not allowed to stray from.

Where to eat/where to stay

Inexpensive and basic (dormitory) accommodation, known as losmen, for travellers who are not that fussed about creature comforts, can be found outside of Besakih on the road to Menang. Some such options are located close to the temple entrance near the souvenir stalls. Visitors will also find several basic warungs there, which sell inexpensive and tasty Indonesian dishes.

and the rajas of Klungkung for that for Shiva. The other two main shrines on either side of the Pura Penataran Agung are, to the west, the **Pura Batu Madeg**, dedicated to Vishnu, and, to the east, the **Pura Dangin Kreteg**, in which Brahma is venerated. On special holidays the shrines are decorated in the symbolic colours of the gods; red for Brahma, white for Shiva and black for Vishnu.

✶✶ THE ASCENT OF GUNUNG AGUNG

Gunung Agung, **the island's highest mountain** (3142m/10,308ft) and the abode of Shiva, can be climbed from several sides, e.g. from Besakih, from Amlapura (about 6 hours) and from Sebudi (near Selat; about 7 hours).

Strenuous mountain tour

The following is a description of the southwestern route from Besakih. Climbers need to be in good physical condition because there are no mountain huts in which to spend the night, meaning the ascent and descent must be made in one day (it can get quite cold during the night and early morning). Sturdy footwear, weatherproof clothing, sufficient food and water are essential. It can be extremely dangerous to wander off the designated paths in this volcanic area; even experienced climbers should take along a guide who knows the terrain. Get as early a start as possible for the ascent of Gunung Agung, preferably around 2am. Even a practised mountain hiker needs between six and nine hours for the ascent alone and at least another five for the descent. The trail begins at the main temple of Pura Besakih and leads through a dense forest, relatively level at first but becoming much steeper later. After about five hours, a rock face is reached. It is known as the Kori Agung and is considered to be the **gateway to the summit region**. It is about two to three hours from this point to the crater's rim, from whose inner wall there are abrupt drops of up to 100m/330ft. The even more strenuous ascent id rewarded by **fantastic views** of large parts of the island.

✶✶ Bukit Badung

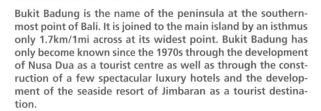

✦ K/L 10/11

Region: Southern Bali
Administrative district: Badung
Altitude: 0–200m/656ft

Distance:
15km/9.3mi south of
Denpasar

Bukit Badung is the name of the peninsula at the southernmost point of Bali. It is joined to the main island by an isthmus only 1.7km/1mi across at its widest point. Bukit Badung has only become known since the 1970s through the development of Nusa Dua as a tourist centre as well as through the construction of a few spectacular luxury hotels and the development of the seaside resort of Jimbaran as a tourist destination.

WHAT TO SEE ON BUKIT BADUNG

The small fishing village of Jimbaran lies on the narrow isthmus lin-   Jimbaran
king the Bukit Badung peninsula with the rest of Bali. For years there was no tourism here to speak of, despite the beautiful beach of
white sand. In recent years, however, some of the most luxurious
hotel complexes on the island have been built in the surrounding
area.

Garuda Wisnu Kencana Cultural Park in Ungasan is a large scale   Ungasan
cultural project with galleries, restaurants, shops and a viewing platform. All sorts of cultural events are staged here in the huge plaza and
the amphitheatre; the focus is to be the world's largest statue, an almost 150m/500ft-high representation of Vishnu riding on the mythical bird deity, Garuda. Because of the concerns of religious dignita-
ries, this monument currently consists of three separate statues, the
20m/66ft »Statue of Wisnu«, the 18m/59ft »Statue of Garuda« and
the »Statue of Wisnu's Hands«, which still have to be stacked and
connected.
❶ daily 8am–10pm, entry: 60,000 rupiah, www.gwk-culturalpark.com

The **sea temple** of Pura Luhur Ulu Watu, near the small village of   **Pura Luhur
Pecatu, sits high atop a cliff that drops abruptly down to the sea. The   Ulu Watu
temple can be reached via the
road branching off in a southwes-
terly direction from the Jalan Bypass (around Denpasar); it is then
only 4km/2.5mi from Pecatu.

Pura Luhur Ulu Watu is considered to be one of the most important temples on Bali. It enjoys the status of a state temple
(sadkahyangan). The shrine is
dedicated to the goddess Rudra
(a manifestation of Shiva), and
the temple site faces the sea. The
richly decorated gates made of
coral stone are particularly notable. There is a **magnificent
view of the sea** from the entrance of the temple, the powerful
surf at high tide battering the heavily eroded cliffs, which are over
80m/260ft high.
❶ Daily 8am–6pm, entry: 30,000 rupiah

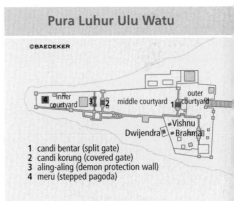

Pura Luhur Ulu Watu

©BAEDEKER

inner courtyard · middle courtyard · outer courtyard · Vishnu · Dwijendra · Brahma

1 candi bentar (split gate)
2 candi korung (covered gate)
3 aling-aling (demon protection wall)
4 meru (stepped pagoda)

A relaxing siesta on the beach at Nusa Dua

Bukit Badung

TOURIST INFORMATION
Badung Government Tourism Office
Jl. S. Parman, Renon
Tel. 03 61 22 23 87

GETTING THERE
Take the Jalan Bypass (approx. 21km/13mi) from Denpasar; it is about 15km/9.3mi from Kuta and Legian, and about 23km/14.3mi from Sanur. There are regular bus services from Denpasar to Tegal; bemos can be found along the road between Denpasar and Nusa Dua. Registered taxis drive between Denpasar, Kuta, Legian and Sanur. Taxi drivers often offer to switch off their meters (particularly in the evening and at night) and name a »fixed« price – presenting a great opportunity for a little haggling.

SHOPPING
Bali Collection
Shoppers can get brand names like Prada, Armani and Versace at quite low prices in the Nusa Dua Tourist Complex. Free shuttle buses ply between the hotels and the shopping complex in the midst of a large park with 150 boutiques, including a good variety of supermarkets, department stores and handicraft shops such as the popular batik shop, Galeri Keris. In addition, dozens of restaurants, cafés and bistros are open late into the night.
(www.bali-collection.com).

WHERE TO EAT
Lotus Garden
£ £ £
Nusa Dua, Jl. Ngurah Rai
Tel. 03 61 77 33 78

On the town's main road, yet still cosy and quiet. Sit surrounded by ponds and water features. Mainly Mediterranean cuisine.

Jimbaran Seafood Restaurants
£ – £ £ £
Jl. Four Seasons, Muaya Beach
Jimbaran Bay
The more than two dozen seafood restaurants get very busy after sunset. Candles and lights exude a romantic atmosphere; diners can hear the lapping of the waves and feel the sand beneath their feet, while ordering the fish, crabs, lobster and calamari that are displayed on ice right by the tables or near the entrance and sold by weight. They are served with starters and salads as well as fruit at the end of the meal.

Kendi Kuning
£ £ £
Jl. Segara Samuh, Benoa
Tel. 03 61 77 57 20
https://www.facebook.com/kendikuning
Walk along the beach from the Nusa Dua hotels to get here. This place serves delicious fish dishes.

Intan Sari Café
£ £
Jl. Four Seasons (Muaya Beach)
Jimbaran
Tel. 03 61 70 52 05
One of many inexpensive restaurants right on the beach that is pariticularly romantic after sunset. The freshly caught fish, crabs, lobster, calamari and mussels are sold by weight and served grilled or fried with salad and rice.

WHERE TO STAY
St. Regis
£ £ £ £
Kawasan Pariwisata Nusa Dua 56
Nusa Dua; Tel. 03 61 8 47 81 11
www.stregis.com/bali
A hotel with six-star luxury whose out-standing restaurant Kayuputi is run by the renowned sommelier Harald Wies-mann.

Banyan Tree Ungasan
£ £ £ £
Jl. Melasti, Banjar Kelod, Ungasan
Tel. 03 61 3 00 70 00
www.banyantree.com
These guest villas of the Asian dream hotel are located on a cliff at Bali's sou-thernmost tip. Snow-white daybeds by the big pool are a fabulous place to kick back and relax. The bar and the restau-rant have spectacular views of the wild cliffs.

The Laguna Resort & Spa
Nusa Dua £ £ £ £
Kawasan Pariwisata Nusa Dua Lot N 2
Tel. 03 61 77 13 27
www.luxurycollection.com/bali
Gently curving, bright blue lagoons with light sandy beaches run through the tro-pical garden of the hotel, whose guests can plunge directly into the water from their rooms.

Amanusa Nusa Dua
£ £ £ £
Nusa Dua Jl. Pura Batu Pageh
Ungasan
Tel. 03 61 77 23 33
www.amanresorts.com
Adrian Zecha, the founder of the Aman Resorts, has once again repeated the mi-racle of creating a perfect hotel. In the middle of the park-like Nusa Dua com-plex, and adjoining the golf course, the tranquil atmosphere extends to beyond the simply styled complex designed to wake up the senses.

Alila Villas Uluwatu
£ £ £ £
Jl. Belimbing Sari
Banyar Tambiyak, Desa Pecatu
Tel. 03 61 8 48 21 66
www.alilahotels.com/uluwatu
The Alila Villas are situated at the wes-tern tip of the Bukit peninsula and near the Uluwatu temple tower on a limesto-ne cliff around 100m/330ft above the sea. The award-winning architecture of the 84 large villas (each with their own pool) with their open designs and loca-tions over different levels and the hotel's ecological ethic contribute to its special atmosphere. There is also a 50m pool on the cliffs, a well-equipped library and the well-run spa.

Karma Kandara
£ £ £ £
Jl. Villa Kandara, Br. Wijaya Kusuma
Ungasan, Tel. 03 61 8 48 22 00
www.karmakandara.com
A hideaway for luxury lovers: 46 villas, all with their own pool, patio garden, pavilions and a contemporary, purist in-terior with living areas that flow into each other. The Di Mare restaurant, situ-ated on a cliff 85m/280ft above the rough sea, is remarkable. It says about itself, immodestly, that it boasts the best location on the island. It is surpassed by the Temple Lounge & Bar above it – an excellent meeting place for a cocktail at sundown or a Moroccan mint tea. Take a lift down the cliffs to the beach and the beach club.

Nusa Dua The east coast of the peninsula has seen the construction of luxury hotels set in beautiful tropical gardens in the tourist centre of Nusa Dua. After the construction of the »Nusa Dua Beach Hotel«, the condition was made that no new hotel building may be higher than the tallest palm tree in its vicinity. It is through the strict observance of this condition and the efforts of architects to follow the traditional Balinese building style that Nusa Dua, with its spacious areas of lawns and parks, appears so elegant and harmonious today. Bali's largest art museum, the Museum Pasifika, has opened in Nusa Dua in an expansive complex opposite the Bali Collection. It exhibits works from Asia and the Pacific area. Several buildings also display works by 20th-century European travellers.

MARCO ⊕ POLO TIP

! *An Oasis for cyclists* Insider Tip

Traffic is quite busy in some of Bali's towns and the manner in which the people of Bali behave on the roads ranges from interesting to dangerous for visitors. Nusa Dua on the other hand is an oasis for cyclists. A well-developed network of paths allows cyclists to get around the park-like area, past hotels and some small Balinese villages in a relaxed manner.

❶ Jl. Amphi, daily 10am–6pm, entry: 100,000 rupiah
www.museum-pasifika.com

Tanjung Benoa, a narrow tongue of land, extends out into the sea on the
Benoa and northeast edge of the peninsula. The harbour of the same name lies
Benoa opposite. **Boats head out to »Turtle Island«**, Pulau Serangan, from
Harbour here.

** Candi Dasa

✦ P 7

Region: East Bali	**Distance:**
Administrative district:	20km/12mi south
Karangasem	of Amlapura
Altitude: sea level	
Population: 3500	

Candi Dasa was first developed for tourism some years ago. Although the beach here is quite narrow, the pleasant and inexpensive accommodation and the good restaurants make the place an ideal base for exploring the east of Bali.

Until a few years ago, Candi Dasa, at the eastern end of Labuhan Amu Bay, was still seen as an insider tip among backpackers. But that was then; now the small fishing village is a lively, albeit largely unspoilt, **holiday centre**. Although apart from the »Amankila« there

Lavish lotus-blossom field near Candi Dasa

are no top class hotels as in Nusa Dua, the infrastructure has been brought up to an acceptable standard. Tourists who prefer peace and quiet and seek lodgings away from the hustle and bustle of the big city of Denpasar would do well to look in Candi Dasa.

One drawback of this resort, which has grown at an unnatural rate, is its beach. Since the relatively unprotected shoreline is occasionally subjected to very strong waves, the sand has simply been washed away. This was largely the result of the destruction of the offshore coral banks through uncontrolled quarrying; the coral was used in the production of lime. A government ban on quarrying came too late, and today the beach is quite narrow. The hotel owners had no other option but to protect their beaches by building very expensive stonewall barriers.

WHAT TO SEE IN CANDI DASA AND THE SURROUNDINGS

Along the road from Klungkung to Candi Dasa, not far from the town of Kusambe, is the cave shrine of Goa Lawah, one of the six sadkahy-angans (state or royal temples) in Bali. It is highly venerated by the Balinese, not least because of the belief in the existence of an underground passage connecting the cave (which has yet to be explored to its end) with the island's holiest temple, Pura Besakih, believed to be the **point of contact between the upper world and the underworld**. Goa Lawah is in fact where Sangyang Basuki lives, one of the two snakes of the underworld. Approximately in the centre of the cave entrance stands a lotus throne (padmasana) reserved for the snake god. **Goa Lawah (Bat Cave)

Candi Dasa

TOURIST INFORMATION
Karangasem Tourist Office
Jl. Ngurah Rai
Amlapura
Tel. 03 63 210 02

Klungkung Tourist Office
Jl. Untung Surapati 3
Semarapura
Tel. 03 66 2 14 48

GETTING THERE
Leave Denpasar and head to Sakah, then turn right towards Blahbatuh and Klungkung; continue along the coast via Padang Bai. There are bus connections from Denpasar-Kereneng several times a day. Bemos can be found along the road.

WHERE TO EAT
The Restaurant £ £ £ £
Amankila, Manggis
Tel. 03 63 4 13 33
An unforgettable evening in one of Bali's best restaurants: fantastic Indonesian cuisine in an attractive setting with Balinese music. Reservations vital!

TJ's Café £ £
Jl. Raya Candidasa
(Hotel Watergarden)
Tel. 03 63 4 15 40
Breakfast consists of muesli, pancakes and scrambled egg; later on in the day why not enjoy Indonesian specialities and Australian steaks?

WHERE TO STAY
Amankila £ £ £ £
Manggis
Tel. 03 63 4 13 33

www.amankila.com
This hotel (35 bungalows), which is part of the legendary Aman chain, combines a purist interior with a hint of Asia. It offers perfect service and an outstanding restaurant. Breath-taking location on a cliff to the west of Candi Dasa with views of Lombok. In addition there is an excursion programme that is individually tailored to each guest.

Puri Bagus £ £ £
Jl. Raya Candidasa
Tel. 03 63 4 11 31
www.puribagus.net
47 villas in the Bali style, situated in an expansive complex. An open restaurant that also arranges private candlelight dinners on the beach. Yoga and spa facilities.

Pondok Bambu **Insider Tip**
Seaside Bungalows £ – £ £
Jl. Raya, Candidasa
Tel. 03 63 4 15 43
www.pondokbambu.com
The pleasantly run hotel with a nice restaurant and small pool is located on the beach and is distinguished by its friendly service and a well tended tropical garden.

Kelapa Mas Home Stay £
Candidasa Beach
Tel. 03 63 4 13 69
Situated right by the narrow beach in a garden with high palm trees and lavish banana plants there are 14 cottages with 22 rooms (fans or air-conditioning). The complex also has an inexpensive restaurant.

Small bats live inside the cave, even right at the entrance, and can be seen crowded tightly together hanging on the rock walls. A small temple has been erected to the right of the mouth of the cave with several wooden merus. Every 15 days, worshippers bring offerings here and in return receive holy water necessary for use in various ceremonies, for example on the rice fields of the surrounding area. Vendors selling incense sticks, batik textiles and crafts can be found at the entrance and in the area in front of the temple. Occasionally it is possible to attend Hindu ceremonies in the temple; entering the cave on the other hand is **taboo**.

A new tourist centre with a large number of mid-range hotels has grown up not far from Candi Dasa – approx. 4km/2.5mi in the direction of Klungkung. It is called **Balina Beach**. The sand is lighter in colour here than in Candi Dasa.

Balina Beach

The Padang Bai ferry terminal at the western end of Labuhan Amuk Bay has ferries serving ►Lombok and the offshore island of ►Penida. The large cruise ships that include a stopover in Bali on their itinerary also anchor in the bay. Thanks to the heavy ferry traffic, there are a great number of around-the-clock bus and bemo services in the town. There are several nice beaches outside Padang Bai.

Padang Bai ferry terminal

Celuk

✦ M 8

Region: Central Bali
Administrative district: Gianyar
Altitude: approx. 100m/328ft
Population: 2000

Distance:
12km/7.5mi north
of Denpasar

There are several places in Bali with the name Celuk. The village described here is just a few kilometres north of the island capital near Sukawati, and is known for its skilled craftspeople.

WHAT TO SEE IN CELUK AND ITS SURROUNDINGS

Gold and silversmith shops are scattered along the main thoroughfare running through the village of Celuk, which itself stretches for some distance along the road. Some have adjoining workshops in which tours are possible. The prices are comparable to those in the main tourist centres. Organized bus tours make scheduled stops in Celuk.

Gold and silver shops

Celuk

GETTING THERE
Take the road from Denpasar towards Sukawati for around 12km/7.5mi. There are buses several times a day from Denpasar to Kereneng; bemos depart from Denpasar, Ubud and Mas as well as along the road to Sukawati.

WHERE TO EAT
The village is frequented almost exclusively by day-trippers who want to visit the many gold and silversmith shops. Fruit, drinks and smaller stacks can be bought from the various open stalls.

Woodcarvers

Celuk is also known for its woodcarvers, particularly those that specialize in wayang figures and wooden topeng masks. Most of the work is original to Celuk, passed down by tradition; but also produced here are wayang figures that are copies of those produced on the neighbouring island of Java. Quite often the masks on offer are mass-produced for tourists. There are some more craft shops in the villages around Celuk, for example in Guang, Batuan and Sukawati. With a little luck, you can find craftsmen in these villages who sell properly produced masks and figures.

*Bali Zoo Park

A former bird park and reptile farm near Singapadu, not far from Celuk and Batubalan, were combined to form the new 3.5ha/8.6ac **Bali Zoo Park**. A tour leads wends its way through the tropical vegetation past monitor lizards, crocodiles, iguanas and snakes, tigers, lions, monkeys and flying foxes. Approx. 350 species of bird, including some magnificent-looking parrots, also call Bali Zoo Park home. There is a petting zoo for little visitors.

❶ daily 9am–6pm, Wed and Sat until 9.30pm, Entry: US$25 (adults/children up to age 12), www.bali-zoo.com

✳✳ Denpasar

 L 8

Capital of Bali and the administrative district of Badung: Region: South Bali	Population: 790,000

Denpasar, or more precisely Ngurah Rai Airport located to the south of it, is usually the first holidaymakers see of Bali. Since the completion of the four-lane Jalan Bypass however, they will notice hardly anything of the hustle and bustle of the capital, heading as they now do directly for one of the tourist resorts.

Denpasar has been the island's capital as well as the seat of the governor of the Indonesian province of Bali and all governmental offices since 1946, a distinction formerly held by ▶Singaraja in the north of the island. In the same year it was given the name Denpasar (new market); prior to this it had been called Badung, like the administrative district in which it is located. The Balinese still prefer using the name **Badung** for their capital. The city lies in the south of the island and has experienced an enormous boom since the 1960s. One of the consequences has been the population explosion that has taken place in and around Denpasar. There are now more than 1,000 people per square kilometre or 2,590 per square mile – in contrast to the western part of the island where only about 250 individuals live in every square kilometre (650 per sq mi). The capital now faces huge problems, including environmental pollution, poor air quality, heavy traffic and an excessive number of people seeking to earn a living in the tourist centres close by. As a consequence, Denpasar continues to expand and in some places has merged with neighbouring independent townships.

Capital of the island

Badung River shows off the idyllic side of the otherwise quite hectic island capital

History   The raja of Badung was one of the first to submit to colonial rule and to formalize this submission by signing a treaty in 1841. He hoped that as a result the Dutch would leave the province of Badung in peace and allow him a degree of independence. This proved to be the case, at least for 63 years.

But a fateful event took place when the Chinese schooner Sri Kumala ran aground off the coast near Denpasar on the night of 27 May 1904. The Balinese looted the ship, whereupon its owner demanded compensation, at first from the Raja Agung Made and, when this proved unsuccessful, from the Dutch.

After unproductive negotiations, the Dutch seized the opportunity and issued the raja with an ultimatum, and at the same time brought in troops and surrounded Denpasar. When the raja refused to give in to the ultimatum, they closed in more tightly and began with the invasion on 14 September 1906. The events that followed on that day contributed to the dark memories the Balinese have of the period of Dutch occupation. When the invaders marched up to the palace of the rajas of Badung, the gates opened and a long procession of people slowly moved out toward the foreigners led by the raja himself, carried on a litter. The procession stopped just a few metres away from the Dutch and a Brahma priest took the raja's jewel-encrusted kris (dagger) and thrust it in his ruler's heart. Following this example, one after the other, men, women and children met their death. For a short time the Dutch stood dumbfounded, but then they took up their rifles and commenced shooting all the Balinese who were not victims of this **ritual mass suicide** (puputan). The palace went up in flames and almost burned to the ground.

The example set by the raja of Badung and his followers was followed the same day by the raja of Pemecutan and later in prison by the raja of Tabanan, whom the Dutch had arrested. In 1908 there was another such puputan in Klungkung in which 250 people died. The Dutch found themselves under international pressure as a result, and in 1914 they replaced the troops with a police force.

Denpasar

TOURIST INFORMATION
Denpasar Tourist Office
Jl. Surapati 7, Denpasar
Tel. 03 61 22 36 02
www.balidenpasartourism.com

Bali Tourism Office
Jl. Parman, Renon

Denpasar
Tel. 03 61 22 23 87

GETTING THERE
By plane
Arrival at Ngurah Rai International Airport located to the south of Kuta. Onward travel by bemo or taxi.

Urban transport

Because of the chaotic transport conditions, the many one-way streets and the lack of parking spots, it is best to avoid driving through Denpasar. The city has very good bus and bemo connections departing from various terminals. It is best to turn to the Tourist Office for up-to-date information.

SHOPPING

In spite of the sometimes busy traffic, a shopping tour of the centre of the Balinese capital is well worthwhile. Instead of looking for tourist-oriented articles found in souvenir shops, shop alongside the local population for things typical of the country: silk cloth, batik, fruit, vegetables, spices, reasonably priced shoes and sandals, and electronic items. Among the most popular shopping streets that also offer Indonesian handicrafts are Jl. Gajah Mada, Jl. Sumatera and Jl. Sulawesi.

Ramayana Bali Mall

Denpasar's oldest shopping mall sells local and Australian branded goods over three storeys as well as a large selection of DVDs and CDs. There are also several cafés and self-service restaurants.

WHERE TO EAT
❶ Atoom Baru £ £
Jl. Gajah Mada 108
Tel. 03 61 43 47 72
A popular place to stop while shopping or visiting the market: a large selection of Chinese dishes. The spicy fish and the seafood are recommended. Wash it down with a cold beer.

❷ Betty £ Insider Tip
Jl. Sumatra 56
Tel. 03 61 22 45 02
A small restaurant, popular with the locals and individual travellers. It serves mie goreng and other Indonesian (rice) dishes.

WHERE TO STAY
❶ Santosa City Hotel £ £
Jl. Patih Jelantik 8, Tel. 03 61 26 47 41
www.santosabalihotel.com
The centrally located establishment has 35 modern, comfortable rooms. There are further creature comforts besides the welcome drink, such as wifi and breakfast served in the room. The deluxe rooms also feature coffee makers and kimonos.

❷ Pemecutan Palace £
Jl. Thamrin 2
Tel. 03 61 22 34 91
The owner of this hotel is, remarkably, King Ida Cokorda Pemecutan XI (►p.171), who you might also run into here. The hotel possesses a nice garden in the Balinese style.

❸ Inna Bali £
Jl. Veteran 3, Tel. 03 61 22 56 81
www.innabali.com
This hotel, which was built as far back as 1927, borders a city park on both sides. It has a pool and a restaurant.

Denpasar

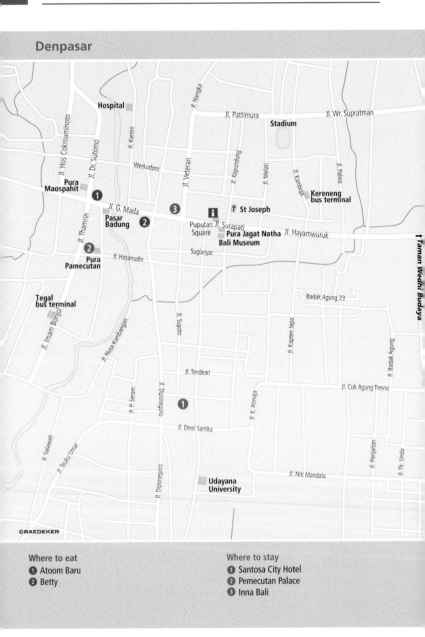

Hospital

Jl. Nangka

Jl. Pattimura

Jl. Wr. Supratman

Stadium

Jl. Hos Cokroaminoto

Jl. Kartini

Jl. Dr. Sutomo

Werkudoro

Jl. Veteran

Jl. Kepundung

Jl. Melati

Jl. Kamboja

Jl. Palwa

Pura
Maospahit ❶

Jl. G. Mada ❸

Pasar
Badung ❷

Kereneng
bus terminal

Jl. Thamrin

✝ St Joseph

Puputan Jl. Surapati
Square **Pura Jagat Natha**
Bali Museum

Jl. Hayamwuruk

Jl. Hasanudin

Sugianyar

❷
**Pura
Pamecutan**

**Tegal
bus terminal**

Badak Agung 23

Jl. Imam Bonjol

Jl. Nusa Kambangan

Jl. Supto

Jl. Kapten Tapa

Jl. Badak Agung

Jl. Tendean

Jl. P. Seram

Jl. Diponegoro

❶

Jl. K. Atmaja

Jl. Cok Agung Tresna

Jl. Dewi Sartika

Jl. Saraswati

Jl. Teuku Umar

**Udayana
University**

Jl. Niti Mandala

Jl. Panjaitan

Jl. Tk. Unda

Taman Wedhi Budaya

©BAEDEKER

Where to eat
❶ Atoom Baru
❷ Betty

Where to stay
❶ Santosa City Hotel
❷ Pemecutan Palace
❸ Inna Bali

WHAT TO SEE IN DENPASAR

A walking tour of Denpasar is not recommended. First of all, the individual sights are located far apart, and these distances are best covered by taxi. Secondly, a walk through the capital's loud streets, jammed with traffic, creates more pain than pleasure.

Take a taxi

The palace of the princes of Badung, into which a small, friendly hotel has been integrated, can be found in the corner formed by Jalan Thamrin and Jalan Hassannudin. Behind the red brick walls are a number of charming buildings set in a lush tropical garden. The owner of the palace, and consequently the hotel, is King Ida Cokorda Pemecutan XI, whom the Balinese greatly respect. The central government of Indonesia, however, has never recognized his coronation in 1989, which was attended by several dethroned kings from Java and Bali. The palace complex, which was almost burnt to the ground after the ritual mass suicide of 14 September 1906, was later rebuilt, but on a smaller scale. The richly decorated entrance gate is impressive, as are a number of fine reliefs, the only surviving remains of the original buildings, to be seen in the rear part of the palace grounds. A collection of lontars (Old Balinese texts on palm leaves) that were saved from the fire are kept in one building; in another are historic gamelan instruments. The luxuriantly blossoming garden forms a sharp contrast to the rumble of traffic outside the palace gates.

**Puri Pemecutan

❶ daily 8am–5pm, donation desired

Measured against international standards, the Bali Museum may be found a little unsystematic. However, the collection is definitely worth a visit. The majority of the exhibits are also labelled in English, making their history, origin and meaning more understandable. The Negeri Propinsi Bali Museum, located on Jalan Wisnu not far from Puputan Square, primarily displays **Balinese art and architecture**. It is housed in three adjacent buildings whose architecture reflects the traditional Balinese building style and which are modelled on both the palace and the temple. The buildings are set in their own grounds in the palace complex entered through a split gate (candi bentar). A second candi bentar opening to the street is permanently closed. Next to it stands a kulkul (bell tower).

**Museum Negeri Propinsi Bali (Bali Provincial State Museum)

The tour of the museum is best begun in the rear building, whose exhibits include a Balinese wedding ceremony (front side) and the tooth filing ceremony (rear), both depicted in glass cases. Take a look at the various wooden models (including a royal throne), carved symbols of Hindu deities and some examples of batik and embroidery, as well as the intricately carved window shutters. The middle building, named Gedung Karangasem after its architectural style, contains finds from the Neolithic period. There is a fine suite of seats and some stone figures on the veranda. The building, by the way, was first built by the Dutch in the form of a hall that was open on all sides; the walls were added later. The third building is richly decorated; it was constructed in the style of the Palace of Tabanan. Inside, in the middle of the room, barong figures are placed on a pedestal. The wooden ceiling beams are very elaborately carved. Between the buildings is a »shower« that the royal family had installed. It is slightly sunken into the ground, making it easy to miss at first glance.

❶ Tue–Sun 8am–3pm, entry: 10,000 rupiah, tel. 03 61 23 50 59

> **!** MARCO ❂ POLO TIP
>
> *Practice makes perfect* **Insider Tip**
>
> It is possible to take part in the public rehearsals of young dancers in the Art Center (daily). The fruits of this hard work can then be seen in the early evening, at around 6.30pm, when dances such as Barong and Kecak are performed.

**Pura Jagat Natha
Just to the right of the main exit of the Bali Museum is the Temple of the Rulers of the Worlds (Jagatnatha), built in 1953. It is dedicated to **Sangyang Widi**, the incarnation of the supreme gods in Balinese Hinduism: Brahma, Vishnu and Shiva. Brahma is worshipped here as the »god of gods«. The symbols for the deity preserved in the temple – Sangyang Widi depicted as a gleaming golden metallic figure sitting on a seven-tiered throne made of coral stone – are venerated, incidentally, not by isolated groups of people but rather by all Balinese Hindus.

*Church of St Joseph
Some 550m/600yd north of the Bali Museum stands the Catholic church of St Joseph, in which Christian images, for example in the stained glass windows, and Balinese sculptural decorations are colourfully mixed.

*Pura Maospahit
Pura Maospahit is one of Denpasar's oldest and most important temples. Its origins date back to the 15th century. As the name indicates, it was founded by the Majapahit dynasty, which originally came from Java, and remains their ancestral temple even today. Over the course of time it has been subjected to remodelling and beautification and many of the original furnishings have been lost.

As the main entrance on Jalan Dr. Sutomo is only open on public holidays, the entrance in alleyway running along the left side of

The Art Center is surrounded by an attractive tropical park where the Festival of Arts takes place

the temple complex must be used. The open door can be found by going some way down the alley designated »Gang III«. There is another entrance into the main part of the temple: go to the end of Gang III and then to the right a short way along the outer wall.

The temple consists of two parts, separated from one another by a high wall. Entrance to the grounds is through a split gate (candi bentar), which is actually the temple's main attraction. The following deities have been carved on the five pillars (from left to right): the god Sangkara (a manifestation of Shiva); the ancient Indian god of the sky, Indra; the god of the dead, Yama; the god of wind, Bayu; the mythical bird and Vishnu's mount, Garuda; the Indian god Kubera (god of wealth); and the sea god, Waruna. There are some sacral structures in the area to the right inside the temple that do not belong to Pura Maospahit, but rather are part of a family temple. At the rear stands the Gedong Maospahit, a shrine for the veneration of ancestors. The ancestors of the East Javanese Majapahit dynasty are venerated in the closed building next to it. It is worth taking a look at the **three thrones for the gods** (pelinggih) decorated with antlers, which are reserved for the ancestors of the Majapahit dynasty.

❶ irregular opening times

*Taman Wedhi Buda-ya Art Center	What makes Denpasar's art centre interesting is its comprehensive collection of Balinese paintings in the main building and an adjoining sales exhibition featuring works by both established and up-and-coming artists (▶ill. p.173).

Behind the building is a **lush tropical garden** with small ponds. There is also an open-air stage by the arts centre where visitors can enjoy dance performances even outside of the annual »**Festival of Arts**«, from mid-June to mid-July.

❶ Mon–Thu 8am–3pm, Fri–Sun until 1pm, entry: free

**Pasar Badung	The **largest market in the capital** is housed in a four-storey building located at the point where Jalan Gajah Mada (one of Denpasar's main traffic arteries) and Jalan Sulawesi converge (▶ill. p.29). The fresh fruit and vegetable market is in the basement of the building, while articles for everyday use can be purchased on the upper floors.

The Pasar Badung has its own house temple (in front of the entrance). Fishmongers' shops can be found on the other side of the building. The reason for them being half hidden is that, according to Balinese-Hindu belief, the sea is occupied by demons and evil spirits; this applies to the creatures caught there too. There are numerous other stalls and markets in the area surrounding the Pasar Badung.

❶ daily 5am–midnight

** Gianyar

M 7

Administrative seat of the district of Gianyar:	**Altitude:** 127m/417ft
Region: Central Bali	**Distance:**
Population: 35,000	26km/16mi northeast of Denpasar

In the 17th and 18th centuries Gianyar was the capital of a powerful kingdom. The city is now the seat of the district that bears its name and lies in well irrigated hill country that is intensely cultivated. Not much is left of the town's former splendour; modern utilitarian buildings now dominate the townscape. Its modest textile and handicraft industries are important to the region.

The city of Klungkung was the capital of the most powerful realm in Bali from the 15th to the 17th century. As Klungkung's authority diminished, the rulers in Gianyar, only 12km/7.5mi away, were increasing theirs. During the Dutch occupation, Gianyar's princes were able to agree terms with the invaders, with the result that Gianyar was spared intervention and the princely family was able to retain its influence.

WHAT TO SEE IN AND AROUND GIANYAR

Puri Gianyar, built by Dewa Manggis IV in 1771, faces the central square. The palace is normally not open to the public, but with a little luck one of the members of the family still living there may open the

**Puri Gianyar

Gianyar

TOURIST INFORMATION
Gianyar Tourist Office
Jl. Ngurah Rai 21
Tel. 03 61 93 40 01

GETTING THERE
Leave Denpasar in a northeast direction to Sakah; turn right and head onwards via Blahbatuh. There are several buses per day from Denpasar to Kereneng. Bemos can be found along the road.

WHERE TO STAY/WHERE TO EAT
Sua Bali £
On the edge of the village of Kemenuh (on the road from Denpasar to Gianyar near Blahbatuh)
Tel. 03 61 94 10 50, www.suabali.com
Less a hotel than accommodation where visitors to Bali can experience socially responsible tourism: it is easy here to live and dine like Balinese people and to get to know locals.

gate. The palace consists of several **traditional Balinese style** pavilions. If you are given the opportunity to view it, take a close look at the superb carvings and the figures in the delightful tropical garden.

*Blahbatuh   Only about 5km/3mi southwest of Gianyar lies the small, quiet market town of Blahbatuh with two particularly interesting temples. Pura Dalem Blahbatuh is located in Benawah on the road leading to Denpasar. Inside is a seated **Buddha (!) in the midst of Hindu figures** – an indication of the tolerance Balinese have in religious matters. The second attraction is Pura Puseh Blahbatuh or Pura Gaduh. It contains the enormous **head of a giant.** According to the locals it is a representation of the prince of demons, Jero Gede Mecaling. He is said to have come to Bali on several occasions in earlier times from the island of ►Penida, wreaking havoc here with his demons and devils.

Gilimanuk

✦ **B 3**

Region: West Bali	**Distance:**
Altitude: sea level	85km/53mi west
Administrative district: Jembrana	of Singaraja
Population: 15,000	

Gilimanuk is the most important ferry and commercial port linking Bali and its larger neighbour, the island of Java. The most westerly town in Bali, Gilimanuk lies on the Bali Strait (Selat Bali), which is only 2.5km/1.5mi wide.

WHAT TO SEE IN AND AROUND GILIMANUK

Port   There are only very few attractions to be discovered in Gilimanuk. However, the bustling activity around the harbour, mostly centred on ferry traffic, is pleasant to watch. Then there is also the night-time market held every evening in the town centre, where there are a few

Gilimanuk

GETTING THERE
The road from Denpasar to Gilimanuk runs in a northwesterly direction, sometimes along the coast (approx. 130km/80mi).
Ferries to the neighbouring island of

Java (Ketapang harbour, approx. 30–45 mins) depart from Gilimanuk (turn left at the end of the main road and follow the signs).
There are regular daily buses and bemo connections from Denpasar to Ubung.

good cookshops. Approx. 500m/550yd east of the harbour is the **Museum of Man (Museum Manusia Purba)**, which displays finds excavated in the vicinity, including exhibits from prehistoric burial sites, pottery and tools.

❶ daily 9am–4pm, entry: 5000 rupiah (donation)

The little village of Palasari with largely Catholic inhabitants is just a short way off the road from Denpasar to Gilimanuk; some 10km/6mi further west is **Blimbingsari**, where mostly Protestants live. The churches of the two villages, both of which were only founded in the 20th century, harmoniously combine the Christian and Balinese cultures.

Palasari

** Kapal

✦ L 7

Region: Southwest Bali
Altitude: 75m/246ft
Administrative district: Badung
Population: 1000

Distance:
15km/9mi north
of Denpasar

There was a time when the people of Kapal were famous for their pottery, but today the village between Denpasar and Mengwi is better known for its temple figures and decorative items made of cement and stone.

WHAT TO SEE IN KAPAL

Shops open to the street line the main road through Kapal. On sale, among other things, are stone figures and house temples. Before making any purchase, do consider the substantial weight of most of these otherwise charming and well-worked objects and the prohibitive expense of shipping them back home.

The Pura Sada (tower) of Kapal is one of the most important temples in Bali. It is the **temple of the founding prince of Mengwi**, whose ancestors originally came from Klungkung. The Pura Sada can be reached by following the main road towards ▶Tabanan and then turning left into a narrow lane (200m/220yd). The buildings that stand today were constructed on old foundation walls, the remains of a shrine built in the 12th century. The temple at first appears to

**Pura Sada
(Prasada)

Kapal

GETTING THERE
The road heads north from Denpasar towards Singaraja. There are good bus connections from Denpasar to Ubung, take a bemo from Denpasar or Mengwi.

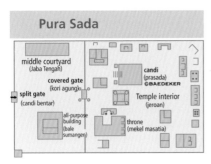

Pura Sada

middle courtyard
(Jaba Tengah)

covered gate
(kori agung)

split gate
(candi bentar)

all-purpose
building
(bale
sumangen)

candi
(prasada)
© BAEDEKER

Temple interior
(jeroan)

throne
(mekel masatia)

have only two parts, since the outer forecourt with a large waringin tree is not enclosed. The entrance into the first enclosed courtyard of the large complex is through a split gate (candi bentar) with a seven-tiered roof thought to date back to the 14th or 15th century. In the inner courtyard, slightly to the left, is the Bale Pesamyangan in which the gods are welcomed to the temple. The original of the massive prasada in Majapahit style probably also dated from the 14th or 15th century. It was completely destroyed in a devastating earthquake in 1917 and not rebuilt until 1948/1949. Whether its current location corresponds to the original site is uncertain. The grimacing demon in the upper part of the pagoda is particularly striking. There is a stone basin in the middle symbolizing the abode of the heavenly nymph Widadari, who is considered to be the mediator between the world of the gods and the world of men. To the right of this are **57 stone thrones for the ancestors** of the Mengwi dynasty and on the eastern side there are three throne seats. In the rear of the temple, other shrines and thrones are dedicated to the divine trinity, Brahma – Vishnu – Shiva.

Pura Desa and Pura Puseh   Another temple that is well worth seeing is located directly on the main road through Kapal. Actually, there are two temples, Pura Desa and Pura Puseh, but the two have been built together in such a way that their original separate identities are only discernible to the initiated. The **richly decorated gate with three entrances, one reserved for each member of the divine trinity, Brahma – Vishnu – Shiva, is quite unusual. There are superbly detailed reliefs depicting parts of the Tantri animal fables on either side of the gate.

Klungkung (Semarapura)

 ✳ N 7

Administrative seat of the district of Klungkung	**Population:** 22,000
Region: East Bali	**Distance:**
Altitude: up to 160m/525ft	23km/14mi east of Ubud

Klungkung, once the governmental seat of a powerful principality, lies at the foot of a region of gently rolling hills. In clear weather, the Gunung Agung volcano forms an impressive backdrop.

Klungkung

TOURIST INFORMATION
Klungkung Tourist Office
Jl. Untung Surapati 3
Semarapura
Tel. 03 66 2 14 48
Fax 2 28 48

GETTING THERE
The road heads east from Denpasar via
Gianyar. There are regular bus connections from Denpasar to Kereneng. Bemos can be found along the road.

WHERE TO STAY/WHERE TO EAT
Cahaya Pusaka Inn £
Jl. P. Diponegoro 135
Tel. 03 61 2 21 18
This small guesthouse with a garden has
basic, inexpensive rooms.

Loji Ramayana Palace Hotel £
Jl. Diponegoro 152, Tel. 03 66 2 10 44
The 9 modern rooms of the hotel are arranged around a courtyard; the hotel's
restaurant serves Chinese food.

Today, Klungkung – which since 1995 has officially gone by the name
of **Semarapura** – is a busy town. It forms an important link between
central Bali and the eastern part of the island, which for a long time
was cut off from the rest of the island, both economically and physi-
cally, following the devastating volcanic eruption of 1963 and the
accompanying earthquakes.

At the close of the 15th century, the Hindus in Java were so persecuted that the only option they had was to flee to the neighbouring island of Bali. Among them was Batu Renggong, the son of Prince
Widjaya. His father, in order to escape imprisonment, had burned
himself alive – a fate his son did not wish to share. With several
hundred followers (among them many priests), he fled to Bali, where
he built a palace in Gelgel, a small place about 5km/3mi south of
Klungkung, declaring himself a Dewa Agung (grand duke) and Gelgel his seat of government. Around 1710, the court moved to the
considerably better situated Klungkung, where Prince Di Made, a
great-grandson of Widjaya, built a new palace. The **Kerta Gosa
Courtroom**, the town's greatest attraction, probably also dates from
this period. Klungkung's importance grew so much in the following
years that this courtroom handled all the important legal disputes on
the whole island of Bali and passed judgement on criminals. Klungkung also played an important role during the attempts by the Dutch
to occupy the island. After the Dutch had brought towns in the north
like Singaraja and Buleleng under their control, a vanguard led by the
merchant **Cornelis de Houtman** reached Klungkung, where they
were welcomed as guests by the Dewa Agung, who had a great interest in the European way of life. A little while later, it was agreed to
establish trading relations. In the 18th century, Klungkung increasin-

History

The Kerta Gosa was built as a royal courthouse in the 18th century

gly lost its importance and influence to nearby Gianyar. Although the Dewa Agung agreed with the rulers of the neighbouring principalities to take concerted action against the Dutch, he did not have the military means to mount a defence against the threatening invasion. As a consequence, after Buleleng fell in the north and Amlapura suffered the same fate in the east, Klungkung became one of the first regions to be conquered by the Dutch. During the course of the invasion in 1908 a terrible event occurred here too that still arouses deep sentiment in the Balinese. When the Dutch reached the palace, the gates swung open and a procession of some 250 men, women and children filed out. When they came to a halt in front of the bewildered Dutch, the Dewa Agung plunged a kris into his breast – an example they all followed (▶Denpasar). This act proved insufficient for the Dutch; every Balinese that had not committed suicide or was badly wounded but still alive was cut down in an ensuing hail of bullets from Dutch rifles.

WHAT TO SEE IN KLUNGKUNG

Modern, functional buildings

Not much remains of the splendour of old Klungkung. The Dutch pulled down almost all of the buildings that represented the Dewa Agung's rule, which leaves the present-day appearance of the city dominated for the most part by modern, functional buildings. It was not until the 1980s that some buildings were repaired or reconstructed. They recall the city's grand past, a time when Klungkung was considered to be the centre of art and culture in Bali and brought forth a great number of important painters.

Spreading out in the centre of town is the Taman Gili (garden of the island), a **well-tended park** whose outline approximately corresponds to that of the Puri Agung, the former princely residence. Standing in the middle of a pond covered in lotus blossom is the Bale Kembang, a small pavilion with beautiful wayang paintings inside.

Taman Gili

The 18th-century Kerta Gosa courthouse is a marvellous sight to behold, particularly because of its **unique ceiling paintings that are also executed in wayang style**. Some artists in and around Klungkung still paint in this style. The ceiling paintings were originally painted on canvas, but in the course of restoration in 1960, they were fixed on more durable sheets of cement. They depict what punishments sentenced delinquents faced. When therefore a condemned man stood in front of his judges, he only had to look up to get an idea of what awaited him after his judgement. Adulterers, for example, had their genitals burned off; women had to look into the faces of their aborted children while walking through an inferno; and thieves were tortured to death in boiling oil. In contrast, heaven and the rewards in store for those who abide by the law during their lives can also be seen. Standing in the centre of the courthouse are six richly decorated chairs and a rectangular table at which the three judges (Pendanda priests) and the assessors sat. There is also a small museum on the premises.

**Kerta Gosa

❶ daily 8am–5.30pm, entry: 30,000 rupiah

AROUND KLUNGKUNG

The small village of Kamasan, some 2km/1.2mi south of Klungkung, is known for its **painters** who still practise the traditional wayang technique. There is also a widely-known art school here that combines traditional and modern painting techniques. Along with textile painting, Kamasan is also noted for its creative **bronze and silversmiths**.

Kamasan

The Seni Lukis Klasik Banda museum is in Banda (Jl. Pertigaan), 5km/3mi west of Klungkung. It is also named the **Gunarsa Museum of Classical and Modern Art** because it was founded by the Balinese artist, Dr. Nyoman Gunarsa. Along with Gunarsa's studio and a

Banda

collection of his work, objects from the 17th through to the 19th century are shown, along with modern and abstract works.

❶ Mon–Sat 9am–5pm, entry: 25,000 rupiah

Kusamba   A few miles down the road from Klungkung in the direction of Amlapura is the small coastal village of Kusamba with its black beach. The inhabitants of this village live primarily from fishing and salt production. On the way to Kusamba, evidence of the violent volcanic eruption of 1963 is still visible.

★★ Kubutambahan

✦ L 1

Region: North Bali	**Distance:**
Administrative district: Buleleng	12km/7.5mi
Population: 20,000	northeast of
Altitude: sea level	Singaraja

Kubutambahan is a typical North Balinese town lying in the middle of a region that has scant rainfall yet is intensely cultivated. There is little here to interest the tourist; the absolute highlight of the town is the temple complex of Pura Meduwe Karang with its floral ornamentation that is characteristic of the region.

WHAT TO SEE IN AND AROUND KUBUTAMBAHAN

★★Pura Meduwe Karang   Pura Meduwe Karang is dedicated to the sun god Surya, the male counterpart of the rice goddess, Dewi Sri. Translated, the name of temple means »to whom the earth belongs«. The local people come here to supplicate for a rich harvest on the surrounding coffee, maize, fruit and vegetable plantations. In the first courtyard (jaba) of the tripartite temple stand three platforms with 13 figures in the lower row, 10 in the centre row and 13 in the back row, all of which represent **characters from the Ramayana epic (▶p.73)**. A four-part split gate (candi bentar) opens into the second courtyard (jaba tengah) with a multitude of figures standing against the wall opposite that separates the third courtyard (jeroan) from the inner sanctum (bebaturan).

Kubutambahan

GETTING THERE
There are good connections from and to Singaraja by bus and bemo.

In the centre of the shrine is a stepped platform on a square base. Standing on it to the left is a gedong pesimpangan, dedicated to Ratu Ayu Sari (one of the manifestations of the earth mother Ibu Prtiwi) and to the right is a gedong pesimpangan for Ratu Ngurah Sari, the protector of the products of the earth. Don't miss the stone relief of a **man riding a flower-bedecked bicycle** on the right-hand side of the shrine. While the locals insist the carving is at least 400 years old, scholars think it depicts the Dutch ethnologist Wijnand Otto Jan Nieuwenkamp, which would explain the cyclist's long nose. While doing scientific research in North Bali in 1904, Nieuwenkamp would travel about by bicycle, a form of transportation completely unknown to the population at the time. The relief is no longer in its original condition as it was damaged in a severe earthquake in 1917. It was altered during later restoration work.

Around 15km/9mi east of Kubutambahan at the village of Pacung a road branches off to the right and leads to Sembiran. The inhabitants of this small mountain village, which possesses around 20 temples, are descended from the Bali Aga, the original inhabitants of Bali, and they speak a **dialect** similar to the Old Javanese language. A further distinctive feature there is their **manner of burying the dead**. While the dead on the rest of Bali (with the exception of Trunyan, ▶p.210) are sooner or later cremated, the people of Sembiran toss their dead into a ravine outside the village. | Sambiran

Kuta

※ K/L 9

Region: South Bali	**Distance:**
Administrative district: Badung	9km/5.5mi
Population: 70,000	southwest of
Altitude: sea level	Denpasar

Back in the 1960s, Kuta, once a fishing village, came to be a tip known only to the first European travellers. Today it is Bali's best-known holiday resort. Kuta lies on the southwest coast of the island, only a few miles away from the international airport.

It was here in Kuta that the now typical so-called »losmen« and »homestay«, accommodation for tourists, were first created. Today, Kuta has merged with the towns of **Legian** and ▶**Seminyak** to the north, and all year round attracts predominantly younger travellers from Australia, Japan and Europe. **There are more than 500 establishments** offering accommodation in all price categories, inclu- | High-class bathing resort

Kuta

TOURIST INFORMATION
Badung Government Tourism Office
Jl. Benasari 7
Kuta
Tel. 03 61 75 61 75
Fax 75 61 76

GETTING THERE
Kuta is located on the road between the airport and Denpasar. Good bus and bemo connections, as well as to other tourist destinations such as Ubud and Lombok (bus/ferry).

SHOPPING
Textiles and leather
Kuta and Legian are the most popular shopping addresses on Bali for textiles. Find countless shops, boutiques and tailor's shops selling international branded goods as well as inexpensive copies, batiks and imaginative fashion in the Balinese hippie style, costumes, trousers and coats made of leather and dresses and shirts made of silk.

Bali Mal Galeria
Jl. Bypass Ngurah Rai
Simpan Dewa Ruci, Kuta
A shopping centre on two floors with many boutiques and outlets (Ralph Lauren, Puma, Adidas) that sell branded goods at inexpensive prices. The large Granmedia Book Shop stocks an outstanding collection of Balinese literature as well as beautiful photographic books. The food court is on the second floor.

Kuta Kidz
Bemo Corner, Kuta
www.kutakidz88.com

A huge, imaginative and colourful selection of clothes for boys and girls at inexpensive prices.

Surfer Girl Insider Tip
Jl. Legian 138, Kuta
You won't find a bigger selection anywhere else: the collections of 82 manufacturers are sold here (e.g. Billabong, Paul Frank, Body & Soul). Surfer Girl has itself become cult, the store's shopping bags are considered a hip souvenir.

GOING OUT
The selection of nightclubs and bars is centred on Kuta. The number one choice for many Kuta fans is still the Hard Rock Café (Jl. Pantai) with new live music every day. There are several other nightclubs and bars along Jl. Seminyak.

WATER PARK
Waterbom Park
Jl. Kartika Plaza
daily 9am–6pm
Entry: 31/19 US$
(adults/children up to the age of 12)
www.waterbom-bali.com
Children, and adults in touch with their inner child, will enjoy the Waterbom Park with its many flumes. Swimming pools and sun loungers under palm trees.

WHERE TO EAT
Made's Warung £ £
Jl. Pantai, Kuta
Tel. 03 61 75 52 97   Insider Tip
www.madeswarung.com
A warung that feels like a little empire: from the ushers on the car parks to the various restaurants that are all gathered

under one roof, to the neighbouring shops for textiles, books and jewellery. Made's has offered an enormous variety of foods, including spare ribs, pasta and blueberry pancakes, for more than 40 years.

Wali Warung ££
Jl. Padma Utara 16
Legian
Tel. 03 61 76 28 60
Wayan and his wife Asa from Sweden

always ensure the best, fresh dishes in their colourful restaurant fitted with bamboo and rattan. Situated in the centre of Legian.

Poppies Restaurant ££
Jl. Poppies 1, Kuta
Tel. 03 61 75 10 59
www.poppiesbali.com
This legendary restaurant will take you away from Kuta's lively streets to a small oasis. Sit in one of the open pavilions

Sun, sea and sand on Kuta Beach

with views of the magical garden. The menu features cocktails as well as fresh fruit juices, Balinese and international cuisine. Gado gado is inexpensive and good, maybe followed by a rich, sweet chocolate cake.

Café Sardinia £ £
Beachwalk, Jl. Pantai, Kuta
Tel. 03 61 8 46 49 66
www.cafesardinia.com
This restaurant is located in the shopping complex »Beachwalk«. It has a terrace to Kuta Beach and to the sea. Besides the pizza, pasta, etc. why not enjoy a latte or a double espresso after your shopping spree or trip to the beach?

TJ's Mexican £ £
Poppies Lane I 24
Kuta
Tel. 03 61 75 10 93
For more than two decades now a loyal following has enjoyed the guacamole, tacos and enchiladas served in the heart of Kuta. On Thursday evenings there is a buffet that is accompanied by Mariachi music.

WHERE TO STAY
Kartika Plaza £ £ £
Jl. Kartika Plaza
South Kuta
Tel. 03 61 75 10 67
www.discoverykartikaplaza.com
This long-established beach hotel (sea views from all rooms) offers a large spectrum of guest rooms, all clean and with a minimalist interior. The beachfront villas are outstanding. They have private gardens and their own pool right on the ocean. Butler service and other luxurious extras. The Discovery shopping centre

next door is connected to the hotel via a walkway.

Hard Rock Hotel £ £
Jl. Pantai
Tel. 03 61 76 18 69
www.hardrockhotels.net/Bali
418 rooms
Asia's first Hard Rock Hotel opened a few years ago next to the Hard Rock Café. It features the typical interior and musician paraphernalia typical of this brand along with various restaurants, a pool and a spa.

Santika Beach £ £ £
Jl. Kartika Plaza
Tel. 03 61 75 12 67
http://santika-kuta-beach.hotelskuta24.com; 164 rooms
The luxurious beach hotel is situated in the middle of a tropical landscape park on the outskirts of Kuta. The »Santika Beach« has a philosophy of tranquillity and sophisticated Balinese elegance. There are two generously sized pools as well as an attractive spa.

Best Western Resort £ £ £
Jl. Kubu Anyar 118, Kuta
Tel. 03 61 76 70 00
www.bestwestern.com
A huge tropical tree with aerial roots several metres long stands imposingly in the hotel's courtyard. Guests can enjoy a coffee or a cocktail at sundown on one of the surrounding rattan chairs. The restaurant by the pool is just as lovely. The lighting after sunset is romantic. The rooms are spacious and tastefully furnished. Be careful upon your arrival since there are three Best Western hotels in Kuta; this one is near the airport (with a shuttle service), but it is 4km/2.5mi to the beach.

Poppies Cottages £ £
Jl. Segara Batu Bolong
(Poppies Lane)
Tel. 03 61 75 10 59
www.poppies.net
A cult meeting place for old Bali hands: this complex in the centre of Kuta with 20 cottages was built 30 years ago by Americans. It has since been modernized and extended several times. The rooms are adorned with Balinese arts and crafts. »Poppies« also has lavish gardens, a pool surrounded by plants and a restaurant that is the hip meeting place in Kuta for breakfast time.

ding the legendary »Poppies«, one of the oldest hotels in the centre of Kuta. Set in beautiful tropical grounds, Poppies has been popular with travellers since it first opened. Since the centre of Kuta received something of a »general overhaul« in 2004, being supplied with a modern sewerage system in the process, and with floral arrangements now increasing its attractiveness still further, the busy shopping streets and alleys are a magnet for ever more travellers from the five-star hotels of Nusa Dua. In the evening, Kuta throngs with thousands of visitors from all over the world.

Kuta Beach, on which a spot in the shade is difficult to come by, is separated from the restaurants and hotels by a busy road. True, it doesn't exactly live up to the clichés of a tropical paradise, but it is nevertheless popular for swimming, sunbathing and surfing. It fills up in the late morning, a **meeting place for young, independent travellers**. At the heart of **Kuta** is Jalan Legian, which stretches several miles to the north. There are countless boutiques, cafés, restaurants, bars and discotheques here. Inexpensive, self-made batik fashion wear is sold at open stalls. In the small spas and wellness salons nearby it is possible to enjoy traditional massage and oil cures – and without breaking the bank. Travel agents offer tours of the island as well as international flights, while tattoo studios compete for business. Moving further north, the restaurants and hotels become more expensive. The **Human Tragedy Monument** commemorates the events of 12 October 2002. It stands on the spot where a bomb attack killed 202 people from 22 countries (▶p.58). Jalan Melasti, which runs east-west and crosses Jalan **Legian**, forms the invisible border of Legian. The beach of the same name is broader here and there is no traffic to disturb the peace and quiet.

Kuta Beach

MARCO ⊕ POLO TIP

! *Everything for beauty*   Insider Tip

There are lots of little spas and beauty salons in Kuta. They offer some outstanding massages and pampering treatments for inexpensive prices. One popular option is the Spa Semara (Jl. Blambangan 4, daily 9am–10pm, www.balispa.net/semara/info.php).

** Lombok

east of Bali

Indonesian province: Nusa
Tenggara Barat
Area: 4725 sq km/1812 sq mi

Altitude: 0–3726m/12,225ft
Population: 3 million
Capital: Mataram

Lombok and Bali were often called the »unequal sisters«, usually in reference to the fact that Lombok, one of the Lesser Sunda Islands to the east of Bali, remained relatively untouched by international tourism. While Bali was known all over the world, Lombok languished in the shadows. Today, all of that is changing.

Once upon a time, only backpackers ventured to Lombok and those who knew it described the island as »Bali as it once was«. In recent years that has become a thing of the past: the island now boasts a good tourist infrastructure. Visitors to Lombok should however prepare for its **peculiarities**. Everything is a little quieter and slower here. The population has not been influenced by tourism nearly as much as in Bali and things more or less tolerated or accepted on the neighbouring island can be considered offensive in Lombok. This is particularly true when travelling in the interior of the island and coming into contact with the Sasaks, Lombok's original inhabitants. With an area of 4725 sq km/1812 sq mi, Lombok is only slightly smaller than Bali. The two are separated by the 40km/25mi wide and up to 3000m/10,000ft deep Lombok Strait (Selat Lombok), which is at the same time a bio-geographical boundary (**»the Wallace Line«**, ▶**p.19**) separating the Indomalayan and the Australasian flora and fauna. The island's most prominent point is the Gunung Rinjani volcano. At a height of 3726m/12,225ft, it is the third-highest elevation in all of Indonesia. Mount Rinjani stretches out in an east-west direction and, counting its foothills, covers almost the whole of the northern half of the island.

MARCO POLO INSIGHT ?

The Wallace Line

Alfred Wallace, a contemporary of Charles Darwin, also developed a theory about evolution. He discovered that the islands to the west and east of the Lombok Strait were unusually different from each other: tropical vegetation, monkeys and tigers were to be found on Bali and the western islands, while Lombok and the eastern islands had a more arid vegetation and a fauna with Australian influences, such as giant lizards and cockatoos.

History Once ruled over by the Balinese princes of the Karangasem dynasty, who considered it merely an adjunct, Lombok was occupied in the

Lombok

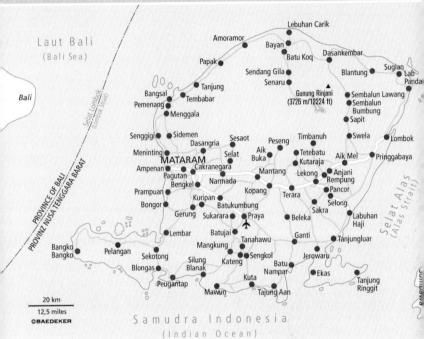

mid-17th century by princes from the island of Sulawesi (Celebes). In 1740, the Karangasem dynasty, who dominated eastern Bali (▶Amlapura), regained control over the western part of the island. The Muslims from southern Sulawesi, however, continued to rule in East Lombok until 1849 when the raja of Karangasem incorporated the whole island into his kingdom.

In 1838, the united Principality of Lombok was established and five years later the princes of Mataram recognized Dutch sovereignty. In 1891 the Dutch crushed a revolt by the Sasak and incorporated the whole of Lombok into the Dutch East Indies. Lombok proved to be an ideal **base for launching Dutch punitive expeditions** against Bali, which the Sasak rulers willingly supported. They welcomed the Dutch forces as a means of freeing them from Balinese hegemony. Today Lombok is part of the Indonesian province of Nusa Tenggara Barat.

Lombok

TOURIST INFORMATION
Lombok Tourism Office
Jl. Raya Senggigi, Km 8
Senggigi, Lombok
Tel. 03 70 6 65 02 38
www.lombok-tourism.com

Rinjani National Park
Jl. Arya Banjar Getas
Lingkar Selatan, Ampenan
Tel. 03 70 6 60 88 74
www.rinjaninationalpark.com

GETTING THERE

Lombok
Lombok can be easily reached from Bali either by planes operated by the Garuda subsidiary »Merpati« (►p.252, flight time approx. 30 mins), by speedboat (approx. 2.5 hrs) or by car ferry (approx. 4.5 hrs). Planes land at Bandara International Airport in the south of the island near Praya, 40km/25mi southeast of Mataram. The Bluewater Express (www.bluewater-express.com) departs twice a day from Serangan on the south coast and Padang Bai on the east cost of Bali to Teluk Kode on Lombok's west coast.
Boats and ferries from Padang Bai on Bali arrive in Lombok at the port of Lembar, approx. 30km/18mi to the southwest of Mataram.
The central bemo station is situated 7km/4.5mi outside of Ampenan and approx. 2.5km/1.5mi outside of Cakranegara.

Gili Islands
Gili Fastboats (www.gilifastboats.com) run between Bali and the Gili Islands (approx. 1 hr), departing from various ports. The Bluewater Express also goes to Gili Trawangan on its way to Lombok.

SHOPPING
Senggigi Art Market
The arts and crafts market (Pasar Seni) of Sengigi in Jalan Raya Senggigi encompasses several smaller shops and boutiques which – tailored to the tastes of the visitors – sell high-quality arts and crafts from Lombok (such as ceramic works adorned with shells and seagrass, black clay pots, woven goods in strong patterns and colours and teak works).

WHERE TO EAT
Asmara £ £ £
Jl. Raya Senggigi
Senggigi
Tel. 03 70 69 36 19
www.asmara-group.com
Visitors have the choice between tables under palm trees or dinging in the restaurant, between Indonesian specialities or pizza and pasta. Upon request there is a car pick-up service. The »Asmara« also has an art gallery.

Dua Em £
Jl. Transmigrasi 99
Mataram
Tel. 03 70 69 67 34
Sit side-by-side with locals to enjoy the national dish ayam taliwang (grilled, marinated chicken with spinach).

Yessy Café £ £
Jl. Raya Senggigi
Senggigi
Tel. 03 70 69 31 48
Great atmosphere in this popular restaurant near the Sheraton hotel.

WHERE TO STAY

Sheraton Senggigi Beach Hotel £ £ £

Senggigi
Tel. 03 70 69 33 33
www.sheraton.com/senggigi
The first five-star hotel on the island is situated right by the white Senggigi Beach. Warm fabrics, chandeliers, rattan and colonial furniture create the atmosphere in the high, open main building. The 154 rooms are situated in low buildings with views of the sea or the tropical park. Even those who are not staying here should stroll through the enchantingly lit gardens in the evening and dine in one of the restaurants. The buffet by the pool is particularly lovely, particularly when it is enhanced by gamelan sounds and dancing.

Qunci Villas £ £ £

Jl. Raya Mangsit
Senggigi
Tel. 03 70 69 38 00
www.quncivillas.com
A small but lovely complex. Guests stay in 20 villas (starting at 40 sq m/430 sq ft) with a modern, purist air. The ikat fabrics, open bathrooms and the view of the tropical gardens and the sea deliver the Balinese atmosphere. After sunset torches light up the pool and garden. Visitors will also enjoy the massage pavilions and the sophisticated restaurant.

Senggigi Beach Hotel £ £

Jl. Pantai
Senggigi
Tel. 03 70 69 32 10
148 rooms
A tranquil, idyllic situation: the expansive complex of the beach hotel is already a bit older but it has a pleasant tropical atmosphere with high coconut palm trees. Frangipani and bougainvillea. It is best to reserve one of the sea-view bungalows rather than stay in the main building.

Insider Tip

Puri Mas Boutique Resort & Spa £ £

Mangsit Beach
Tel. 03 70 69 38 31
www.purimas-lombok.com
Private and individual: the Dutch owner, a retired professional dancer, has created a gem in the local style. Immediately beyond the gate, ornamented in dramatic wood carvings, visitors enter an enchanted world. The 17 rooms are distributed across small houses with their own veranda. They are fitted with Indonesian antiques. Hindu deities guard the tropical garden that borders the sea with just a narrow section of beach.

Maskot Beach Resort £

Jl. Raya Senggigi
Senggigi
Tel. 03 70 69 33 65
Fax 03 70 69 32 36
21 delightful bungalows on the beach of Senggigi with lots of watersports facilities. The small resort restaurant serves Balinese as well as »American style« breakfasts, fruit juices and dishes typical of the country.

Dharmarie £

Senggigi Beach
Tel. 03 70 69 30 50
Small, inexpensive complex right on the beach. Simple bungalows with air-conditioning interspersed by lawn and tropical flowers. Reduced prices for longer stays.

Population   Approximately 3 million people live on the island of Lombok; 85% of them are **Sasak**, the indigenous inhabitants. The Sasak people are thought to have originally come from northwest India, and possibly also from Burma (present-day Myanmar). This occurred some time around the 14th century. A possible indication of Burmese origin is the great similarity of Sasak traditional clothing to that of mountain tribes living in today's Myanmar. The Sasak primarily live from agriculture. The great majority of the Sasak people are **Muslims**; only about 10% of Lombok's population profess the Hindu faith. The different influences can still be clearly recognized today in the language, culture and traditions of the island.

Some 30,000 Balinese live in Lombok today. Just as in Bali, rice cultivation plays an important role here, but the rice terraces are not nearly as artfully and systematically arranged. In addition, there are vegetable and tobacco plantations, but little produce is exported as the harvests are almost exclusively used for domestic consumption.

Villages and   Even though there has been a discernible trend in recent years tohouses   ward urbanization in Lombok, the majority of the Sasak still live in typical villages. One characteristic feature of these traditional-style settlements is the **rice house** (lumbung). Normally square in shape, these houses are constructed exclusively of the natural materials clay and wood and raised up on stilts. The roofs are usually made of grass, but rice straw can be used as well. The lumbung is a very practically designed structure. Domestic and working animals are housed below, the family lives in the middle and provisions are stored under the high, semicircular roof. Sasak houses are also used as models when designing new hotels.

Religion   In contrast to the Balinese, the majority of the population in Lombok had **converted to Islam** by the 16th century. Apart from an insignificant Hindu minority living mainly in the western part of the island, most of the indigenous Sasak today remain faithful to Islam. Occasionally, especially in the mountain villages in the northern part of the island, there are those who profess the old **Wetu Telu religion**, a form of Islam with elements of Hinduism and an ancestor cult, which involves the veneration of natural shrines.

MATARAM • AMPENAN • CAKRANEGARA

Mataram   Mataram (population: 340,000) is the capital of the island of Lombok and the administrative centre of the Indonesian province of Nusa Tenggara Barat. Although today Mataram and its neighbours, the originally independent towns of Ampenan and Cakranegara, have

A dream beach on Lombok – and not a soul in sight

merged together to the point where their borders have all but disappeared, they have each been able to retain something of their original character. **Ampenan** has remained the port because of its location next to the ocean, but has largely lost its significance. As has always been the case in **Cakranegara**, the Chinese who settled here over the course of the centuries dominate commercial life in the markets and bazaars, which explains why the locals derisively call the place »Chinatown«.

Apart from the museum in Mataram, there are hardly any places of interest in Mataram – Ampenan – Cakranegara to speak of. There are, however, some easily accessible sights in the surrounding area that are worth the trip.

*Lombok Museum	The Lombok Museum is a must for anyone interested in the history of the island, and particularly in the history of its people. In addition to a number of documents and writings, its exhibits include tools, implements, weapons and examples of the decorative arts. Traditional Sasak house architecture is illustrated with a number of models. Most of the displays are explained in both Indonesian and English. ● Jalan Panji Tilarnegara 6, Sun–Thu 8am–2pm, Fri until 11am, entry: 3000 rupiah
*Meru Temple	The Meru Temple, built in 1720 by the Balinese Prince Karang, is also worth a visit. In the innermost part of the extensive temple are several merus dedicated to the Hindu trinity of Shiva, Vishnu and Brahma.
*Lingsar Temple	The Lingsar Temple, located not far north of Cakranegara at the village of Narmada, is venerated by both faithful Hindus and believers in the Wetu Telu religion. On a certain day at the beginning of the rainy season (October–December) the Lingsar Temple attracts throngs of **pilgrims from both religions**. A split gate (candi bentar) opens onto a broad roadway with a pond to the right and left. Standing to the left about halfway down the roadway is a Hindu temple on a square base (no entry allowed) with four shrines (the one on the left faces Gunung Agung, the abode of the gods on neighbouring Bali). A separate shrine is for members of the Wetu Telu religion. Beyond are pools used by worshippers for their ritual ablutions.
Mayura-Water Palace	Close to Jalan Seiaparang are the ruins of the Mayura Water Palace built in 1744 as part of the palace of the Bali princes. Standing in the middle of an artificial lake is an open-sided pavilion accessed by means of a narrow causeway. It was used both as a meeting place for the Hindu princes and as a courtroom.
Pura Segara (Water Temple)	Northwards along the coast is the Pura Segara or Water Temple. There are several small fishing villages along the way with colourfully painted wooden boats. A Chinese and a Muslim cemetery are located in the vicinity of Pura Segara.

SENGGIGI • SUKARARA

Senggigi	Just a few years ago only local children played on the beach here, but now **Senggigi Beach has become a tourist centre** (18km/11mi north of Ampenan). The resort has several decent hotels surrounded by a number of bars and restaurants. The attractions however are li-

mited to the bathing facilities and the beach itself, which is plagued by hordes of pedlars who descend on the holidaymakers, especially in the evening hours.

The small village of Sukarara lies a good 25km/15.5mi southeast of Mataram and is known for its traditional-style hand-woven textiles. These skilfully worked fabrics, often taking months to produce, are offered for sale directly in the village at prices fully justified by the skilled work involved.

Hand-woven fabrics in Sukarara

✱✱ CLIMBING TOUR OF GUNUNG RINJANI

An ascent of the Rinjani volcano, the third highest mountain in the Indonesian Archipelago, is one of the most memorable experiences possible in Lombok. Any tour planned for this worthwhile climb should allow for sufficient time to enjoy the magnificent volcanic landscape of the area, which has been a nature reserve since 1984.

There are several different routes to the summit of Gunung Rinjani (3726m/12,224ft), which is revered by both the Sasak and the Balinese as a sacred mountain. The relatively easy climb from Senaru in the central north of the island is recommended. Not only are a number of local guides available here, but it is also highly likely that there are other tourists willing to join forces and form a group. Most guides will also see to arranging the necessary equipment. A bus or bemo can be taken from Mataram to Anyar. From here it is only a few miles to Senaru. It is best to spend the night in Senaru and get an early start on the 12km/7.5mi hike to Segara Anak Cater Lake the next morning. The ascent, best begun early in the morning before sunrise, is quite easy; just follow any of the mostly well-travelled paths with trail markers beginning in Sengara that are numbered from 1 to 200. An ascent all the way to the summit of the volcano requires not only ample time but also good physical condition. The summit can be reached from the crater lake in about 4.5 hours. From the summit there is not only a **fantastic view** of the crater lake and the entire island of Lombok, but you can also see all the way to Bali and its highest mountain, Gunung Agung. Except during the rainy season, the descent from the crater's rim down to the crater lake can be made in a good three hours. A trail from the lake leads in about 1.5 hours to a highly sulphurous hot spring that has a temperature upwards of 70°C/158°F; the spring is the source of the small Kali Putih river (white river). Primitive camping sites are provided here, as well as on the shores of the crater lake, making it possible to extend the tour for several days.

Holy mountain

The Gili Islands – A Divers' Paradise

The coastal strips around Bali and Lombok have some of the world's best diving spots to offer, but they are not such an obvious destination for divers as the Maldives and Mexico. However, divers all around the Gili Islands enjoy warm, clear waters, a species-rich underwater fauna as well as wrecks and caves.

During the trip out to the coral reefs it is possible to see turtles and sharks; when diving down to the reef, you will be surrounded by colourful fish. The diversity of tropical reef fish in this area is indeed unique. Underwater photographers will be particularly happy because many fish are not disturbed by divers.

The reefs have very different structures: in addition to flat regions with soft corals and sections with channels, caves and arches there are also reefs that should be visited only by experienced divers.

Mantas and Mola mola

The waters off Bali's east coast offer good conditions. The turquoise depths attract divers with a large variety of exotic fish and a largely intact coral world. See manta rays, schools of large tuna fish and mola mola, the ocean sunfish so famous among divers.

The Gili Islands are synonymous with fascinating diving experiences (gili = island). They consist of three small islands to the northwest of Lombok: Gili Trawangan, Gili Meno and Gili Air. It is easy to get to them by speedboat from Bali (approx. 1hr) or from Lombok. The car-free Gili Trawangan has several excellent dive resorts and dive bases. The lovely »Villa Ombak« has a sophisticated design and was built in the typical Balinese style, combining a rustic ambience with luxury and a closeness to nature. It too arranges dive trips and makes equipment available.

Gili Biaha

The exotic underwater panorama of the Gili Islands surprises European divers and thrills snorkellers too: the coral reefs are home to very different inhabitants.

Gili Biaha for example, nothing more than a rock in the Strait of Lombok, can boast a steep underwater cliff that drops off in steps, a veritable playground for reef sharks among others. The white-tip reef sharks, which grow to almost 2m/6ft and sleep motionless below overhangs, have developed a special breathing technique that allows them to no longer have to swim in order to channel water over their gills.

Thanks to their location in the middle of the open ocean, it is possible to encounter manta rays and ocean sunfish when diving around Gili Biaha. Floating in the current, the manta rays have cleaner fish take care of them. In the middle of coral gardens divers will encounter a large number of other small and tiny marine inhabitants.

The Gili Islands attract divers with their fascinating underwater world

Gili Tepekong

Gili Tepekong is the name of the small rocky island off the eastern coats of Bali (approx. 15 mins by boat from Padang Bai) that excites experienced divers with cliffs, caves and coral scree; however, there are some dangerous currents here. Dive sites near Gili Tepekong start at a depth of seven metres. Here too, with a bit of luck and a knowledgeable guide divers will see sleeping whitetip reef sharks, which only hunt at night. The reef extends across three rocks and is an ideal spot for this shark species that lives in the entire Indo-Pacific. What divers love about Gili Tepekong is that they can see the entire palette of tropical reef fish and many different coral formations in one spot.

Gili Selang

Gili Selang is the name of the small island in northeast Bali between Amed and Gili Biaha. It is separated from Bali proper by a channel around 15m wide and 6m deep. Dives here tend to start at a lagoon on the island's north side, a natural treasure trove full of corals and colourful reef fish. While the lagoon is relatively shallow, the reef drops off steeply to great depths on the south side of Gili Selang. This is where the big fish are to be found. There is a wreck around which divers will find a wide variety of coral species that are surrounded by schools of fish.

A view of Gunung Riniani and Lake Segara Anak

GILI ISLANDS

Popular trips for holiday-makers on Lombok The three small islands of Gili Air, Gili Meno and Gili Trawangan lie only a few miles off the northwest coast of Lombok. They can be reached by boat from the small port town of Pemenang. The crossing takes between 20 minutes and an hour. The Gilis – as water sports enthusiasts from all over the world have been calling them for ages – offer **fantastic beaches** and an **underwater world that is mostly still intact**. All motorized traffic is banned. The traditional cidomos (horse and cart) serve as transportation. Most of the lodgings offer only modest comfort but are cheap. The best spots for diving and snorkelling are to be found on Gili Trawangan, which, with its 300ha/740ac, is the largest of the Gili Islands (▶MARCOPOLO Insight, p.196).

** Mengwi

━━━━━━━━━━━━━━━━━ ✧ **L 7**

Region: Southwest Bali   **Distance:**
Administrative district: Badung   16km/10mi
Population: 20,000   northwest of
Altitude: 95m/310ft   Denpasar

Mengwi was once the chief town of the principality of the same name. Its rulers played a role in Bali's history insofar as they were continually having to come to terms with other powers – at first in a power struggle with the princes of Klungkung and Gianyar and later with the Dutch colonial rulers, to whom they rapidly acquiesced. In 1891 the rulers of Tabanan and Badung divided up the principality amongst themselves, putting an end to its independent status.

WHAT TO SEE IN AND AROUND MENGWI

Pura Taman Ayun (Garden Temple in the Water) is one of Bali's six state temples making it one of the most important temples on the island. The imposing temple complex – one of the largest on the island – is **set on an island in a river**. The inner temple is also surrounded by a moat. Having passed through a split gate (candi bentar), a large fountain dedicated to the underworld can be seen in front of the entrance to the inner temple. The innermost temple, entered through a covered gate (candi korung), has no less than 27 structures of differing importance and purpose. The great significance of the Pura Taman Ayun can be recognized by the fact that it is not only used to worship the deities for which the temple was built, but also those who come to visit from other shrines during their celebrations. This includes, for instance, the gods who make their home on Gunung Agung and Gunung Batur. A meru next to the enclosure wall is dedicated to the rice goddess Dewi Sri, and the third bale on the left-hand side is held to be home to a number of gods. Pura Taman Ayun was built in 1634 during the reign of Raja Gusti Agung Anom and given its present appearance around 1937.

**Pura Taman Ayun

Mengwi

GETTING THERE
There are regular bus and bemo connections from Denpasar to Ubung. Bemos can also be found along the road to Mengwi.

The museum's two pavilions can be reached by a small ferry. The museum displays pictures and models detailing the Manusia Yadnya ceremonies.

Manusia Yadnya Museum

*Monkey forest of Sangeh

Like so much in Bali, the monkey forest of Sangeh, 20km/13mi north of Denpasar and 10km/6mi from Mengwi, has become very commercialized. Even before reaching the forest where **hundreds of monkeys live wild**, visitors are subjected to a plethora of souvenir shops lining the path leading from the car park. According to legend, the monkeys are the living progeny of Hanuman, the monkey king, a central figure in the Indian epic, the Ramayana (▶p.73). They are therefore considered sacred, and venerated in Pura Bukit Sari, a temple in the middle of the forest thought to date from the 17th century. Even more impressive than the temple are the massive trees towering around it, which are found nowhere else in Bali. Their origin is unknown. Beware – the monkeys can sometimes be rather aggressive. This is particularly true of mothers with young. It is best to keep a safe distance to avoid getting bitten. Handbags should be kept closed and cameras put away during the walk through the forest. People who wear glasses should be aware that the monkeys like to

Surrounded by broad moats populated by water lilies, the Pura Taman Ayun has the feel of a small island

play with a borrowed pair. Feeding the animals can also present problems. The monkeys have a tendency to grab food out of visitors' hands when they approach with a bag of nuts or with bananas. Some animals will pursue tourists in order to get at the tasty treats more quickly.

In Marga, situated 15km/9.3mi northwest of Mengwi, is the **Margarana National Memorial** that commemorates the battle for independence against the Dutch on 20 November 1946. Next to it are the cemetery for the 1371 fallen Indonesians and a memorial museum.

Marga

❶ Daily 9am–4pm, entry: free

** Negara

————————————————————— ⟡ D 5

Administrative seat of the district of Jembrana
Region: West Bali
Altitude: 120m/395ft

Distance: 33km/20mi southeast of Gilimanuk
Population: 25,000

Most of Bali's Muslims live in Negara, right in the middle of one of the island's most thinly populated regions. This undoubtedly has to do with its relative proximity to the neighbouring island of Java, which has a predominantly Islamic population. Negara has hardly any tourist attractions but is widely known for the water-buffalo races that take place in the city between July and October.

Negara

TOURIST INFORMATION
Jembrana Government Tourist Office
Jl. Surapati 1
Negara
Tel. 03 65 4 12 10

GETTING THERE
Head 97km/60mi west from Denpasar towards Gilimanuk. There are regular buses from Denpasar to Tegal. It is best to take bemos from Gilimanuk or Pulukan.

WHERE TO EAT
Makan Wirapada £
Jl. Ngurah Rai 107, tel. 03 65 4 11 61
The hotel restaurant serves good, simple Indonesian dishes.

WHERE TO STAY
Jimbarwana £
Jl. Udayana 2, tel. 03 65 4 10 60
This hotel has 49 comfortable rooms, a café and a restaurant, a well-tended pool and a children's pool.

WHAT TO SEE IN AND AROUND NEGARA

The small town has a number of attractive houses typical of the type of construction used in this part of Bali. There are also several mosques that can be visited outside of prayer times, but do ask permission to enter first.

**Water Buffalo Races Twice a year, the otherwise sleepy little town of Negara comes to life. For about the last hundred years or so, in mid-August and between September and November, water-buffalo races, humorously also called »Balinese Ben Hur races«, have been held here. Thousands of visitors converge on the city, many of whom are intent on having a

Ben Hur on Bali: lavishly adorned buffalo teams put on exciting races

flutter. Hotel receptions or the tourist office in Denpasar can supply the exact date. During the races, pairs of buffalos pull two-wheeled carts that carry jockeys trying to urge the clumsy-looking beasts to greater speeds. Amazingly, the water buffalo are capable of reaching speeds of **up to 30mph/50kmh** along the 2.5 km/1.5mi race course.

A small, private gamelan museum with a beautiful collection of regional gamelans (►p.70 and MARCOPOLO Insight, p.204) can be tracked down in **Sangkar Agung** by following the signs saying »Jegog Suar Agung«. The village is a little way off the road to Denpasar, approx. 12km/7.5mi to the southeast of Negara.

Gamelan museum

Meanwhile, the main road to Denpasar continues through the small town of Pulukan, which is particularly popular with travellers wishing to get off the beaten track. The lodgings available here are admittedly only modest, but surfers will appreciate the good waves.

Pulukan

✶✶ Peliatan

✦ M 7

Region: Central Bali
Administrative district: Gianyar
Altitude: 66m/217ft
Population: 2000

Distance:
2km/1.2mi south
of Ubud

Peliatan is popular with visitors to Bali who favour idyllic country charm over the bustle of the tourist centres. Two of Bali's most famous dance groups call Peliatan home. At certain times their rehearsals in the royal palace of Puri Agung are open to the public.

WHAT TO SEE IN PELIATAN

Peliatan's temples are of little cultural or historical significance. An exception is **Pura Pande**, the »Temple of the Blacksmiths«, which has an exceedingly attractive covered gate (candi korung) of red brick and white tuff. Beyond it is a Garuda figure on a wall that protects against demons (aling aling). A further protective wall stands in front of the steps leading into the inner courtyard.

Agung Rai's painting gallery, the largest of its kind in Bali, located on Jalan Rengosekan, is a must for art lovers. Agung Rai (born 1955), a descendant of a royal family, has been a committed collector of Balinese art for many years. It is thanks to him that many local artists

✶✶Agung Rai Fine Art Gallery

Traditional Balinese Music

You will encounter gamelan music everywhere on Bali. Western ears may need to get used to the unusually off-tone music and endlessly repeating rhythms at first. But with time you can recognize the melodies of the different instruments, which can be meditative or quick depending on the region.

Listen to and watch gamelans

Gong (A)
Marks the end of a section of music.

Kempuls (B)
small gongs

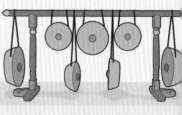

Slenthem (C)
Has a sound box made of bamboo pipes

Gender (D)
Like the slenthem, but with higher tones and twice as many sound plates

Celempung (E)
Instrument with 26 strings, a kind of zither

▶ **Types of tones**
There are two types of tones in gamelan: the Sléndro system, which consists of five tones, and the Pélog system, which consists of seven tones. The Pélog tones are called:

Penunggul	1
Gulu	2
Dhadda	3
Pélog	4
Lima	5
Nem	6
Barang	7

Pélog Bonang

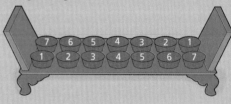

Pélog in western musical notation

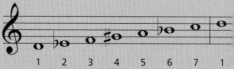

Kenong (F)
kettle gongs

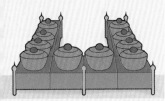

▶ Layout of a gamelan orchestra

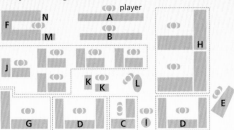

player

Gambang (G)
Like a xylophone, 17 to 20 wooden sound plates, melody instrument

Bonang (H)
Consists of 10 to 14 bronze kettles, elaborates the melody

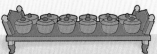

Suling (I)
Bamboo flute

Saron (J)
Metallophone with 6 to 7 sound plates, plays the main melody

Kendang (K)
Drum, makes the rhythm, is played by the conductor

Rebab (L)
Two-stringed instrument for bowing, sounds like a violine

Kempyang (M) & Kethuk (N)
small kettle gongs

▶ Notation
Unlike the Western system notes are written as numbers.

1 5 6 1   5 6 1 2

3 5 3 2   1 6 3 5

2 2 . 3   5 6 5 3̂

1̄2 . 2 1   6 5 3 ⑤

Dot over a number One octave higher

Dot under a number One octave lower

Downward circumflex Is played by the kenong

Upward circumflex Is played by the kempul

Circled number Gong

Plus over number Is played by the kethuk

Simple dot Pause or fading tone

Line over several numbers Notes are played twice as fast

Peliatan

GETTING THERE
The road to Peliatan heads northeast from Denpasar towards Ubud. There are regular bus and bemo connections from Denpasar to Kereneng and from Ubud.

have had the opportunity of presenting their work to a wider public and are able to live off the sale of their paintings. The gallery owner reinvests the proceeds from the pictures sold in new paintings, constantly increasing the considerable size of his collection. The **Agung Rai Museum of Art** (ARMA) with works by Walter Spies, Rudolf Bonnet and Le Mayeur (►MARCOPOLO Insight, p.214) now belongs to the Fine Art Gallery on the Jalan Pengosekan, as do the Café Arma, the ARMA Thai Restaurant and the ARMA Resort with 23 rooms.

Agung Fine Art Gallery: Jalan Pengosekan, daily 8am–5pm, entry: free, www.agungraigallery.com

Agung Rai Museum of Art: daily 9am–6pm, entry: 25,000 rupiah www.armabali.com

Museum Rudana

Another museum that largely focuses on modern art is the Rudana Museum on Jalan Cok Rai Pudak 44, which is surrounded by a lovely garden. Modern Balinese paintings are displayed on the first two floors and numerous classic works are to be found on the third. Adjoining the museum is the Rudana Fine Art Gallery.

❶ Mon–Sat 9am°5pm, Sun noon–5pm, entry: 20,000 rupiah www.therudana.org

✳ Penelokan

✳ **N 4**

Region: North Bali	**Distance:**
Administrative district: Bangli	40km/25mi north
Altitude: 1452m/4764ft	of Ubud
Population: 1000	

Translated, the name Penelokan means something like »beautiful view«. And that is by no means exaggerated. The panorama enjoyed here consists of a fascinating landscape with Lake Batur stretching out below and the summit of the Gunung Batur volcano towering above.

Once, both Penelokan and the village of Batur (►p. 209) lay directly at the foot of Gunung Batur. The inhabitants patiently accepted the considerable damage caused by the volcanic eruptions in 1917 and 1926 before they decided after the latest eruption in 1963, which oc-

Experience Penelokan

GETTING THERE
After Penelokan head from Denpasar to Bedulu, then take the road towards Lake Batur. There are buses several times a day from Denpasar-Kerereng. All larger towns have bemo and bus connections to Penelokan and/or Kintamani.

WHERE TO EAT
Lake View Restaurant £ £
Lake View Hotel
Penelokan, Kintamani
Tel. 03 66 5 25 25
The hotel restaurant serves up typical Balinese fare along with an excellent view of Gunung Batur and the crater lake.

WHERE TO STAY
Lake View Hotel £ £
Penelokan, Kintamani
Tel. 03 66 5 25 25
www.lakeviewbali.com
In its fantastic location on the edge of the crater, the »Lake View« features stylish rooms with views of the volcano and the lake. Many guided hikes and excursions to the surrounding area can be booked in the hotel. There are also regular cultural and musical events.

curred at roughly the same time as the Gunung Agung eruption, to resettle the village on a less dangerous spot higher up on the rim of the crater.

WHAT TO SEE IN AND AROUND PENELOKAN

The awe-inspiring view of the volcano, Gunung Batur, and Lake Batur, impressive though it is, is about all that Penelokan has to offer. Any sights of interest were completely destroyed in the eruptions of 1926 and 1963. One of these was a temple dedicated to the goddess Dewi Danu containing a shrine that was highly venerated because of her function as a tutelary of the seas and the waters of Lake Batur. As if by a miracle, it was spared by the flows of lava and is today in Pura Ulun Danu Batur. The village has many restaurants, souvenir shops and stands and countless numbers of souvenir hawkers move from place to place, sometimes pestering the visitors here.

Penelokan is a good starting point for a four-hour **hike up the Gunung Abang volcano**, which, at 2153m/7064ft, is a good 400m/ 1300ft higher than Gunung Batur rising up on the opposite shore of Lake Batur. Gunung Batur can also be easily climbed from Penelokan.

**Gunung Abang

With an area of some 140 sq km/54 sq mi, the Batur crater **is one of the world's largest volcanic craters**. It was formed millions of years ago by the collapse of the magma chamber after the volcano vent

**Danau Batur (crater lake)

Excursion boats on Lake Batur, with Gunung Batur rising up behind

had been partly emptied through an eruption. Lake Batur formed in roughly the centre of the caldera and today has a maximum depth of 100m/330ft.

Gunung Batur A tour to the summit of Gunung Batur (also called Gunung Lebah or »Mountain in the Depths«) offers the chance to experience some fabulous landscapes. The climb can be made in three hours at most, even by the less experienced, provided you have good footwear because of the loose lava rock. Since the mountain is often already veiled in thick clouds in the morning hours, it is best not to set off too late. First, take the road from Penelokan down to Kedisan and follow it to Toya Bungkah, a village on the western shore of the crater lake known for its hot sulphur springs. A **well marked trail begins south of Toya Bungkah and leads up the volcano. While hiking through the marvellous scenery, do not stray from the path because the danger of fumaroles lurks on all sides. There is a stunning view from the summit of the barren landscape with its bizarre lava formations, the valley and Gunung Abang opposite. Those wishing to hike around Gunung Batur should have a good head for heights. In some spots the route heads over ridges with frighteningly deep abysses on both sides. An alternative route up Gunung Batur involves a three-hour climb from the village of Pura Yati. For reasons of safety, it is best to

make the ascent **accompanied by a person who knows the territory**. There are plenty of Balinese interested in guiding visitors on the
three-hour tour.

6km/4mi along road no. 35 to the northwest of Penelokan, just before reaching the bustling market town of Kintamani sprawled out
along the road, lies the village of Batur, which has some inexpensive
accommodation on offer. The highlight here is the significant **Pura
Ulun Danu Batur** temple complex. The buildings are grouped
around a shrine in the form of an eleven-tiered meru dedicated to the
goddess of the lakes and rivers, Dewi Danu, that survived the volcanic eruptions of 1926 and 1963. There are several other merus for-
ming an impressive backdrop, especially in the morning and evening.
The temple complex of black lava rock underwent several years of
restoration and expansion. It now encompasses nine main temples
with a total of 285 shrines and pavilions that are dedicated to the
Hindu deities of Shiva, Brahma and Vishnu. Of particular note are
the demons depicted in the entrance area, which are considered to be
guardians and protectors against evil spirits. The temple grounds offer a superb view of the surrounding mountain scenery. Batur was
threatened by the volcanic eruption of 1917 and then partially destroyed nine years later by lava flows. The villagers then abandoned
their original village and built new homes on higher ground, which
seemed safer to them. When Gunung Batur erupted once again in
1963, the move proved to have been a wise one. The flow of lava did
not reach the new village site.

Kintamani

Up on Mount Penulisan (1745m/5725ft), some 5km/3mi north of
Kintamani, is the temple complex of Pura Tegeh Koripan, the high-
est-lying shrine on Bali. The path up to the complex has close to 350
steps; it is a climb best made only by visitors in suitable physical condition. The ideal time to visit is either early morning or late afternoon. The temple complex, which offers a fine view across the surrounding countryside, dates back to the 11th century and probably
served as a royal temple of the Warmadewa dynasty from Pejeng. The
Pura Tegeh Koripan temple is entered through two split gates. There
is an interesting **stone cube** in front of the entrance on the left-hand
side along with the surviving fragments of a lingam; both cube and
lingam are highly revered. Standing inside the temple are a number
of bales containing stone figures, some presumably dating from the
Hindu-Javanese period in Bali. Of particular note are the figures of
the divine couple, Vishnu and Lakshmi, holding a four-leaf lotus
blossom in their hands. Other interesting figures depict Shiva, Par-
vati, Ganesha and a four-headed Brahma. Standing in the middle of
the courtyard is a throne reserved for Shiva, the lord of the mountain,
when he attends cult ceremonies.

*Pura Tegeh
Koripan

Trunyan   The village of Trunyan on the eastern shore of Lake Batur can be reached in 20 minutes by motorboat from Toya Bungkah. It is inhabited by **Old Balinese** (Bali Aga), who live comparatively traditional lives and have only recently begun taking an interest in tourism.

** **Penida**

✦ O–Q 9/10

Administrative district:
Klungkung   **Altitude:** 0–529m/1,735ft
Area: 322 sq km/124 sq mi   **Population:** 48,000

Lying 8km/5mi off the southeast coast of Bali is Penida (Nusa Penida), an island some 22km/13.5mi by 16km/10mi which actually belongs to a group that includes the considerably smaller islands of Ceningan and Lembongan located off to the northwest. The islands are populated predominantly by Muslims.

Surfing and   The limestone massif that forms the core of the island of Penida
diving   reaches a height of 529m/1736ft. None of the three islands have any agricultural value as the permeable karst soil is hardly suitable for cultivation. The main source of the modest income there is **fishing**.

Penida and Lembongan

GETTING THERE
Penida
Speedboats depart Padang Bai (southwest of Amlapura) several times a day to get to Toyapakeh in approx. 40 mins. From Kusamba, around 6km/3.5mi southeast of Klungkung, the outriggers that depart every morning take around 2.5 hours to Sampalan or Toyapakeh.

Lembongan
To get to Nusa Lembongan (dock at Jungutbatu), you will either have to depart from Toyakapeh (on Penida) or Sanur (on Bali) by outrigger or on a small motorboat (negotiate the price!).

WHERE TO EAT / WHERE TO STAY
Nusa Lembongan
Resort £ £ £ – £ £ £ £
Tel. 03 61 72 58 64
In addition to a beach in Sanghiang Bay and a view of the Agung volcano, this hotel offers tranquillity, relaxation and a lot of water sports. Very good Indonesian and international cuisine is to be enjoyed on the terrace with wonderful views of the beach and the ocean. There is also a pleasant bar nearby.

Bungalows Pemda £
Sampalan (opposite the police station) 14 basic rooms, but with magnificent sea views

Visitors to the island prefer the north coast, an ideal location for surfers and divers.

Penida formerly served as the **place to which convicted criminals from Klungkung were exiled**. Believing as they do in spirits, the Balinese are highly suspicious of Penida Island. As they tell it, the **giant, Jero Gede Mecaling,** an exceptionally evil spirit, lives on the island and has already managed on a couple of occasions to cross the Badung Strait with his band of evil spirits and wreak terror and destruction in Bali. Only after the Balinese fashioned a similarly looking figure of a demon and set it up on the coast did the giant stay away. Even today, on the eve of Nyepi, the festival celebrating the New Year (►MARCOPOLO Insight, p.98), when the Balinese carry gigantic figures of demons through their village to burn them, they mainly have the terrifying giant Jero Gede Mecaling in mind.

WHAT TO SEE ON THE ISLAND OF PENIDA

Those making the crossing to Penida from Kusamba first set foot on dry land in the island's main town, Sampalan. A lively market is held daily near the harbour, but there is not much else of interest here. | Sampalan

The Pura Taman Dalem Penataran Agung temple is situated in the harbour village of Ped between Sampalan and Toyapakeh on the island's north coast. The holy temple shrine stands in a square lotus pond about 50m/164 ft from the beach. | Ped

Located some 5km/3mi southeast of Sampalan is the Goa Karangasari cave with an **underground freshwater lake**. The entrance to the system of caves is somewhat concealed and the cave entrance itself only measures 2.5m/8ft across. Inside, the cave opens up to an impressive 15m/50ft in height with a series of small passages leading off it (bring a powerful torch or hire one from the locals offering their services as guides on the road outside). A walk through the whole cave will lead to the opposite exit in a steep rock wall. | ****Goa Karangasari**

There are a number of nice beaches on the west coast of Penida. The beach at Toyakapeh is particularly attractive to swimmers, snorkellers and divers, but beware, the tides here are quite strong. Occasionally there are dangerous underwater currents, and sharks are sighted from time to time as well. | Beaches

Swimming is not possible on the island's south coast, but the steep cliffs rising sharply up to 200m/656ft above the crashing breakers are impressive. | Seaside cliffs

NUSA LEMBONGAN

*Beaches   The island (population 3500) earns a living from day trippers who
come to snorkel, swim, surf, dive and then return to Bali after 5pm.
There are few cars; three-wheeled taxis are the main form of transport. The main village on the 4km x 2km/2.5mi x 1.2mi island is
Desa Lembongan. The houses are enclosed by decorated stone
walls. Mangos and banana trees can be seen in the gardens. The women of the island harvest algae from the ocean to use as fertilizer or,
finely ground, for cosmetics and medicinal treatments or to sell to
chemical factories. The ruins of a Hindu temple, **Pura Pancak**, are

Outriggers take tourists to the small island of Lembongan

perched on a 50m/164ft-high hill, from which there is a fine panorama of the sea and even the Gunung Agung volcano in Bali. The main attraction, however, is the **»Underground House«**, which took one man 15 years to chisel out beneath the ground. It has rooms, hallways, stairs, a kitchen and a bath, with shafts providing light and air. Reasonable accommodation offering comfort and relaxation can be found in Sanghiang Bay and Nusa Lembongan Resort. A pedestrian bridge connects Nusa Lembongan to the neighbouring island of Nusa Ceningan.

Sanur

✦ **M 9**

Region: South Bali	**Distance:**
Administrative district: Badung	7km/4mi
Altitude: sea level	southeast of
Population: 15,000	Denpasar

Things are somewhat quieter in Sanur than in Kuta and Legian, even though the town just southeast of Denpasar has experienced a boom in recent years.

The basis for this boom had been established much earlier, though, when the Grand Bali Beach Hotel was built in 1967, the first hotel in Bali that reached an international standard. This concrete monolith dominated the area and was the reason that the building codes in Bali were changed to restrict the height of new structures to that of the tallest palm tree in the vicinity. A coral reef lies off the beach and can be reached by outriggers (jukung). Sanur's lagoon is good for swimming except at low tide; the current is dangerously strong beyond the reef.

Compared to Kuta and Legian, Sanur is considered to be **a somewhat finer class of resort** and, accordingly, luxury hotels line the beaches. That may be the reason that the sand here is also a little cleaner. The **spectacular sunrise on Nusa Penida** should not be missed!

Not far from the Grand Bali Beach Hotel is the house of the Belgian painter, Le Mayeur, who died in 1958. It has been turned into a museum (▶MARCO POLO Insight, p.214).
   Le Mayeur House

🅞 daily 8am–2pm, entry: 10,000 rupiah

Bali's oldest artefact is a stone pillar that can be found on the southern outskirts of town behind Pura Belangjong. It has an inscription in Sanskrit and is estimated to be more than 1000 years old.
   Stone pillar

A Balinese Love Story

One of the most famous love stories between a foreigner and a Balinese was that of the Belgian painter Adrien Jean Le Mayeur (1880–1956) and the legong dancer Ni Pollok. The couple resided in a villa in Sanur, which was turned into a museum after Ni Pollok died.

It all happened in 1933. Ni Pollok, Bali's foremost legong dancer and a celebrity on the island, turned 16 and was soon to be too old to dance the legong, because, according to the prevailing opinion, the best dancers were to be found in the age group 12 to 17. When, by chance, the delicate beauty met the Belgian painter Adrien Jean Le Mayeur, who had come to the island a year earlier, the two fell in love. Ni Pollok became Le Mayeur's model and the one year the painter from far away had wanted to spend on the island turned into many decades. Two years after the first meeting, the artist and the legong dancer married.

A Bali Style Villa

Ni Pollok purchased land in Sanur and the two of them decided to build a house. She and Le Mayeur, a graduate of a technical school and self-proclaimed hopeless romantic, resolved to design the property in traditional Balinese style. The famous sculptor Ida Bagus Made Pantri assisted them in any way he could and, taking their time, they started construction. Time was of such little consequence that it was not until two decades later that the construction team were in agreement – their project was completed.

Teak wood and magnificent carvings characterize the interior. Some wooden blinds feature carved scenes from the Ramayana, the huge Indian Hindu epic. It is said that the completion of a single ornamented table took more than half a year. Le Mayeur was a perfectionist: the windows were placed so that each one appears like a painting, revealing a scene of his creation in the garden, such as a special flowering tree, an artwork or the pond guarded by lotus blossoms.

Enthusiastic Visitors

Mayeur became a renowned and highly regarded artist, whose fame spread far beyond the borders of Indonesia. The exhibitions of his paintings in Singapore (1937), Kuala Lumpur (1941) and Singapore (1941) were extraordinary successes. In 1951, National Geographic magazine dedicated a story to Le Mayeur and remarked that the hospitality of the Belgian-Balinese couple was exceptional. Indeed, numerous visitors, including many foreigners taking a holiday in Bali, came and went to and from the couple's villa, being served trays of delicacies by the lady of the house and her servants. Le Mayeur and Ni Pollok were even able to welcome Sukarno, Indonesia's first president, and the Indian Prime Minis-

Legong dancers in magnificent costumes

ter Nehru in Sanur in 1956. Supposedly it was Sukarno who inspired the childless couple to erect a museum on their marvellous property after their deaths.

Le Mayeur Museum

The painter died two years later and was buried in Brussels. Ni Pollok lived in Sanur until her death at the age of 68 in 1985. The Le Mayeur Villa on the beach went to the state, and was made into a museum. Along with a large number of Indonesian art treasures and antiques, there are 88 of Le Mayeur's colourful paintings on display. The two most famous are of his favourite subject – his wife. The Le Mayeur Museum is located 200m/220yd north of Grand Bali Beach Hotel in Jl. Hang Tua in Sanur and is open daily 8am–2pm; entry fee: 10,000 rupiah.

Sanur

TOURIST INFORMATION
Denpasar Tourist Office
Jl. Surapati 7
Denpasar
Tel. 03 61 22 36 02
www.balidenpasartourism.com

GETTING THERE
Regular bus connections from Candi
Dasa, Kuta Lovina, Padangbai and Ubud.
Bemos can be flagged down along Jl.
Danau Tambligan and Jl. Danau Poso.
The island of Lembongang (▶Penida) can
be reached by outrigger or motorboat
from Sanur. The cross from the northern
end of the beach takes about one hour.

WATER SPORTS
Sanur is a centre for a wide variety of
water sports. Besides the beachfront hotels, there are a number of small businesses and private individuals offering
diving and snorkelling trips and windsur-
fing courses. Trips lasting several hours
in one of the many outrigger canoes are
very popular (do not forget sun protection). Jet skis and paddle boats are also
offered for hire. With the capital close
by, the beaches are quite busy at weekends and the number of stands offering
snacks, batik and arts and crafts, already
quite numerous on weekdays, increases
even more. Among the places that can
be recommended for surfing instruction
and diving courses is:

Ena Dive Centre & Marine Adventure
Jl. Tirta Ening 1, Sanur
Tel. 03 61 28 88 29
www.enadive.co.id

WHERE TO EAT
Lotus Pond £ £ – £ £ £
Jl. Danau Tamblingan
Tel. 03 61 28 93 98
Serves dishes from all regions of Asia
and puts on dance performances from
time to time.

Restaurant Penjor £ £
Jl. D. Tamblingan 141
(200m/220yd north of the Hyatt)
Tel. 03 61 28 82 26
The »Penjor« puts on traditional dance
performances several times a week.

Warung Mamarita £
Jl. Danau Tamblingan 152
Tel. 03 61 28 79 69
Serves delicious calamari dshes and
freshly caught grilled fish, upon request
also the Balinese classic babi guling (sucking pig).

WHERE TO STAY
Bali Hyatt Hotel £ £ £
Jl. Danau Tamblingan 89
Tel. 03 61 28 12 34
www.bali.resort.hyatt.com; 389 rooms
A successful synthesis of luxury, torpical
ambience and Balinese decor, along with
an atmosphere good for body and soul.

Inna Grand Bali Beach Hotel & Spa £ £ – £ £ £
Jl. Hang Tuah, Tel. 03 61 28 85 11
www.innagrandbalibeach.com; 574
rooms
Hardly any visitor will get past this hotel:
it is the seat of several airline companies.
The hotel, housed in the island's only
skyscraper, has comfortable rooms that
are unfortunately somewhat sterile in

their decor. Several restaurants, cafés, bars and shops.

Sanur Beach Hotel £ £ £
Jl. Danau Tambligan
Tel. 0361 28 80 11
http://www.sanur-beach-hotel.com
One of Bali's oldest hotels: a luxury resort on the southern beach of Sanur in the middle of a wonderful tropical garden that is romantically lit after sunset.

Paradise Plaza £ £
Jl. Hang Tuah 46
Tel. 03 61 28 17 81
This complex, surrounded by a lot of water, is particularly family-friendly: children

like the »Camp Splash« with water slides and good opportunities for playing. There are an excellent spa and good restaurants for the grown-ups.

Segara Village £ £ £
Jl. Segara Ayu
Tel. 03 61 28 84 07
www.segaravillage.com
Stone gods, flower arrangements and the scent of the lotus blossom: the reed-covered bungalows of this hotel complex built on the beach in the style of a Balinese village are very comfortable, with modern interiors. There is a spa along with several restaurants and bars.

A trip to Bali Orchid Garden (3km/1.8mi north) is a wonderful place for an outing. It can be found 3km/2mi north of Sanur. Thousands of these elegant plants can be admired there. The shop on the premises sells orchid honey and other orchid products.   **Orchid Garden**

❶ Jl. Bypass Topathi, daily 8am–6pm, entry: 1000,000/50,000 rupiah (adults/children up to the age of 12), www.baliorchidgardens.com

Padang Galak lies only a few miles north of Sanur. Every year in July, it attracts tourists and Balinese alike when the large **Kite Festival** takes place. Initially, the object of this event was to give a boost to the flagging art of Balinese kite making, but the contest has developed into a major tourist attraction. The black beach is a favourite meeting place for surfers.   **Padang Galak**

** Seminyak

✴ K 2

Region: South Bali	**Distance:** 13km/8mi southwest of Denpasar
Government district: Badung	
Altitude: sea level	**Population:** 35,000

In the 1970s the former home or rice farmers and fishermen turned into a hideaway for stars; Mick Jagger, the Guinness family and members of the English aristocracy checked into private luxury villas and the town developed into a destination for a trend-conscious public interested in luxury.

Seminyak

TOURIST INFORMATION
Government Tourist Information Centre
Jl. Benasari 7
Kuta
Tel. 03 61 75 40 92

GETTING THERE
Seminyak likes away from the road from the airport to the capital of Denpasar. Good bemo connections to Kuta-Legian and Denpasar.

SHOPPING
The fashion on sale in the boutiques of Seminyak is created by designers from Asia and Australia and is among the most exclusive and expensive in Bali. Teak furniture and decorative objects are appreciated by the many foreign nationals living in Seminyak and the neighbouring town of Canggu.

WHERE TO EAT
Gateway of India £ £
Jl. Abimanyu 10
Tel. 03 61 73 29 40
www.baliindianfood.com
Simple interior but the best Indian cuisine on the southwest coast, e.g. kadai chicken.

Gado-Gado £ £ £ £
Jl. Camplung Tanduk 99
Tel. 03 61 73 69 66
www.gadogadorestaurant.com
This restaurant has been considered one of the best in Seminyak for more than 20 years. The exquisite beach location and the smart interior contribute to this reputation. Enjoy a cocktail in one of the open lounges before being seated for dinner: crab ravioli, seafood risotto and lamb chops – everything here is excellent.

Ku De Ta £ £ £
Jl. Laksmana
Tel. 03 61 73 69 69
www.kudeta.net
This Asian-Italian restaurant is excellent but the actual meeting place is the associated smart lounge bar on the ocean. Treat yourself to one of the outstanding drinks or champagne cocktails.

Warung Ocha £ £
Jl. Raya Seminyak 52
Tel. 03 61 73 62 22
Inexpensive prices, top quality and a pleasant atmosphere in the small, snug patio garden explain the great popularity of this restaurant. In addition to fresh fruit and vegetable juices, diners are attracted by cocktails and a large selection of Balinese and Indonesian dishes, international classics and fresh baked goods.

WHERE TO STAY
The Oberoi
£ £ £ £
Jl. Kayu Aya
Tel. 03 61 73 03 61
www.oberoihotels.com/oberoi_bali
75 rooms
One of the island's best hotels for more than 30 years. It is stylish, like all the hotels of this Indian luxury chain. The amphitheatre restaurant puts on Balinese dances three times a week during the buffet; the Kura-Kura restaurant is both romantic and luxurious. It is just a stone's throw from the ocean.

The Legian £££served
Jl. Kayu Aya
Seminyak Beach
Tel. 03 61 73 06 22
www.ghmhotels.com
Asian minimalism, shiny, dark tropical hardwood and lavish flower arrangements shape this wonderful beach hotel that was designed by architectural legend Ibrahim Jaya. It has 67 suites of which the smallest measures 99 sq m/1066 sq ft and the terraces have daybeds with views of the sea. After sunset The Legian reveals itself in all its beauty, when countless lights illuminate the gardens and the ocean. Understated, perfect service, Swiss management.

The Elysian £££
Jl. Saridewi 18
Tel. 03 61 73 09 99
https://theelysian.com

In a hidden spot in the second row: this boutique hotel has 26 villas decorated in the modern Asian style. It has its own pool in the shielded garden. The spa, private cabanas by the 25m hotel pool and the outstanding restaurant »Rush Bamboo« will spoil discerning guests. Upon request visitors can have food prepared for them on the terrace of their villa.

Bali Agung Village ££
Jl. Sari Dewi
Tel. 03 61 73 03 67
www.bali-agung.com
Stonemasonry, reed-covered roofs and Balinese interior decorating details: the stylish yet inexpensive complex, the rooms and »deluxe villas« lovingly furnished with four-poster bed and historical prints spoil guests with their quiet location (a few minutes to the beach), pool bar and restaurant.

The development into a tourist destination began with the opening of the sophisticated, beautiful »Oberoi« hotel in the middle of a lavish tropical park by the sea. Today, the transition from ▶Kuta to the adjoining Legian and Seminyak is almost seamless. The Jalan Melasti, which runs in an east-west direction, forms the invisible boundary between Legian and Seminyak, the seaside resort that has made a name for itself through luxurious hotels, good and expensive restaurants and boutiques. Seminyak, ironically called by some the »Beverly Hills« of Bali, is particularly busy during the peak season. Seminyak Beach is wide and has fine sand, and the tranquillity is not interrupted by vehicle noise. Unfortunately frequently underwater currents (marked, among other things, by flags) interfere with swimming pleasures; families with young children have to be particularly careful or fall back on the hotel swimming pools. These are among the best on the island, hidden in expansive tropical settings at the northern end of Seminyak.

Bali's »Beverly Hills«

The trend towards the quick and the cheap is unmistakable. In addition to bars where tourists can »party« around the clock, there are souvenir shops and inexpensive café-restaurants.

✷✷ Singaraja

✦ K 2

Administrative seat of the district of Buleleng	**Population:** 100,000
Region: North Bali	**Distance:** Approx.
Population: 100,000	80km/50mi north of Denpasar
Altitude: 15m/50ft	

Singaraja, the seat of the administrative district of Buleleng and the second largest city in Bali, lies on the north coast of the island. There are large-scale coffee plantations in the surrounding fertile countryside. The new seaport further west plays an important role in the commodities trade with other Indonesian islands.

History   The area around present-day Singaraja was probably already settled by the 10th century. The settlement did not gain any importance, however, until the reign of Raja Panji Sakti in the 16th century, when the raja had his residence, Singaraja (Lion King), built there in 1604 and the village was named after it. The district of Buleleng takes its name from a cereal variety that was cultivated in the region in the late Middle Ages. Singaraja played no small part in the Dutch efforts to bring Bali under their rule. After several failed attempts, the Dutch managed to capture the stronghold in 1849. The town was later made the seat of the Dutch colonial government and remained the island's capital until 1946 (after that ▶Denpasar became the capital).

WHAT TO SEE IN SINGARAJA

The original town of Singaraja has **numerous houses in the Dutch colonial style**. It lies slightly inland and is bordered to the north by the city districts of Pegulangan and Pabeanbuleleng. The place makes a decidedly quieter impression than the current capital of Denpasar. Pabeanbuleleng boasts a charming Chinese temple (usually closed) at the old harbour, two small mosques and a large, bustling market (Tama Lila) held daily in Jalan Ahmad Yani.

✷✷Pura Dalem   Pura Dalem, **one of the most interesting Hindu temples in the north of Bali**, can be found in Jalan Gajah Mada. The temple is entered through a small split gate (candi bentar) which leads into the first temple courtyard. To the left is another gate, elaborately decorated, which reveals the second courtyard that is, surprisingly, set about 2m/6ft lower. Standing to the left is the Bale Gong, and to the right the Bale Pemalaiyagan, in which the gods are welcomed by the wor-

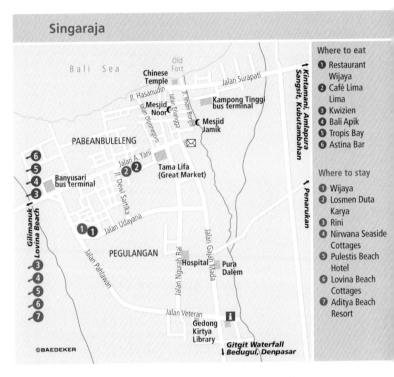

Singaraja

Bali Sea

Old Fort

Chinese Temple

Jalan Surapati

Jl. Hasanudin

Jalan Erlangga

Jalan Imam Bonjol

Jalan Diponegoro

Mesjid Noor

Kampong Tinggi bus terminal

Mesjid Jamik

PABEANBULELENG

Jalan A. Yani

Jl. Dewi Sartika

Tama Lifa (Great Market)

Banyusari bus terminal

Jalan Udayana

Jalan Pahlawan

PEGULANGAN

Jalan Ngurah Rai

Jalan Gajah Mada

Hospital

Pura Dalem

Jalan Veteran

Gedong Kirtya Library

Gilimanuk Lovina Beach

Penarukan

Kintamani, Amlapura Sangsit, Kubutambahan

Gitgit Waterfall
Bedugul, Denpasar

©BAEDEKER

Where to eat
1. Restaurant Wijaya
2. Café Lima Lima
3. Kwizien
4. Bali Apik
5. Tropis Bay
6. Astina Bar

Where to stay
1. Wijaya
2. Losmen Duta Karya
3. Rini
4. Nirwana Seaside Cottages
5. Pulestis Beach Hotel
6. Lovina Beach Cottages
7. Aditya Beach Resort

shippers during the temple festivals. On the right side of the wall separating the first and second courtyards is a wooden seat for the priests with a stand for the offerings. Five steps at the end of the temple lead up to a stone terrace with gedongs for a number of different deities. Take a look at the finely executed **erotic reliefs** throughout the whole temple complex.

The Gedong Kirtya Library stands at the east end of Jalan Veteran in the Sasana Budaya complex, the old palace of the kingdom of Buleleng in the south of the city. A visit can be recommended to those with a burning interest in Balinese history and, preferably, some knowledge of Dutch. Besides **some 3,000 manuscripts written on lontar palm leaves**, the library founded by the Dutch in 1928 also houses countless diaries, newspapers and periodicals as well as 8200 historical books from the period of the Dutch occupation. The books are, however, in a poor condition. Only the palm leaf manuscripts are stored in tin boxes, everything else is stacked on open shelves – and pretty haphazardly at that, seemingly lacking any form of classifica-

**Gedong Kirtya Library

Singaraja

TOURIST INFORMATION
Buleleng Tourist Office
Jl. Ngurah Rai 2, Singaraja
Tel. 03 62 2 51 41

Tourist Information Service
Jl. Raya Lovina-Singaraja, Lovina
Tel. 03 62 4 19 10

GETTING THERE
The road to Singaraja runs from Denpasar northwards via Mengwi and Bedugul, or, much more attractively, from Denpasar to Kapal, then westwards via Antosari to Pengastulan and onwards along the coast via Lovina Beach. There are daily bus connections from Denpasar to Ubung. Bemos drive along the coastal road to Lovina Beach.

GOING OUT
Even though much quieter than the »Bermuda Triangle« of Kuta, Lovina has plenty of options for listening to live music in the evenings. In addition to the restaurants bars and cafes also put on music events that change week upon week.

SHOPPING
The night market by the Banyusari bus station (Jl. J.A. Yani) also has a large number of snack bars.

WHERE TO EAT
Most of Singaraja's restaurants are on the main road J.A. Yani and serve Chinese fare.

❶ *Restaurant Wijaya* £ – £ £
Jl. J. Sudirman 74
Singaraja, Tel. 03 62 2 19 15
Even diners not staying at the hotel like to eat in the best restaurant in town. In addition to Indonesian dishes it serves sandwiches, soups and salads.

❸ *Kwizien* £ £ – £ £ £
Jl. Raya
Lovina
Kaliasem
Tel. 03 62 4 20 31
The focal point lies on European cuisine: from Norwegian salmon to Greek salads and lamb dishes to pasta and French pies. Sophisticated picture gallery.

❺ *Tropis Bay* £ £
Lovina Beach
Kalibukbuk
Tel. 03 62 4 20 90
The open corner restaurant is one of the best and most beautiful restaurants in town and also exceptionally reasonably priced. Enjoy a meal here with views of the ocean.

❻ *Astina Bar & Restaurant* £ £
Lovina
Jl. Mawar
Kalibukbuk
Insider Tip
Tel. 03 62 4 11 87
Pleasant, open garden restaurant that is part of a small hotel (with nine cottages). Dine on benches and chairs in the Dutch colonial style, surrounded by lavish tropical vegetation. Free wifi and the occasional Balinese dance performances attract diners, as do the inexpensive prices and the large selection of dishes and drinks.

❹ *Bali Apik* £
Jl. Bina Ria
Lovina

Kalibukbuk
Tel. 03 62 4 10 50
Meeting place for younger independent travellers who appreciate the delicious breakfast and the inexpensive snacks.

❷ *Café Lima Lima* £

Jl. J. A. Yani, Singaraja
Tel. 03 62 2 17 69
This nice café serves fresh, simple dishes.

WHERE TO STAY

Most visitors prefer hotels in Lovina since they are quieter, more comfortable and less expensive.

❸ *Rini* £

Lovina Beach, Kalibukbuk
Tel. 03 62 4 13 86
www.rinihotel.com
The surrounding tropical gardens, dense bougainvillea hedges and high palm trees impress guests as does the well-tended pool. The guest rooms, all with their own small terrace, are basic, somewhat dark but well looked after.

❹ *Nirwana Seaside Cottages* ££

Lovina Beach, Kalibukbuk
Tel. 03 62 4 12 88
Long-term guests and independent travellers on their way through to Pemuteran and to the national park stay in this basic, tropical-romantic hotel. Friendly employees, inexpensive prices for the accommodation and the food make up for some of the shortfalls.

❺ *Pulestis Beach Hotel* £ – ££

Lovina Beach, Kalibukbuk
Tel. 03 62 4 10 35
A large terrace in front of the (basic) rooms, a lavish garden and a well-tended pool, restaurant and café, all close to the beach and near the Dolphin Statue. The enterprising owners offer organized trips and a taxi service to the nearby destinations.

❶ *Wijaya* £

Jl. J. Sudirman 74
Singaraja
Tel. 03 62 2 19 15, Fax 2 58 17
The 26 rooms of the »Wijaya« (with bath and air-conditioning) are arranged around a courtyard.

❻ *Lovina Beach Cottages* £ – ££

Jl. Raya Kalibukbuk
Pantai Lovina
Tel. 03 62 4 12 85
The hotel in the Balinese style is situated near the centre of town by the dark beach. 32 simple rooms with a safe, air-conditioning and coffee maker. The boats for dolphin watching trips start outside the hotel. Internet access, pool, water sports activities.

❷ *Losmen Duta Karya* £

Jl. J. A. Yani 59, Singaraja
Tel. 03 62 2 14 67
12 rooms with bath and air-conditioning or fan, small courtyard, attentive service.

❼ *Aditya Beach Resort* ££

Lovina, Kaliasem
Tel. 03 62 4 10 59
http://adityalovinabali.com; 80 Z.
Small bungalows right on the beach. Well-tended, simple interiors, a quiet atmosphere, swimming pool. Popular restaurant with sea views. Lots of other inexpensive accommodation (known as homestays, losmen) can be found in the centre of Lovina.

Lovina Beach with its dark sand tends to be fairly quiet

tion. Those with time to spare or wishing to use a rainy day to explore the history of the island just might make a revealing discovery in the Gedong Kirtya Library. The staff allow access to almost everything in the library. It is customary to sign the guest book before leaving.

ⓘ Mon–Thu 7.30am–3.30pm, Fri 7am–12.30pm, entry: 10,000 rupiah

AROUND SINGARAJA

Lovina Beach   A little less than 10km/6mi west-southwest of Singaraja, stretched along the Bali Sea coastline, is the seaside resort of Lovina Beach with a number of new hotels. Even if the quality of the beach is not particularly outstanding – it is **quite narrow and its sands are dark** – a beach holiday here has its attractions as it is much quieter than the overcrowded beaches in the south of the island.

Lovina is made up of several villages, which are **predominantly vi-** **Lovina**
sited by independent travellers looking to book several days of
cheap lodging. Guesthouses, small hotels and restaurants line Jl. Raya
Singaraja, the main street in the town centre, as well as the road leading to the beach, Jl. Rambutan. Bordering to the east is the village
of Banyualit, where the hotels are crammed along Jl. Lovina. Brightly coloured fishing boats lie on the beaches and »beach boys« urge
the tourists to buy souvenirs, take a tour on the water or head into
the mountains. Snorkel tours to the clear waters of the offshore **coral**
reef are proffered on the beach. **Dolphin watching is also on offer**.
Dolphins will usually be sighted during the course of a one-hour
tour, and they then accompany the boat.

Komala Tirtha can be found by turning off the main road from Lo- **Komala**
vina Beach shortly before coming to Singaraja and following the **Tirtha**
signs for a few miles. Komala Tirtha has a hot sulphur spring and
enjoys a delightful setting in a forest. Visitors can bathe in the spring's
pool for a small fee.

Gitgit waterfall is located **in dense jungle** near Bedugul near the vil- ***Gitgit**
lage of Gitgit, located some 10km/6mi inland to the southeast of Sin- **waterfall**
garaja (▸ill. p.120). A path, about 800m/880yds long with a number
of steps, leads from the car park past rice fields, clove trees and
through tropical vegetation. There are stalls offering food to feed the
numerous monkey families, along with patchwork quilts and handicrafts. The spray from the waterfall can already be felt just beyond
the ticket booth were the admission fee is paid. The cataract plum-
mets from a height of about 35m/115ft into a gorge with a stream.
»Showering« and swimming are allowed.
❶ Access daily 9am–5pm, entry: 10,000 rupiah

Standing near the village of Sangsit, about 6km/4mi northeast of **Sangsit**
Singaraja, is the lavishly decorated **Pura Beji**, a temple dedicated to
the fertility and rice goddess Dewi Sri. It belongs to a rice farmers'
cooperative (subak) and exhibits **both Hindu and Chinese-style**
elements. The tripartite split gate opening into the inner temple
courtyard is lavishly ornamented. The faces of grimacing demons
framed by finely crafted lotus blossoms can be made out on its exterior. Beyond is an aling aling, a protective wall to keep out demons,
flanked by two snakes. The diversity of architectural ornamentation
typical of northern Bali is continued inside. Rising above the temple complex is the gedong of the goddess Dewi Sri. Three figures from
the Ramayana can be seen to the right and left on the exterior wall
when leaving the temple. Though the other temple in Sangsit, **Pura**
Dalem, is otherwise plain, the finely detailed stone reliefs are note-
worthy.

Sukawati · Batuan

✳ M 8

Region: Central Bali
Administrative district: Gianyar
Altitude: 95m/312ft
Population: 12,000

Distance:
approx.
17km/10.5mi
northeast of Denpasar

Sukawati is two towns in one. Centuries ago it grew so closely together with Batuan, the town bordering to the north, that only people from the two towns can tell where the boundary between them is. Prince Marakata issued a decree in 1022 ordering that the towns be separated, but nothing much really happened. Today, the large number of Chinese living in Sukawati are putting their stamp on the town.

WHAT TO SEE IN SUKAWATI AND BATUAN

Old tradition

Sukawati and Batuan are **renowned for their many craftsmen**, who offer their wares in the shops lining the thoroughfares. The production of decorative arts has a tradition here. In former times, noted artists stayed in the royal palace of Sukawati. The »**Art Market**« (Pagar Seni) in downtown Sukawati is an interesting place to visit: numerous dealers offer sculptures, puppets, woodcarvings, fans, costumes and all manner of other goods here in a two-storey building. The towns and villages all around Sukawati and Batuan, such as Puaya, are also home to many artisan businesses selling their artistic products.

Sukawati and Batuan

GETTING THERE
From Denpasar head northeastwards towards Gianyar. There are regular bus connections from Denpasar-Kereneng. Bemos can be found along the roads from Denpasar and Gianyar.

Batuan style

The town of Batuan has garnered a certain amount of fame through the distinctive style of painting named after it. This style, which gained significance around 1920, has its focus not so much on religious mythical subject matter but rather on **expressionistic depictions** of the life of the Balinese people. Up until then, artists had considered and painted objects only as a decorative accessory to the much more important underlying intent; now the focus shifted and they concentrated their attention on the person or landscape as subject matter. It is assumed that the impetus for this change in style during the Dutch colonial period was primarily the new rulers, who commissioned works from the local artists and made European painting techniques and equipment available to them. The Batuan style later gained greater influence when painters were among the first tourists arriving in Bali from around the world, and they instructed the islanders. Two of them were the still highly esteemed painters Walter Spies (►Famous People) and Rudolf Bonnet.

** Tabanan

K 7

Administrative seat of the district of Tabanan	**Population:** 12,000
Region: South Bali	**Distance:**
Altitude: 105m/345ft	24km/15mi northwest of Denpasar

Tabanan, the seat of the district of the same name, is located in the fertile region north of Denpasar known as the »Rice Basket of Bali«.

Tabanan's rulers played an important role during the Dutch attempts to occupy Bali. Tabanan was able to maintain its power over the centuries and under its ruler Gusti Pandji Sakti (c1700) became one of the most influential principalities in Bali. When the Dutch landed on the coast on 22 June 1846, the Balinese defences lasted only a few days, though it must be said the rulers had gone into hiding in the hills. It is recorded that one of the rajas said: »While I live the state shall never recognize the sovereignty of the Netherlands! Rather let the kris decide.« And decide it did! When the Dutch finally succeeded in taking Tabanan and stood before the palace, the members of the royal family seized the kris (dagger) and committed ritual suicide (puputan). | History

WHAT TO SEE IN TABANAN AND AROUND

The city has a number of temple complexes, but the really special sights are more to be found in the surrounding area. The busy market (pasar) near the bemo station is worth a visit. Tabanan is otherwise known for having a **good gamelan orchestra**. There is also a Christian mission station. On the eastern edge of town is the small but interesting **Subak Museum** with displays featuring models and farming implements that illustrate rice cultivation in Bali. | Temples, markets and music

 no regular opening hours

The road heading north from Tabanan toward Singaraja passes through a truly **breathtaking mountain landscape** with artfully | **Country-side

Bali Rice Terraces

Bali's lush green rice terrace are lined up on mountain slopes like artistic landscape gardens. The rice farmers harvest up to three times a year. About 5% of Indonesia's rice production comes from Bali, which only makes up about 0.3% of Indonesia's land. This is due to the success of Subak system, which only exists on Bali.

▶ **»Subaks« as World Cultural Heritage**
A village cooperative called a »Subak« takes care of water distribution as well as building and maintenance of the irrigation system of the rice terraces. In 2012 five rice growing regions that are controlled by Subaks were listed as UNESCO World Cultural Heritage.

Temple complex
Pura Ulun Danu Batur

● Lake Batur

Catur region
Angga Batukaru   *BALI*

Pakerisan Valley

Temple complex
Pura Taman Ayun

▶ **Rice varieties**
Three varieties of rice are raised on Bali.
They vary in taste and have different uses.

White rice
Most common for everyday use, both for eating and for daily offerings.

Black rice
Gives sweets a unique taste, but it is also used to make tea.

Red rice
The rarest and most expensive variety is mostly used in ceremonies and also to make tea.

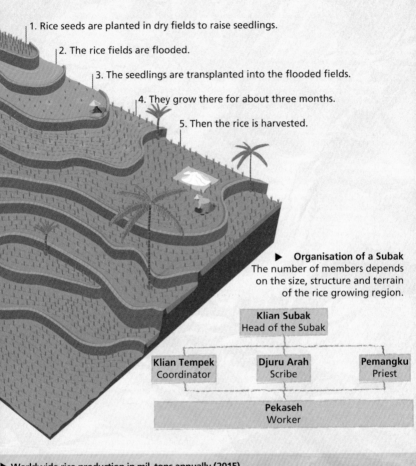

1. Rice seeds are planted in dry fields to raise seedlings.

2. The rice fields are flooded.

3. The seedlings are transplanted into the flooded fields.

4. They grow there for about three months.

5. Then the rice is harvested.

▶ **Organisation of a Subak**
The number of members depends on the size, structure and terrain of the rice growing region.

| Klian Subak |
| Head of the Subak |

| Klian Tempek | Djuru Arah | Pemangku |
| Coordinator | Scribe | Priest |

| Pekaseh |
| Worker |

▶ **Worldwide rice production in mil. tons annually (2015)**
Indonesia stands third in worldwide rice production. Bali contributes 5% of this.

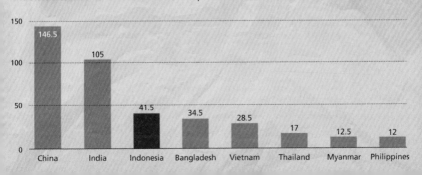

China	India	Indonesia	Bangladesh	Vietnam	Thailand	Myanmar	Philippines
146.5	105	41.5	34.5	28.5	17	12.5	12

Tabanan

TOURIST INFORMATION
Tabanan Tourist Office
Jl. Gunung Agung
Tel. 03 61 81 16 02, Fax 81 27 03

GETTING THERE
To get to Tabanan, leave Denpasar in the direction of Gilimanuk and Negara. There are good daily bus and bemo connections from Denpasar-Ubung.

WHERE TO EAT
There are a few simple warungs in the centre and around the market.

WHERE TO STAY
Puri Anyar £ £
Baturiti, Kerambitan
(7km/4.5mi west of Tabanan)
Tel. 03 61 81 27 74
Guests and visitors to the Puri Anyar, a 17th-century palace, are regularly able to experience the »Palace Nights«, featuring traditional dances and Indonesian culinary specialities.

Alila Villas Soori £ £ £ £   Insider Tip
Banjar Dukuh
Desa Kelating
Kerambitan
Tabanan
Tel. 03 61 8 94 63 88
www.alilahotels.com/soori
The west coast, still largely untouched by tourism, is home to an unusual designer hotel, embedded in among rice fields that extend all the way to Mount Batukau and to the black volcanic beach. Soo K. Chan, the owner of the award-winning architectural office SCDA from Singapore designed this boutique hotel for himself (with a rare »Green Globe« certification for maintaining environmentally friendly standards). Its qualities only become clear little by little. A private, exclusive ambience that blends in with its environment in an ideal way. The dinner in the Coast Restaurant is unsurpassable. It can be enjoyed on a terrace just a few metres from the spray of the ocean waves.

arranged rice terraces and little villages with friendly inhabitants. It is worth taking a little extra time on this route to enjoy the many impressive sights this charming countryside has to offer.

**Kerambitan A few miles seaward is Kerambitan, a village of considerable size. There are two interesting former royal residences here, Puri Anyar and Puri Gede. Both palaces lie directly on the road.

Puri Anyar is actually a faithful reproduction of the original 17th-century building that was destroyed for the most part during an earthquake. The palace complex, which is structured into several courtyards, was already opened to the public in 1967. It is now a hotel with rooms offering a view of a magnificent tropical garden.

The second palace in Kerambitan, **Puri Gede**, stands opposite Puri Anyar. It was built in the 18th century in typical Bali style.

One of the island's six state temples, Pura Luhur Batukau, is located at the foot of Bali's second tallest mountain, the 2276m/7468ft-high Gunung Batukau. The temple is located about 28km/17mi from Tabanan along a well developed road. The expansive temple complex was built in a **romantic jungle setting**. The central shrine faces Gunung Batukau. A small pura dalem stands to the left of the entrance into the first temple precinct. The stone throne for the goddess Batari Uma (here in the manifestation of Durga) with a Vishnu figure mounted on the mythical bird, Garuda, is worth a closer look. The temple is divided into two courtyards and on both sides of the first one are bales that are used for preparing the flower and fruit offerings. A traditional split gate (candi bentar) with ornate reliefs forms the entrance to the second section. Towering upwards inside the second courtyard are several merus with a varying number of pagoda roofs (tumpang) dedicated to different deities. The highest (centre) has seven steps and belongs to Batara Panji Sakti. Left of it is a meru with three tumpangs dedicated to the gods of the five directions, Shiva, Vishnu, Ishvara, Brahma and Mahadevi. Pura Batukau attracts thousands of pilgrims from all over the island who make offerings to the gods for several days every year in March. At those times, the otherwise seemingly remote temple is festooned with colour.

Insider Tip

! MARCO POLO TIP

A visit to the spice garden

Pepper, vanilla, ginger, cinnamon and cocoa; Balinese spice gardens will whisk you away to an aromatic world of intoxicating fragrances. Exotic shrubbery and vegetation abound; take a sniff here and a whiff there, sample strange fruit with a completely unknown name or sip a cup of freshly prepared cocoa. Ready packaged spices, coffees and teas can be purchased afterwards.

**Pura Luhur Batukau

Bubbling away some 7km/4.5mi south of the little town of Wangayegede are the hot sulphur springs of Yeh Panas. A **spacious bathing complex** has recently been built here and provides a large pool for swimming. In addition, private fenced-in »séparées« with effervescent baths can be hired.

*Yeh Panas Hot Springs

If there is one sight among Bali's innumerable attractions that no visitor should miss, then it is surely Pura Tanah Lot (»Land in the Sea«). Every evening, coach-loads of tourists bussed in from Kuta, Legian and Sanur file through a labyrinth of lanes, full of souvenir dealers, to experience one of nature's grand spectacles. The **fascinating sunset** behind the backdrop of the relatively small temple on the rocky cliffs off the coast is a sight to behold. Pura Tanah Lot, which can be reached on foot at low tide, was erected by Pedanda Sakti Bau Rauh. Forced to flee to Bali from religious persecution on

**Pura Tanah Lot

the neighbouring island of Java, he erected several temples on the island. There is a shrine in his honour in Pura Tanah Lot. The highest structure in the temple complex, which is closed to non-Hindus, is a five-step meru (tumpang), the seat of the divine trinity. A sacred snake »lives« in one of the other shrines. The best view of the temple and the sunset is from a specially built **visitors' terrace**. As it is usually full to the last seat, it is advisable to get there early before the tour operators' large omnibuses arrive.

❶ Daily 9am–7pm, entry: 30,000 rupiah

You can only get to Pura Tanah Lot with dry feet at low tide

** Tampaksiring

─────────────────── ✳ M 6

Region: Central Bali
Administrative district: Gianyar
Altitude: 630m/2065ft
Population: 1000

Distance:
78km/48mi
northeast of
Denpasar

If it were not for Tirtha Empul, one of Bali's most important spring temples, the modest market village of Tampaksiring would never appear on any tourist map. Having said that, the villagers of Tampaksiring are also known for their fine wood and horn carvings that can be purchased all over Bali but are best bought right here in the village, where they are cheapest.

WHAT TO SEE IN AND AROUND TAMPAKSIRING

Tampaksiring has a **Vishnu shrine**, Pura Desa. The complex, which has two courtyards, lies on the main road heading north; in the first courtyard stand a couple of pavilions decorated with beautiful carvings and reliefs.

*Pura Desa

Like Tampaksiring, the small village of Pujung is known for the **high quality of its wood carving**. The countryside around Pujung is fantastic, above all when bathed in the light of early morning. It is worth getting up early just to enjoy a walk here at that time of day.

*Pujung

2.5km/1.5mi down the road heading south from Tampaksiring towards Gianyar is an **unusual kind of religious architectural site**. Deep down below in the narrow valley of the river Pakerisan is an ensemble of three groups of rooms or cells resembling a hermitage and another three groups of monuments all hewn from rock. The Balinese call the site Gunung Kawi, which means »Mountain of the Poets«. According to a number of inscriptions, Anak Wungsu, once the ruler of a large part of Java, along with his four wives and another four concubines, is commemorated here – legend has it that the eight women were voluntarily burned to death after Anak's death. If this is true, then the complex assuredly dates back to the 11th century, either to the time Anak was alive or relatively shortly after his death. The narrow footpath from Tampaksiring down to Gunung Kawi first leads to a group of four monuments. The small Pakerisan river cuts through particularly appealing terrain at this point. To the left on the opposite river bank is the group of five monuments; the one positioned a bit higher up could have been for Anak Wungsu. To the right

**Gunung Kawi

of the group of five is a complex with monks' cells and in the middle is a monolith whose significance has yet to be determined. A tenth monument (possibly for one of Anak's high officials) can be found by following the Pakerisan gorge further southward. There are more monks' cells (second and third hermitages) carved out of rock above the river on the east bank as well as some a little further south of the tenth monument.

*Pura Gunung Kawi Sebatu

The terraced complex of the **spring sanctuary** Pura Gunung Kawi Sebatu is best reached by turning right just outside of Tampaksiring and following the signs (approx. 2.5km/1.5mi). Three pools form an ensemble. Added to that is the shrine in the shape of a square pond, in the centre of which stands a small, open shrine with a stone throne. Even though the finely-worked **water spouts** are overgrown with thick moss, the exceptional quality of their craftsmanship is recognizable. The actual spring temple of Pura Sakti Puseh, standing to the side, is always closed.

**Pura Tirtha Empul

The origin of the Pura Tirtha Empul spring sanctuary is tied to a legend. It seems at one time there was a great drought when the demon Vitra had seized power over all of the water in the lakes and rivers and kept them locked away. This brought Indra into action, who thrust a lance into the ground where Tirtha Empul stands today and once again opened the springs. Indra has been considered the »protector of water« ever since. The centrepiece of the spring temple is a lake whose waters, flowing through a total of **31 elaborately designed spouts**, feed four bathing basins. The left pool is reserved for men and the right one is for women to perform ritual ablutions. Once a year, the villagers symbolically cleanse their pots, bowls and water jugs. The »five holy waters«, Pari Suda, Panglukatan, Sudamala, Tirtha Teteg and Bayan Coko, are collected in the small basin to the far right. A gedong standing in the pool's centre is reserved for the god of the spring shrine. Many visitors take the holy water with them from the spring for use in rituals such as rites of passage.

Tampaksiring

GETTING THERE

The road to Tampaksiring departs Denpasar via Celuk in a northbound direction. There are several buses a day from Denpasar. There are good bus and bemo connections from Ubud.

Wisma Negara (Sukarno's former summer residence)

Located above the spring temple is Wisma Negara. The founder of the Indonesian state, President Sukarno (►Famous People), had the palace built as his summer residence in the 1950s. It has two sections separated by a narrow valley cleft but connected by a footbridge. Today the building, furnished in the modern style, serves as an **Indone-**

Girls praying in the Pura Tirta Empul spring shrine

sian government guesthouse. It is occasionally open for tours, but identification papers are required. Its extensive park offers a nice view of the spring temple down below in the valley.

One of the oldest settlements in Bali is Taro (10km/6mi northwest of Tampaksiring). It has an impressive temple, **Pura Gunung Raung**, whose form is supposed to resemble the mountain of the same name in East Java. The place is also noted for its **albino cows**, which are loaned out for religious ceremonies. They can be seen grazing south of the village just outside the **Elephant Safari Park**, where it is possible to take a look at the countryside from the back of a Sumatra elephant.

*Taro

★★ Tenganan

✳ P 6

Region: East Bali
Administrative district:
Karangasem
Altitude: 242m/794ft

Population: 450
Distance:
4km/2.5mi north
of Candi Dasa

The inhabitants of the village of Tenganan have a special ethnicity. Up until the 1980s, this tiny fraction of the Balinese population lived in total seclusion. Tenganan lies at the southern foot of the central volcanic massif whose highest elevation is Gunung Agung.

Special inhabitants

The inhabitants of Tenangan claim to have been created by the god Indra himself and to be a chosen people. As proof of this, they refer to the »Usana Bali«, the Balinese story of creation written on palm leaves as early as the 14th century, which mentions that the exactly 30 families in the village are the **descendents of the gods**. The **Bali Aga** (Old Balinese) of Tenganan form an independent community – much like those in Trunyan (▶p.210) – consisting of a number of groups organized according to strict rules. There is no private property here; everything belongs to the community. As early as about the age of eight, boys and girls must, after a transitional period of a year, join a group (Truna or Daha). From then on, the parents and family play only a minor role. The group assumes the responsibility of raising them to be fully-fledged members of the community (krama desa). Factors such as age, sex, profession and abilities are decisive when they are later sorted into the »right« group, where they remain for the rest of their lives. As the »darlings of the gods«, the Tengananians see the purpose of their lives not in physical labour but rather in leisure – and in preserving old traditions and arts and crafts. They let others work for them. The rice fields around the village are cultivated by outsiders who relinquish a part of the harvest as rent. This leaves the villagers free to devote time to playing gamelan music, weaving artistic textiles – this is the only place where the **art of the double ikat** is still practised (▶p.67 and MARCOPOLO Insight, p.108) – or to copying ancient manuscripts. Whoever leaves the community (e.g. marries a person from another village), loses all rights enjoyed as a native of the village. Although still tolerated in Tenganan, they must

Tenganan

GETTING THERE
Depart Candi Dasa in a northwesterly direction. There are no regular bus or bemo connections. There are motorbike taxis (ojeks) waiting by the side of the road.

move to the eastern part of the village, the Banjar Pande, and they are also no longer permitted to participate in religious ceremonies.

WHAT TO SEE IN TENGANAN

As recently as the 1980s, Tenganan was a village where visitors were highly unwelcome, but since then the Bali Aga have come to realize that good money can be made with tourism and the prosperity they already enjoy can be increased even more. The village is only open to visitors as part of a guided tour in return for which a donation is expected. Visitors are banned from the village's sacred temple com-

**General layout of the village

Tenganan is the only location where double ikat fabrics are made

pounds. After the guided tour it is possible to visit one of the courtyard houses and purchase fabrics (including the famous double ikat) as well as woven basketry. **No motor vehicle traffic** is allowed in Tenganan. The village consists of three avenues running parallel to each other in an imaginary line from Gunung Agung to the sea. Lining these streets are the kampongs (family compounds) with their rice-straw thatched residential and functional buildings. It is quite possible nowadays for the residents to invite visitors in to take a look around. In the western part of the village are those buildings in which groups of boys and girls meet, as well as the Bale Agung, where the married, full members of the village community gather. Further up from the village stands the shrine dedicated to the Old Balinese Prince Pangus, Pura Sembangan, and Pura Santi, the seat of the deities of Gunung Agung.

** Ubud

✦ **M 7**

Region: Central Bali	**Population:** 30,000
Administrative district: Gianyar	**Distance:** 25km/15.5mi northeast of
Altitude: 92m/302ft	Denpasar

Ubud, Bali's »artistic heart« in the centre of the island, nestles in a very appealing tropical setting with lush green rice terraces and almost impenetrable forests and wild gorges. The irrigation of the soil, principally achieved by means of an ingenious system of canals, has enabled Ubud's population to live from farming for centuries. Today, however, the livelihood of the city's inhabitants is based largely on tourism.

Bali's centre of art and culture

Ubud is considered to be Bali's centre of art and culture. Many of the artists living here still derive inspiration from the beautiful landscape all around the city. Some of them – including painters, sculptors, and woodcarvers – have joined together in **artists' communities**. Ubud and it environs are regarded as the »shopping centre« for traditional Balinese arts and crafts. With a little luck, it is still possible to acquire an authentic antique and take it home – after obtaining the necessary export permits. Aside from the numerous artistic attractions, Ubud itself has only a few sites of historical and cultural interest. However thanks to all the accom-

> **!** *Yoga, dance & Balinese cuisine* Insider Tip
>
> MARCO◉POLO TIP
>
> Ubud is a stronghold of exciting workshops and lectures about Bali's culture, ranging from hour-long talks to week-long courses. Tourist offices will have a list of events.

Art temple in Ubud: the Blanco Museum

modation available, it is an **ideal base for daytrips** into the surrounding countryside to visit, for example, the monkey forest, the great white egrets of Petulu or the craftsmen of Mas.

WHAT TO SEE IN AND AROUND UBUD

The museum named after the Balinese painter Suteja Neka (born 1939) will particularly appeal to those with a special interest in the development of **painting in Bali**. Neka received his artistic training in part from his father, who, although a gifted sculptor and an active member of Bali's first artist society, did not gain much of a reputation until his later years. Suteja Neka's breakthrough came in 1966, when his and his father's works were exhibited at the opening of a hotel in Sanur. He subsequently taught young Balinese the basics of painting. In addition, he collected art works in Bali, including pictures by **Walter Spies** (▶Famous People), Rudolf Bonnet and Miguel Covarrubias, as well as numerous works by Balinese artists. The Neka Art Museum

**Neka Museum

Ubud

TOURIST INFORMATION
Ubud Tourist Office
Jl. Raya
Ubud
Tel. 03 61 97 32 85

GETTING THERE
The road from Denpasar to Ubud runs northeastwards via Kesiman and Sukawati. There are several bus connections a day from Denpasar to Kereneng; bemos also leave Denpasar on a regular basis.

EVENTS
Ubud is the centre of traditional cultural events. Every evening, either in one of the twelve large temples located in and around Ubud, in a park or in a hotel a ceremony or performance is held under the stars. These include kekac, fire and trance dances, gamelan music, Ramayana ballets and legong dances. The variety is considerable and the events are of exacting artistic quality. A list is available in the tourist office on Jalan Raya.

WELLNESS
Numerous hotels and guesthouses in Ubud offer Balinese massages; there are even spas that specialize in them. Plenty of advice and addresses can be obtained just by walking along the streets of the city centre. Some of the most beautiful and most expensive spas are in the five-star hotels. Make your appointment early, as some treatments can only be booked when there is little demand from the hotel guests. Ketut Arsana, a famous Balinese healer, has been in the business for a long time. The master himself can be found working along

with his many personally trained employees at »Ubud Body Works«, where creams, soaps and massage oils, as well as Jamu herbal medicines, popular throughout Indonesia, can be purchased.
Jl. Hanoman 25
Tel. 03 61 97 57 20
https://www.ubudbodyworks.com

SHOPPING
The region is a true Mecca for aficionados of the decorative arts. Ubud is famous for the high quality of the paintings on show in the city, while outstanding silversmiths are at home in the village of Celuk; Mas has its woodcarvers, and Batubulan is the village of stonemasons.

WHERE TO EAT
❷ *Casa Luna* £ £
Jl. Raya Ubud
Tel. 03 61 97 74 09
www.casalunabali.com
The favourite spot of many foreign nationals and locals that has gained its popularity because of its ambience and the quality of the food. On two floors that are open to the tropical forest and decorated with antiques and Indonesian teak furniture, it serves freshly baked cakes and pies, fruit juices and Indonesian and Western dishes. Free wifi, regular music events and poetry readings.

❸ *Pesto Café* £
Monkey Forest Rd.
(next to Tama Gallery)
Tel. 03 61 97 58 84
Balinese specialities and Mediterranean dishes are served on Monkey Forest

Road. There are also good vegetarian snacks.

❶ *Sweet Komang's Gallery Café* £
Jl. Bisma 102
Tel. 03 61 97 71 04
A German-Balinese business in a side street near the town centre: Adi's Gallery puts on exhibitions of modern Balinese art where the works are for sale, while the lady of the house prepares Indonesian dishes, sweets, tea and coffee.

❹ *Murni's Warung* £ £
Jl. Raya Campuhan
Tel. 03 61 97 52 33
www.murnis.com
This traditional café-restaurant with its magical views of the tropical forest is located not far from Tjampuan Hotel by the bridge across the river.

WHERE TO STAY
❶ *COMO Shambhala* £ £ £ £
Banjar Begawan
Desa Melinggih Kelod
Payangan (north of Ubud)
Tel. 03 61 97 88 88

www.comohotels.com/comoshambhalaestate
Shambhala is a term from Buddhism and means »place of blessedness« – no overstatement for a hotel that many consider the most beautiful in Bali. Even just the location on Begawan Giri, the »mountain of the wise man«, is unique. In addition there is the spring the Balinese consider sacred; it bubbles up below the hotel. This establishment offers, among other things, customized Ayurveda, yoga and wellness treatments by qualified instructors and teachers (►MARCO POLO Insight, p.244).

❼ *The Chedi Tanah Gajah* £ £ £ £
Jl. Goa Gajah, Tanah Gajah
(4km/2.5mi southeast of Ubud)
Tel. 03 61 97 56 85
www.tanahgajah.com
Just 20 villas and suites situated in among a five-hectare garden surrounded by rice fields. The discreet complex was designed in the 1980s by Hendra Hadiprana, an architect and artist very successful in Indonesia, for himself and his family. It is filled with artistic treasures and antiques from their private collection. The resort also has the atmosphere of a private visit to rich friends on Bali. The »Chedi« also possesses its own amphitheatre where regular dance performances are shown.

❸ *Uma Ubud* £ £ £   *Insider Tip*
Jalan Raya Sanggingan
Banjar Lungsiakan
Kedewatan
Tel. 03 61 97 24 48
http://theumaubud.com
A luxurious hideaway in a dense tropical, green setting above the river Oos (ap-

prox. 20 minutes' walk from the centre of Ubud) that perfectly embodies the synthesis between contemporary minimalism and the rich Balinese artisanry. The »Garden Rooms« possess open courtyards with a koi pond, bedrooms with four-poster beds and a bathroom in a dramatic black and white with an outside shower. The restaurant »Kemiri« is one of the best in Ubud and serves modern, light southeast Asian cuisine.

❻ Four Seasons at Sayan £ £ £ £
Sayan, Ubud, Gianyar
Tel. 03 61 97 75 77
http://www.fourseasons.com/content/fourseasons/en/properties/sayan/
18 suites and 42 villas
Spectacular architecture in the mountains on the edge of the village of Sayan near Ubud. The hotel's open lobby, with views of rice terraces and coconut palm trees, is accessed via a bridge. The rooms of the »Four Seasons« are extremely comfortable. The open restaurant with views of the dense jungle serves Indonesian specialities. A circular pool seems to float above the valley of the Ayung river (►MARCOPOLO Insight, p.244).

❹ Tjampuhan £ £ – £ £ £
Jl. Raya Campuhan
Tel. 03 61 97 53 68
www.tjampuhan.com
Monument of the local hotel industry: the Tjampuhan, opened as far back as 1928, is based in a princely estate and is one of the most stylish hotels in Ubud. Lots of stone steps join up the 63 cottages, natural stone grotto and spring-water pool of this hotel complex that is itself situated in a dense, green setting.

❷ Ulun Ubud £ £ £
Jl. Raya Sanggingan
Tel. 03 61 97 50 24, https://ulunubud.id
Charming hotel in the style of a Balinese village in the middle of lavish green. A dramatic view of the Tjampuhan river far below, colonial ambience with four-poster beds, mosquito nets and antiques.

❺ Puri Saren Agung £
Jl. Raya Ubud, Tel. 03 61 97 50 75
Stylish and yet inexpensive: the accommodation in the palace in the centre of Ubud is simple and the rooms have some antique furniture. Lively and not always quiet, but a stay here will definitely be unforgettable.

has a total exhibition area of 6900 sq m/74,300 sq ft, spread out over four buildings standing in a beautiful garden. Temporary exhibitions are featured in a fifth building. A richly illustrated museum guide that not only provides information about the works on show but also includes the artists' biographies is available at the ticket office.

❶ Jl. Raya Campuhan, Kedewatan, Mon–Sat 9am–5pm, Sun noon–5pm, entry: 75,000 rupiah, www.museumneka.com

*Blanco Museum Art lovers should not miss visiting the house – now a museum – of the painter **Antonio Maria Blanco** (►Famous People), who died in 1999. The house stands in a magnificent tropical garden not far west of the city centre. The museum provides a glimpse of the multi-faceted work of the exalted artist, who, during his lifetime, understood

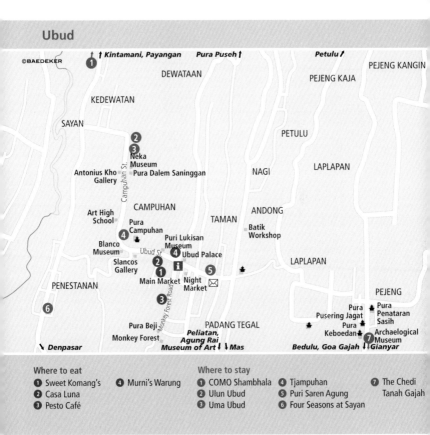

Ubud

©BAEDEKER

↑ Kintamani, Payangan   *Pura Puseh* ↑   *Petulu* ↗

PEJENG KANGIN

DEWATAAN   PEJENG KAJA

KEDEWATAN

SAYAN   PETULU

Neka Museum

Antonius Kho Gallery   Pura Dalem Saninggan   NAGI   LAPLAPAN

Campuhan St.

Art High School   CAMPUHAN   TAMAN   ANDONG

Pura Campuhan   Batik Workshop

Blanco Museum   Puri Lukisan Museum

Ubud St.   Ubud Palace

Slancos Gallery

PENESTANAN   Main Market   Night Market   LAPLAPAN

PEJENG

Monkey Forest Road

Pura Beji   PADANG TEGAL   Pura Pusering Jagat   Pura Penataran Sasih

Monkey Forest   Peliatan,   Pura Keboedan   Archaeological Museum
Agung Rai

↘ *Denpasar*   *Museum of Art* ↓ ↓ *Mas*   *Bedulu, Goa Gajah* ↓↑*Gianyar*

Where to eat
❶ Sweet Komang's   ❹ Murni's Warung
❷ Casa Luna
❸ Pesto Café

Where to stay
❶ COMO Shambhala   ❹ Tjampuhan   ❼ The Chedi
❷ Ulun Ubud   ❺ Puri Saren Agung   Tanah Gajah
❸ Uma Ubud   ❻ Four Seasons at Sayan

exceptionally well how to reach a worldwide, artistically-minded public. Blanco's property, which was provided him by the son of a Balinese prince, is now the centre of the **Blanco Art Foundation**. It sup-
ports many talented young artists; one of the ways it achieves this is
by organizing group exhibitions.

❶ Daily 9am–5pm, entry: 50,000 rupiah, www.blancomuseum.com

The private museum Puri Lukisan (Palace of Painting) in the main
road, Jl. Raya Ubud, was founded in 1954 with the support of the
Dutch painter Rudolf Bonnet (died 1978), who also became its first
curator. It is dedicated to the history and tradition of Balinese painting
and woodcarving. A museum shop and café can also be found here.

❶ daily 8am–4pm, entry: 10,000 rupiah, http://museumpurilukisan.com

Museum Puri Lukisan

Wellness Oases

The air is filled with lemon grass and other exotic aromas, quiet game-lan music lets your mind wander to peaceful spheres. The hands of the masseuse glide gently across your back… a typical Balinese massage is always a pleasure – in contrast to a Thai massage or the traditional Swedish massage, which can at times be quite painful.

Bali is a veritable wellness Mecca. Almost every hotel and guesthouse will have its own spa or a room or an outside pavilion where beauty and wellness treatments are offered. In addition to Balinese massages there are Indonesian ones – the movements are somewhat different here. There are Thai massages and Swedish ones and those where ayurvedic oils are applied. Guests can also enjoy reiki and shiatsu treatments, cosmetic cleanses and almost anything else that is relaxing or beautifying.

Wellness in the Jungle

The best and undoubtedly the most beautiful among Bali's many outstanding spa resorts is the »COMO Shambhala Estate«, a fifteen minute-drive to the north of Ubud. It emerged from the former hotel Begawan Giri and is now a flagship establishment of the award-winning holistic Health Company COMO Shambhala. Even just its location is unique, in a 10-hectare jungle valley where a sacred spring rises. The residences have been built into the steep hillside and consist of several suites, resembling architectural miracles. They blend perfectly in among the tropical vegetation in between lilly ponds. It is possible to relax in a bath in the water garden that was chiselled out of a piece of stone weighing six tons.

Guests are advised about which yoga and stress-release workshops are suitable for them. There is also the option to relax in the meditation temple, which has views of the jungle. In addition to body-oriented workshops there is an emphasis on the opportunity for inner change.

Associated with the resort are for example Rovert Thurman, an American author and university professor who subscribes to Tibetan Buddhism, and Rodney Yee, a yoga instructor famous in the United States, who runs retreat weeks on certain dates.

Ayurveda by the Agung

The »Four Seasons at Sayan« near Ubud is also lastingly impressive. Its spa combines ayurvedic and classic Balinese elements. Medicinal plants, traditional oils etc. are used. In addition to treatments with a meditative air there are also peelings and massages. After that guests can sit on the outside terraces of the spa and enjoy the magical views of the tropical gorge high up above the bubbling Ayung. There are two plunge pools to relax in as well. One oasis in the classical Balinese look is the hotel spa of the »Bali Hyatt« in Sanur: air-conditioned spa villas covered in palm leaves surround an

Dense jungle surrounds the »COMO Shambhala Estate« near Ubud, one of the most beautiful spas on the island

enchanted patio with orchids, stone guard statues and koi ponds. To start the treatments, ginger tea and guava juice is served, then it is time to head to the massage bed in a batik kimono. While listening to Asian lounge music, you can enjoy a gentle, stroking massage or a deep tissue massage, aromatherapy treatments and peeling. Hotels of the moderate price range also often possess nice, good quality spas and oases in the classic Balinese look. There are spa villas covered in palm tree leaves that surround tropical patios with orchids and lilly ponds.

COMO Shambhala Estate, Banjar Begawan, Desa Melinggih Kelod, Payangan, Gianyar, tel. 03 61 97 88 88, www.comohotels.com/comoshambhalaestate

Four Seasons at Sayan, Sayan, Ubud, Gianyar, Tel. 03 61 70 10 10 und 97 75 77, http://www.fourseasons.com/content/fourseasons/en/properties/sayan/

Bali Hyatt, Jl. Danau Tamblingan 89, Sanur, Tel. 03 61 28 12 34, www.bali.resort.hyatt.com

There are several groups of crab-eating macaques living in an outdoor enclosure at the end of Monkey Forest Road

Monkey forest

The monkey forest can be easily reached on foot. It is located south of the city centre and although not nearly as large as the forest of Sangeh (►p.200), it is situated in a more beautiful landscape. After leaving the unavoidable peanut and souvenir hawkers behind, the path leads to an enormous waringin tree with a stone monkey sitting underneath. Pura Dalem Agung Padang Tegal, the **shrine** in the monkey forest, always has hundreds of little monkeys romping about on it. They are eager to take any food offered but occasionally can become aggressive. Spectacle wearers in particular should be on their guard. The monkeys have even been known to grab the contents of trouser pockets and handbags. The temple is a good example of southern Balinese religious architecture. Take a closer look at the covered gate (candi korung) and the bell tower (kulkul) with its phallus-shaped clapper, resting on a stepped base and richly decorated with reliefs.

AROUND UBUD

Bird-watchers should not miss making a detour to Petulu, which is   Petulu
only about 3km/2mi north of Ubud. Towards evening, huge flocks of
great white egrets, held sacred by the Balinese, settle on the trees in
the vicinity.

A good 4km/2.5mi south of Ubud is the small village of Mas, which   Mas
is first and foremost famous for its exceptionally skilled inhabitants.
The shops and showrooms of numerous **woodcarvers**, sculptors and
other craftsmen can be found scattered along the main road. The
workshops, in which it is possible to watch the artists at work, are
often right next-door. Some woodcarvers teach courses, both for beginners and the advanced. At the end of the village are the shops of
the furniture makers, who produce tables, chairs and sitting room
suites of bamboo and rattan.

PRACTICAL INFORMATION

How best to get to Bali? What are good sources of information about the island? How should you behave in a temple? What is »good day« in Indonesian? This chapter has the answer to these and many more questions.

Arrival · Planning the Journey

By air There are flights to Ngurah Rai International Airport near Denpasar from the UK and USA. The major airlines on this route are Malaysia Airlines, Qatar Airways, Singapore Airlines, Cathay Pacific, KLM, Thai Airways and Qantas. The distance from London to Denpasar by air is about 12,500km/7770mi, and the flight time (in the air) is about 14 hours. Most flights make intermediate landings in Doha, Bangkok, Kuala Lumpur, Singapore or Jakarta. These stopovers can often be **extended** into short stays if desired.

The price for a scheduled economy-class return flight from London to Bali is about £600/$1200. Qantas flies direct from Sydney to Denspasar. Singapore Airlines, Qantas and Japan Airlines fly there from the USA. Qantas also fly from Canada. The carriers mentioned above operate numerous routes in the Asiatic region so that a flight to Bali is also possible from all major cities in East, South and Southeast Asia. All-in package deals and various bargain offers are much cheaper; see the airlines' websites.

Garuda Indonesia, the state airline, maintains a dense network of routes that includes the airport in Denpasar in Bali. Along with numerous intercontinental connections (including London, Sydney and Los Angeles), there are regular flights to Indonesian airports such as Jakarta, Palembang, Surabaya and Yogyakarta, as well as neighbouring Malaysia, the city-state of Singapore, Bangkok, Manila, Hong Kong and Tokyo. The smaller airlines providing air travel within the Indonesian archipelago alongside Garuda Indonesia are »Merpati« and »Lion Air«. As a rule, the **price of a ticket** in Asia is cheaper than in Europe. However, the flights are likely to be fully booked, if not overbooked, before and after a national holiday.

At the airport Ngurah Rai Airport is named after a Balinese freedom fighter. It is located about 12km/7.5mi south of **Denpasar** and around 3km/2mi south of Kuta. Flights within Indonesia are handled in the left-hand part of the airport building (Domestic Airport) and international flights in the right (International Airport). The centre is reserved for arrivals, and the arrival hall has a counter for enquiring about and reserving hotel rooms. Upon request, transport to the hotel can also be arranged. There are also several bureaux de change in the arrival hall. Normally, the hotel or the tour operator provides the **transfer** from or to the airport. Otherwise there is a »Koperasi Taxi Service« counter in the airport building. This is a cooperative of taxi drivers that organizes the transfer between the airport and destinations in Bali at set prices. The price for each ride can be found on a notice displayed at the counter, where it is also paid. The taxi driver is then only given the receipt.

AIRPORT
Ngurah Rai International Airport
Denpasar
Tel. 03 61 75 10 11
www.baliairport.com

AIRLINES
Garuda Indonesia
Jl. Sugianyar 5, Denpasar
Tel. 03 61 22 53 20
www.garuda-indonesia.com
In Kuta:
Kuta Paradiso Hotel
Tel. 03 61 75 11 79
In Sanur:
Bali Beach Hotel Arcade
Tel. 03 61 28 79 15

Cathay Pacific
Wisthi Sabha Building
Ngurah Rai International Airport
Denpasar
Tel. 03 61 75 39 42
www.cathaypacific.com

KLM Royal Dutch Airlines
Ngurah Rai International Airport
Denpasar
Tel. 03 61 75 61 26
www.klm.com

Lion Air
Bandara Ngurah Rai
Denpasar

Tel. 03 61 76 51 83
www.lionair.co.id

Malaysia Airlines
Ngurah Rai International Airport
Denpasar
Tel. 03 61 9 36 69 25
www.malaysiaairlines.com

Merpati Nusantara Airlines
Jl. Melati 51, Denpasar
Tel. 03 61 23 53 58, www.merpati.co.id

Qantas
Bali Beach Hotel, Sanur
Tel. 03 61 28 92 80
www.qantas.com.au

Qatar Airways
Discovery Kartika Plaza Hotel
South Kuta Beach, Kuta
Tel. 03 61 75 22 22
www.qatarairways.com

Singapore Airlines
Ngurah Rai International Airport
Goi Building 2nd Floor
Tel. 03 61 9 36 83 88
www.singaporeair.com

Thai Airways
Grand Bali Beach Hotel, Sanur
Tel. 03 61 28 81 41
www.thaiair.com

The best way to get **to Lombok** is via Bali. Bandara International Airport, which opened in 2011, is located on the island, which neighbours Bali to the east. The airport itself is in the south of the island near Praya, 40km/25mi to the southeast of Lombok's capital of Mataram. There are several planes a day operated by the regional airline »Merpati« between Ngurah Raj airport and the one on Lombok. The flight time is approx. half an hour. A sufficient number of taxis are available for getting to the desired hotel upon arrival. The local representatives of tour operators will be waiting outside the arrival hall for travellers with package arrangements. There is a counter in the arrival hall to provide independent travellers with information about vacant hotel rooms. **Porters** offer assistance in both airports; the charge is determined by the number of bags to be carried. Even if the airline ticket has »OK« printed on it, the flight must be confirmed with the airline by telephone or in person at least two days before the **return flight** or the seat reservation can be cancelled. Check-in time for international flights is two hours before departure; one hour is normally enough for flights within Indonesia. An airport tax must be paid in cash before flying; at present it is about 150,000 rupiahs (£10 or $13) for international flights and 30,000 rupiahs for domestic flights.

By train and ferry from Java
It is possible to travel to Bali via the Indonesian island of Java, but it is time consuming. Trains leave regularly from Jakarta and Yogyakarta to the ferry port of Ketapang (not far north of Banyuwangi) at the eastern end of Java (travel time approx. 16 hrs). Change there for one of the car ferries that cross regularly several times daily to Gilimanuk on the west tip of Bali (crossing takes approx. 30 to 45 min). As there is no railway on Bali, the rest of the trip is by bus.

TRAVEL DOCUMENTS

Passport
Citizens of the UK, Republic of Ireland, USA, Canada, Australia and New Zealand wishing to enter Indonesia must have a passport that is valid for six months beyond the time of entry. Since 2012 even children under the age of 16 have required their own passport.

Visa
The visa is stamped in the passport on arrival, and is valid for 30 days. It costs US$25, which must be paid in cash in dollars, other major currencies can be exchanged. Visitors wishing to stay longer need to apply for such a visa from the Indonesian embassy before travelling. Indonesian authorities will demand proof of possession of a paid return or onward flight or passage by ship.

Vaccination guidelines
At present, a certificate of vaccination is not required of travellers entering Indonesia directly from Western Europe. In case of a stopover in an area infected with yellow fever, namely various African countries as well as India, Nepal, Myanmar, Sri Lanka and others, it is best to consult the Indonesian embassy or consulate (▶Information) about the current situation. Occasionally a smallpox vaccination is required that should not be older than three years – even though the World Health Organization has declared the earth to be free of smallpox. It is recommended to be vaccinated against cholera and to take anti-malarial drugs when travelling outside the tourist areas, as well as during the rainy season.

CUSTOMS REGULATIONS

The following are duty free: items for personal use in reasonable quantities, cigarettes (at most 200), 50 cigars, 100g/3.5oz tobacco, 2l/68fl oz wine or spirits, two cameras with film, and a film or video camera.
The importing of drugs, Communist literature and pornographic materials is absolutely prohibited, likewise hunting weapons and ammunition. It does not usually take a visitor to Bali long to get through customs.

Entry into Indonesia

Consumer goods purchased in Indonesia may be exported in any amount, as may souvenirs. The export of antiques is subject to special regulations; detailed information is available from the Bali Government Tourism Office (►Information).

Departure from Indonesia

It is permissible to enter the country with an unlimited amount of foreign currency. The import of more than 100 million rupiah (approx. £6000/$8000) per person has to be declared; permission is needed from the Indonesian Central Bank to export more than 100million rupiah.

The importing of plants, animals or animal or plant products that are under protection according to the CITES agreement (also known as the »Washington Endangered Species Act«) is prohibited. This includes – in reference to Bali and Indonesia – coral (particularly black coral), reptiles (especially geckos), turtles and tortoises (also tortoiseshell).
Persons arriving in the European Union (EU) by air or ship from non-EU states may bring travel souvenirs and gifts up to a total value of €430/£345. In addition, persons over 15 years of age may import 500g/1.1lb coffee or 200g/7oz soluble coffee, 50g perfume and 0.25l eau de toilette; persons over 17 years of age may bring in 1l/34 fl oz spirits with more than 22 % alcohol content by volume or 2l/68fl oz spirits with a maximum of 22 % alcohol content by volume or 2l/68fl oz sparkling wine, 2l/68fl oz wine, and 200 cigarettes or 100 cigarillos or 50 cigars or 250g/8.8oz smoking tobacco.

Re-entry into the EU

Electricity

The mains supply throughout Bali is 220 volts AC (50 Hertz). Fluctuations in current should be expected. Plug sockets conform to the European norm; visitors from the UK or USA should bring an adapter.

Emergency numbers

General emergencies Tel. 112	**Fire brigade** Tel. 113
Police Tel. 110	**Ambulance** Tel. 118
Tourist police Tel. 22 41 11	**Indonesian Red Cross** Tel. 03 61 48 02 82, 22 64 65

Etiquette

Begging   Primarily in the places frequented by tourists, children and sometimes also sick or disabled people do beg in Bali. Especially in the case of children (who are increasingly being abused by adults who send them out to beg or to sell grossly over-priced merchandise), tourists should refrain from giving money so as not to support their social neglect. Children are also pleased with little things like a bar of soap or a ballpoint pen.

Drugs   As in almost all Asian states, the consumption of drugs and especially drug dealing is punished with severe penalties in Indonesia – and thus also in Bali. The importing or exporting of any and all controlled substances is strictly forbidden; possession of illegal drugs is also punishable by law. As a rule, the long prison sentences resulting from violations of the narcotics laws apply to foreigners as well; in very serious cases the death penalty is applied. No help can be expected from homeland consulates in cases of drug offences. Under no circumstances agree to transport anything home as a favour for someone. Attempts have often been made to exploit travellers as drug couriers.

Photography and film cameras   Generally, the Balinese are happy to be photographed, but it is always best to ask permission first (a simple motion with the camera is usually enough), and if the response is a declining gesture, simply accept it. Those who do not want to be photographed will not do it for money either; strict Hindus are occasionally camera-shy. There can be moments during temple festivals when using a flash can cause great annoyance among the believers. It is difficult to prescribe the correct behaviour in such instances because it could vary from village to village and temple to temple. For this reason it is always best to ask permission before pressing the shutter. It should go without saying that tourists should not offend people by photographing them while they are practising their religion.

Unfortunately, in Bali as elsewhere, women travelling alone must reckon on being an object of interest for male tourists, and be prepared to deal with their advances. There is hardly any danger of this from the local male population. Even so, women should not undertake walks alone, especially at night, and not into uncertain terrain.

Information for women

Light and airy clothing is recommended all year round. However, warmer items (such as sweaters and cardigans) should be taken along for the »cooler« months and for trips into the mountains. Clothing that covers bare arms and legs is recommended for evenings on the beach to protect against annoying insects. Respect for the religion of the Balinese **forbids entering their sacred sites dressed in things like shorts or T-shirts**. Women should definitely cover their shoulders and men wear long trousers. Before entering a temple site, wrap a temple sash, called a selendang, about the hips. The wearing of a sarong is obligatory when attending a temple festival – for all tourists, male and female alike! Selendangs and sarongs can either be purchased right at the start of your stay in Bali or hired for a small sum at the temple entrance.

Clothing

The left hand is considered unclean. Do not proffer or take anything with the left hand. The exchange of intimacies in public is improper. Nude bathing is banned and considered to show disregard for Balinese sensitivities. Climbing on temple walls or, even worse, temple figures, is strictly forbidden and punishable with stiff fines. This is an offence that confronts the local population with a well-nigh unsolvable problem: a temple that has been desecrated in this manner has, to a large extent, lost its spiritual character. A temple visit (see dress code above) by people with open wounds (this includes menstruating women!) is strictly forbidden: violations are considered sacrilegious and desecrate the temple. Restoring it to its original, sacred condition requires highly elaborate rituals.

Taboos and sacrilege

Although the bill in most restaurants and hotels already includes a service charge of between 5 and 10 percent, it is customary when satisfied with the service to give an additional tip or to round up the bill. Giving a small gratuity to porters and chambermaids at the beginning of the stay is a good idea, and if satisfied with the service at the end of the holiday, another tip is in order. Taxi, bus and bemo drivers are not normally tipped.

Tipping

Rules of behaviour

Tolerant as the Asians are toward the visitors from the West, there are some forms of behaviour that bring even the legendary composure of the Balinese to boiling point. Even if the offending tourist does not notice it, he has lost face and the Balinese consider him to be a person of little account. When conversing, exercise **elegant reserve**. Wild gesticulating or pointing at other people is considered improper. Intimate subjects are not the stuff of conversation, even among friends. Questions about income or one's personal situation, for instance, are answered evasively. And never forget that important part of every conversation: the smile. The rule is: the more non-committal the answer, the friendlier the smile. If invited to a Balinese home, it is customary to bring along a **small gift**. The lady of the house is always pleased with a bunch of flowers, and if there are children, remember to bring sweets. Shoes are removed before entering the home.

Health

HEALTH PRECAUTIONS

A holiday in the tropics demands some preparation before leaving and a certain amount of caution once there to ensure that the trip is a positive experience. Consult your family doctor before departure: he or she will advise you on avoiding health risks.

Traveller's first aid kit

Because the risk of infection is greater in the tropics, a first-aid kit plays a much greater role when on holiday in Asia than when travelling within Europe or other temperate zones. It should contain scissors, tweezers, cotton wool, two gauze bandages, a package of bandaging materials, two first aid dressings, sticking plasters, disinfectant and medicines against fever, pain, diarrhoea, constipation, travel sickness and infection. Along with sunscreen, an insect repellent is important.

Vaccinations

The Indonesian authorities do not require that European visitors have any specific vaccinations as long as they have not passed through areas infected with certain diseases. However, protection against tetanus and poliomyelitis is recommended. It is best always to carry a medical certificate listing possible allergies and intolerances as well as your blood group. Furthermore, an inoculation against hepatitis A, whose pathogens are transmitted through the unhygienic preparation of food and drink (particularly ice!), is advisable. Sensitive tourists should have themselves immunized with gamma globulin before departure. The National Travel Health Network

DENTIST
Nusa Dua Dental Clinic
Jalan Pratama 81A
Nusa Dua
Tel. 03 61 77 13 24

HOSPITALS ON BALI
Bali International Medical Center
Jalan Bypass Ngurah Rai
Kuta, Tel. 03 61 76 12 63
http://.bimcbali.ccom

Dharma Ushada Hospital
Jl. Panglima Sudirman
Denpasar, Tel. 03 61 22 75 60

SOS Medika Klinik Bali
Jl. Bypass Ngurah Rai 505
Kuta, Tel. 03 61 71 05 05
www.sosindonesia.com

and Centre in London (www.netdoctor.co.uk), funded by the Department of Health, promotes clinical standards in travel medicine.
Information on recommended vaccines country by country is available at www.tmb.ie. Cases of malaria have recently been on the rise
again in Southeast Asia. The use of anti-malarial drugs, especially
when travelling outside the tourist centres, is recommended.

It takes time for the body to adjust to the tropical climate. It is best to   **Adjusting to the climate**
avoid physical exertion the first couple of days, and to minimize ex-
posure to the intense rays of the sun. It is essential to take a sun lotion
with a high sunscreen factor: Bali is after all located not far from the
equator. Treat air conditioning with caution. Even if the artificially
produced cool air feels initially pleasant in contrast to the tropical
temperatures outside, there is an acute danger of catching a cold for
those that remain in »air-conditioned« – which often means chilly
– rooms for longer periods of time. When sleeping at night, the air
conditioning should be turned down.

The danger of becoming infected with HIV/AIDS in Indonesia is   **AIDS**
relatively great for those who engage in those activities known to
carry a risk of infection. Only the well-known precautionary
measures can help protect against the transmission of the virus. The
use of condoms reduces the risk during heterosexual and homosexual
intercourse, and disposable syringes should be used only once for
injections.

Food from snack bars is generally safe for tourists to eat, but do pay   **Food**
attention to cleanliness. Fruit must always be thoroughly washed before eating. Avoid, as a matter of principle, the consumption of raw
foods, unpeeled fruits, ice cream, and beverages served in glasses
with a lot of ice. Caution is advised in the consumption of alcohol in
the tropics. Heat can intensify its well-known unpleasant side effects.

IN CASE OF ILLNESS

Pharmacies   There are numerous pharmacies on Bali, above all in places frequented by tourists, recognizable by the signs »Apotik« or »Toko Obat«.
They stock a selection of the usual medicines, some though with
names only customary in Asia.

Those dependent on certain medicines (or requiring contraceptives)
should bring an ample supply from home or ensure by comparison
with an original package that the preparation available in Indonesia
is identical to the one needed. If in doubt, go and see a doctor. Medicines are – as everywhere in Asia – significantly cheaper than in Europe.

Doctors and   Particularly in the tourist centres, there is sufficient medical provi-
hospitals   sion in both Bali and Lombok. There are doctors in private practice
in the cities and villages, though very few of them speak much English. English-speaking physicians in the employ of large hotels can be
summoned to reception when needed. In an emergency, the tour
operator's local representatives are also ready to arrange for a suitable
doctor or dentist.

There are no hospitals in Bali capable of handling very severe injuries
or life-threatening illnesses. It is therefore advisable in such cases to
consider being transported to Jakarta or Singapore. In cases of serious illness, your consulate or embassy (▶p. 254) should be notified
without fail.

Ambulance   The ambulance service in Bali and Lombok is, by Western standards,
Service   rudimentary. Expect to wait quite a long time in cases of accidents
outside of the tourist centres, although generally you can depend on
the local Balinese who are anxious to help. Should there be a need for
an early return flight for medical reasons, a flying ambulance must be
requested from home. Return transport can be very expensive, so it
is advisable to take out travel health insurance that covers return
transport for medical reasons.

Information

There is currently no Indonesian tourist office in the UK. Information can be obtained from the Indonesian Embassy in London. The
Garuda Indonesia Office in Sydney Australia promotes tourism in
Indonesia, as does the Indonesian Tourist Office in Los Angeles. All
addresses are listed below. In addition, a wealth of information about
Bali and Indonesia, as well as hotel directories and personal travel
reports, can be found on the internet.

TOURIST INFORMATION
OFFICES IN BALI AND LOMBOK
Bali Tourism Board
Jl. Raya Puputan 41
Renon, Bali 80235
Tel. (0361)235600
Fax 239200
www.bali-tourism-board.com

Bali Government
Tourism Office
Jl. S. Parman 1, Niti Mandala Renon,
Denpasar 80235
Tel. (0361)222387, fax 226313

Lombok Regional
Tourism Office Jalan
Langko 70, Mataram
Tel. (0370) 631730   Fax 631866
Opening hours: Mon–Sat 8am–3pm

TOURIST INFORMATION
OFFICES IN AUSTRALIA
AND THE USA
Garuda Indonesia Office
4, Bligh Street, PO Box 3836
Sydney 2000
Tel. 232-6044, fax: 2332828

Indonesian Tourist Office
3457 Wilshire Boulevard
Los Angeles, CA 90010
Tel. 213 387 2078

DIPLOMATIC AND
CONSULAR REPRESENTATION
In the UK
38 Grosvenor Square
London W1K 2HW
Tel. 020 7499 7661
Fax 020 7491 4993
www.indonesianembassy.org.uk

In the Republic of Ireland
Honorary Consul

25 Kilvere Rathfarnham
Dublin
Tel. 353 852 491

In the USA
2020 Massachusetts Ave NW
Washington DC 20036
Tel. 202 775 5200
www.embassyofindonesia.org

In Canada
55 Parkdale Ave
Ottawa, Ontario K1Y 1E5
Tel. 613 724 1100
www.indonesia-ottawa.org

In Australia
8 Darwin Ave
Yarralumla, ACT 2600
Tel. 02 6250 8600

In New Zealand
70 Glen Road
Kelburn, Wellington
Tel. 04 4758 697
https://www.embassypages.com/missions/embassy5033

*Diplomatic Representation
in Bali*
Foreign embassies are based in Jakarta.
In Bali, the following consulates can provide assistance in the case of an emergency:

UK
Jl. Tirtanadi 20
Sanur
Tel. 270601

USA
Jl. Hayam Wuruk 188
Renon, Denpasar
Tel. 233605

Australia
Jl. Hayam Wuruk 88B
Renon, Denpasar
Tel. 241118
www.dfat.gov.au/bali
The Australian consulate shares responsibility for Canadian citizens, and can also offer assistance to citizens of the Republic of Ireland and New Zealand.

INTERNET
www.bali-board.com
English-language website of a tour operator in Bali with an extensive service, ranging from guided tours to transportation.

www.balidiscovery.com
On its Bali forum, the travel network offers discussions, reports and advice from travellers to Bali.

www.baliguide.com
English-language website by expats living on Bali with background information on the island, numerous practical travel tips and suggestions for private villas and hotels.

www.bali-paradise.com
English-language website with an abundance of tourist information and links to beaches, restaurants, crafts, shopping, activities, tours, festivals and much more besides.

Language

Bahasa Indonesia   In contrast to many other Asian languages, the local language »Bahasa Indonesia« (Bahasa for short), which is closely related to Malay, is relatively easy for Europeans to learn. Malay **grammar** is quite simple. For example, plurals are expressed by simply doubling the singular (»bulan« = month; »bulan-bulan« = months) – although in certain circumstances a doubled word can also take on a completely different meaning. Bahasa Indonesia has no articles. »How much does the room cost?« is in Bahasa »Berapa harga kamar kosong ini?« (= »How much cost room?«). Verbs are not conjugated; the context of the sentence indicates what the inflected form would be. Possessive pronouns are postpositional: »my room« is »Kamarku« (end syllable »ku« = »my«).

Bahasa Indonesia demonstrates some peculiarities regarding **pronunciation**. A »c« is always pronounced as »cha« (»candi« is thus »chandi«); a »z« is always devoiced (= »s«).

A formal **salutation** is not customary in Indonesia. There are also no corresponding expressions. A favourite way of opening a conversation is to ask the other person's name (»Siapa namayana?«) or place of origin. Sometimes a question concerning general well-being is asked (»Apa khabar?«), which can be answered either with »Bagus, bagus« (= »good, good«) or with »Khabar baik« (= »I feel fine«). Indonesia is largely an Islamic country, and this has resulted in several

Arabic words entering the language. For example, the word »sela-mat!« (= »May your deeds be blessed!«), which is always linked to a time of day or a request.

Indonesian phrases

At a Glance

Yes	Ya.
No	Tidak.
Perhaps	Mungkin./Bis jada./ Barangkali.
Please	Silankan (offering, inviting).Tolong (ask for help). Kembali (you're welcome/ think nothing of it).
Thank you	Terima kasih.
Many thanks.	Terima kasih banyak.
You're welcome	Sama-sama.
Sorry!	Maaf!/Sorry!
Pardon?	Maaf, bagaimana?
I don't understand you.	Saya tidak mengerti.
I speak only a little ...	Saya hanya bis jada berbicara sedikit ....
Do you speak ...	Apa Bapak/Ibu/kamu berbicara bahasa ....
English?	Inggris?
French?	Perancis?
German?	Jerman?
Would you please help me?	Apa Basak/Ibu bisa menolong saya?
I would like ...	Saya mau ...
I (do not) like that.	Saya (kurang) menyukainya.
Do you have ...?	Apa di sini ada ...?
How much does it cost?	Berapa harganya?
What time is it?	Jam berapa sekarang?

Becoming acquainted

Good morning!	Selamat pagi!
Good day!	Selamat siang! (11am to 3pm)
	Selamat sore! (3pm to 6pm)
Good evening!	Selamat malam!
Hello!/Hi!	Halo!
My name is ...	Nama saya ...
What is your name (please)? (informal)	Siapa nama Bapak/Ibu?
How are you?	Apa kabar Pak/Ibu?
Very well, thank you.	Terima kasih.
And yourself? (infomal)	Dan Bapak./Ibu/kamu?

Goodbye	Sampai jumpa lagi!
Good night	Selamat tidurr!
Cheerio!	Permisi!/Ayo!/Bye!/Daag!/ Mari!
See you later	Sampai nanti!
See you tomorrow	Sampai besok!

Getting around

left/right	kiri/kanan
straight ahead	terus, lurus
near/far	dekat/jauh
Please, where is ...?	Maaf, di mana ...?
How far is it to ...?	Berapa jauhnya ke ...?
Which bus goes to ...?	Bus mana pergi ke ...?
Where can I buy a ticket?	Di mana saya bisa membeli karcis?
Where is the next taxi stand?	Di mana pangkalan taksi terdekat?
to the train station/... hotel	Ke stasiun/hotel.
to ... (please)	Ke ...

At the petrol station

Where is the next petrol station (please)?	Di man pompa bensin terdekat?
I would like ... litres	Saya mau ... litre
... two-star petrol/regular	... premium.
... super	... premix.
... diesel	... solar.
... mixture	... bensin campur.
Fill it up, please.	Isi penuh.

Emergency

Help!	Tolong!
Watch out!	Awas!
Careful!	Hati-hati!
Please quickly call	Tolong cepat panggil
... an ambulance	... ambulans.
... the police	... polisi.
... the fire department	... pemadam kebakaran.
It was my/your fault.	Ini kesalahan saya/Bapak/Ibu.
Please give me your name and address!	Tolong berikan saya nama dan alamat Bapak/Ibu.

Dining/Shopping

Where do I find	Di mana ada
... a good restaurant?	... restoran yang baik?
... a typical restaurant?	... restoran yang khas?
Please reserve (for us)	Saya mau memesan

a table for tonight for a party of four.	meja untuk vier orang untuk malam ini.
Do you have vegetarian dishes/diet-low calorie food?	Apa ada hidangan tanpa daging/untuk diet?
Could we have a little more rice/water?	Apa bisa mendapat nasi/ ar lagi?
Cheers!	Cheers!/Prost!
Enjoy your meal!	Selamat makan!
Not too spicy, please!	Tolong jangan terlalu pedas!
Can we have the bill, please.	Saya mau bayar.
The meal was excellent.	Makanannya enak sekali.
That is for you.	Ini untuk Bapak./Ibu.
Where are the toilets?	Di man kamar kecil?
Where do I find	Di mana saya bisa membeli
... a chemist's shop?	... apotik?
... a bakery?	... toko roti?
... a batik shop?	... toko batik?
... a camera shop?	... toko alat-alat foto?
... a department store?	... pasar swalayan?
... a travel agent?	... biro perjalanan?

Numbers

0	nol	19	sembilan belas
1	satu	20	dua puluh
2	dua	21	dua puluh satu
3	tiga	30	tiga puluh
4	empat	40	empat puluh
5	lima	50	lima puluh
6	enam	60	enam puluh
7	tujuh	70	tujuh puluh
8	delapan	80	delapan puluh
9	sembilan	90	sembilan puluh
10	sepuluh	100	seratus
11	sebelas	200	dua ratus
12	dua belas	1000	seribu
13	tiga belas	2000	dua ribu
14	empat belas	1000	sepulu ribu
15	lima belas		
16	enam belas	1/2	seperdua, setengah
17	tujuh belas	1/3	sepertiga
18	delapan belas	1/4	seperempat

Accommodation

I reserved a room with you.	Saya telah memesan kamar die sini.
Do you still have a vacancy	Apa di sini masih ada kamar kosong
... for one night?	... untuk satu malam?

... for a week?	... untuk satu minggu?
... with bath?	... denang kamar mandi?
How much does a room cost with ...	Berapa harga kamar dengan ...
... breakfast?	... makan pagi?
... half-board?	... makan pagi dan malam saja?
... full-board?	... tiga kali makan?

Doctor

Could you recommend a good doctor?	Apa Bapak/Ibu tahu seorang dokter yang baik?
I have an upset stomach.	Perut saya tidak enak.
I have diarrhoea.	Saya diare.
I have a fever.	Saya demam.
I have pains here.	Saya sakit di sini.
I cannot tolerate the heat/food.	Saya tidak tahan makanan itu/panas.

Bank

Where is a bank (please)/ a bureau de change/money changer?	Di mana ada bank/money changer di sini?
I would like to exchange ... euros into rupiahs.	Saya mau menukar ... Euro dalam Rupiah.

Literature

Illustrated Books

Joyce Jue Savouring Southeast Asia. Time Life UK (2000). A successful example of a new generation of cookery books that offer information about the country and its people with large format photographs along with the recipes. Because the culinary traditions of other Southeast Asian countries are greatly valued in Bali, the similarities in the recipes are not restricted to the typical use of ingredients such as rice, coconut milk, fresh herbs and exotic spices; rather numerous dishes exist that have an »international« character. This book presents a collection of 130 recipes together with a wealth of information about eating traditions and related cultural history. Local products and customs are described, as well as selected restaurants. The glossary introduces the basic preparation and special ingredients of Southeast Asian cuisine.

Angelika Taschen (ed.): Inside Asia (2 vols.). Taschen (2005). For leafing through, reading, obtaining information, planning, and dreaming. The renowned Swiss photographer, Reto Guntli, Asia expert and enthusiast since his childhood, travelled for months through the region searching for subjects to photograph that express the essence of what constitutes life and living in Asia, namely the calmness and harmony with all sentient and feeling beings. Bali captivated him once more through the warm-heartedness of its people, its tropical nature and the spirituality possessed by everything on the island. These two magnificent volumes will provide lasting enjoyment for anyone interested in Asian culture.

Angelika Taschen (ed.): Living in Bali. Taschen (2005). »When it comes to Balinese houses, walls are not compulsory, wood is every-where, earth tones are dominant, and thatched roofs abound«, report the authors of this opulent volume that portrays 19 magnificent houses, villas and hotels. Inspiring photographs of private living spheres allow the viewers to immerse themselves into the diversity of Balinese living. Concise commentaries in three languages provide interesting explanations of each interior. Along with famous hotels such as Begawan Giri Estate, smaller, delightful guest-houses are also highlighted, as well as the houses of local and foreign artists who have lived in Bali for years.

> **MARCO ⊕ POLO TIP**
>
> *Holiday reading* — Insider Tip
>
> Almost every place visited by tourists has a well-stocked second-hand-bookshop, and most of the books are in English. The booksellers also operate a part-exchange system: bring in the book that you're finished with, and get at the very least a hefty reduction on the one you take away.

Vicki Baum: Love and Death in Bali (previously published as A Tale from Bali). Tuttle Publishing, US (2010). Vicki Baum (▶Famous Persons) spent several months in Bali in 1935; she delved into the history of the island, observed life there and intensely studied Balinese culture. With this novel, first published in German in 1937, and later translated, Vicki Baum helped a European reading public gain an insight into the exotic island for the first time.   Novels

Media

There are a number of radio stations in Bali that normally broadcast the news in English on the hour. Those with a shortwave radio should be able to receive the BBC World Service and Voice of America. As the frequencies change, check the transmission schedule online before leaving home: www.bbc.co.uk/worldservice and www.voa.gov respectively.   Radio

Most of the larger hotels in Bali and numerous others offer satellite television with programmes in English. Furthermore, English-language films shown on Indonesian television channels are not dubbed,   Television instead having subtitles. The news in English is broadcast daily at 6.30pm by RCTI, a private TV station.

Newspapers and magazines   Among the more than 70 dailies published in Indonesia, three are in English and available throughout the country. Although no direct censorship exists, a myriad of press laws are meant to prevent reports critical of the system. The Jakarta Post is in the main newspaper available in Bali, though usually not until around noon. International newspapers and magazines are only available at the newsagents of the larger hotels, and are very expensive. Several monthly or bimonthly magazines, containing features, travel articles and what's-on guides, are targeted specifically at tourists. These include Bali and Beyond, Bali Echo, Hello Bali, Bali Tribune and Bali Travel News.

Money

Currency   The Indonesian currency unit is called the rupiah (Rp.). The coins come in denominations of 25, 50, 100, 200 and 500 rupiahs. The Indonesian banknotes have values of 100, 500, 1000, 2000, 5000, 10,000, 20,000, 50,000 and 100,000 rupiahs.

Exchange rate   The exchange rate for banks is officially set by the authorities. This rate is used by Bank Negara Indonesia's (BNI) official bureau de change at the airports as well as in the bank's branches in the island's interior. On the other hand, it is quite possible that other money changers may offer a somewhat better rate. The variation becomes obvious after arriving at Ngurah Rai airport, where the money changers inside the airport itself sometimes offer a distinctly worse rate than those outside the arrival hall. Only exchange money in hotels in emergencies, because the rate there is generally less favourable. By the way, it is only possible to sell back rupiahs by presenting a receipt for a previous exchange.

?   *Exchange rates*

MARCO ⊕ POLO INSIGHT

- 10,000 Rupiah = GBP 0.51
  1 GBP = 18,800 Rupiah
- 10,000 Rupiah = USD 0.75
  1 USD = 12,900 Rupiah
- 10,000 Rupiah = 0.98 AUD
  1 AUD = 9,800 Rupiah
- 10,000 Rupiah = 0.94
  1 CAD = 10.200 Rupiah

Means of payment   It is recommended to bring some **rupiahs in cash** from home to cover the initial expenses incurred upon arrival (taxi, bus, tips, etc.). Pay special attention to the quality of the banknotes, at home as well as in Indonesia. They must be in good condition, as damaged or heavily soiled notes of any currency will not generally be accepted.

Taking along **travellers' cheques** is also recommended. The built-in insurance provides rapid assistance in case of loss or theft – though only when the instructions have been followed with care (above all, keep cheques and purchase receipts separate). Cash can be withdrawn from cash machines (ATMs) all over Bali with a **debit card** bearing a Maestro symbol. The usual **credit cards** such as American Express, BankAmericard/Visa, MasterCard/Eurocard and Diners Club are accepted mainly in the areas frequented by tourists in Bali and Lombok. If a credit card is lost, contact the card issuer at home or the local representative without delay.

Negara Indonesia and **Dagang Negara banks** are recommended on Bali and Lombok for all ordinary banking transactions. There are branches in the larger towns. It is possible to transfer money by telegraph to Indonesia, but it takes at least two days. A passport must be presented when collecting the money.

MARCO ⊕ POLO INSIGHT **?**

Lost or stolen card

There is a number on the back of every credit card which should be called in the case of the card being lost or stolen – it is a good idea to make a note of this number as well as those given by the bank. Some emergency contact numbers are listed below:
HSBC: tel. +44 (0) 1442 422 929
Lloyds TSB Bank: tel. +44 (0) 1702 278 270
Barclays Bank: tel. +44 (0)1904 544 666
NatWest Bank: tel. +44 (0) 142 370 0545
Citibank: tel. +44 (0) 207 500 5500
MasterCard: tel. 0800 96 4767 (UK) or 001 63 67 22 71 11 (USA)
American Express: tel. +44 (0)1273 696 933
Visa: tel. 0800 89 1725 (UK) or 800-8-11-824 (US)
Contact details in Bali
American Express: Jl. Legian Kuta 80, Kuta, tel. (0361)758781
Mastercard: Bank Central Asia, Jl. Raya, Kuta 55, Kuta, tel. (0361)762247
Diners: Jl. Diponegoro 45, Denpasar, tel. (0361)235559

Personal Safety

Bali is no »island paradise« as far as security is concerned. Still, the rate of crime is no higher here than in other places in the world frequented by tourists. The visitor should not fail to take necessary precautions, remembering the motto »opportunity makes a thief«. After all, a holidaymaker often carries more cash on him than a simple hotel worker can earn in a month (or longer). Do not flaunt your superior standard of living and leave your valuables in the hotel safe. Also, it is best to carry only as much money around with you as you expect to spend. Always leave your room keys at the hotel reception.

Don't flaunt luxury

Precautionary measures
For security purposes, travel documents should be photocopied before leaving home and the copies taken along and kept separate from the originals. In case of loss, this greatly facilitates their replacement. When using travellers' cheques, remember to store the purchase receipt apart from the cheque forms; only then is the insurance coverage guaranteed. Most of the large hotels offer **free safe-deposit boxes** or even room safes, although they accept no liability at all for any theft occurring in the rooms. Neck pouches or special belts next to the body to hold money and other valuables, invisible from outside, provide security from pickpockets, who are certain to be active at all the marketplaces and anywhere that large crowds of people gather. There are no official lost property offices in Bali; even bus companies do not offer this service. Lost articles, if turned in, can be picked up at the nearest police station (▶ p. 265)).

Official security advice
There has been some success in the investigation into the 2002 terror attack in Bali resulting in numerous arrests and convictions, although some of the extremists identified as the masterminds are still at large. The attacks in Bali confirm that there are groups in Indonesia who have the capability and motivation to carry out (suicide) attacks. Such acts of terrorism will most likely continue in the future. Areas considered to be at particular risk are Jakarta and, in Bali, the places frequented by foreigners or identified with Western countries such as hotels, embassies, shopping centres and tourist facilities. Up-to-date travel and security advice can be obtained from the websites of the UK Foreign Office or the US Dept. of State.

Post · Telecommunications

Post office
As a rule, the Indonesian post office in Bali and Lombok operates dependably. It normally takes seven to ten days for postcards and letters to reach Europe. Indonesian letter boxes are red, and collection times are listed on a sign on the front. It is also possible to give letters to the hotel reception for posting. The main post office in Denpasar is located in Jl. Raya Puputan; there are more post offices in Sanur (Br. Taman), in Kuta (Jl. Raya Kuta Gung Selamat) and in Ubud (Jl. Payangan). Business hours are usually Mon–Thu 8am–2pm, Fri 8am–11am, Sat 8am–12.30pm.

Telephoning
Telephoning in Bali and Lombok can occasionally be quite arduous because the lines are often overloaded. There are **card telephones** almost everywhere across both islands. Telephone cards can be purchased in post offices and call shops, as well as in hotels and supermarkets. A personal **mobile phone** is more handy but also quite

TELEPHONE DIALLING CODES
From abroad
... to Indonesia:
Tel. 00 62
... to South Bali:
Tel. 00 62 361
... to North Bali:
Tel. 00 62 362
... to West Bali:
Tel. 00 62 365
... to East Bali:
Tel. 00 62 363
... to Klungkung:
Tel. 00 62 366
... to Lombok:
Tel. 00 62 370

from Bali and Lombok
... to UK:
Tel. 0 01 44
... to US and Canada: Tel. 0 01 1
... to Ireland: Tel. 0 01 353
...to Australia: Tel. 0 01 61

TELEPHONE DIRECTORY ENQUIRIES
National
Tel. 100

International
Tel. 101

expensive. Information about roaming tarifs can be obtained from the mobile companies at home. There is **no specific local area code** for Bali, but a distinction is made between the five regions when calling from abroad.

Many large hotels offer an (expensive!) direct dial service from Bali to Europe and other desinations by IDD (International Direct Dialling). It is also possible to make calls abroad in all post offices on the island, although there are often long waiting times. Normal overseas calls are decidedly cheaper, as is the sending of faxes via the state-sponsored Wartel Telecommunications Service. A three-minute call to Europe costs about 30,000 rupiahs; a local call from a public telephone costs 1000 rupiahs (more expensive in hotels). **H ome Country Direct Service Reverse-charge calls** are somewhat problematic. A hefty connection fee will be charged in a public telephone office, or wartel, if they allow such calls at all. It is best to use a public telephone and ask to make a reverse-charge call either via the Indonesian operator (dial 101) or by using the Home Country Direct Service to talk directly with an operator from your home country. The Home Country Direct Service can be accessed from any phone capable of IDD. Dial 001 801 and then the country code (44 for the UK).

The best service with regard to communication, telephones and faxes, and one that is also relatively inexpensive is offered by internet cafés. Alternatively, faxes can be sent from the Wartel offices located in the larger towns, recognizable by their white signs with black let-   Fax and internet tering and a blue logo. Fax machines can be found in almost every hotel. They are available to hotel guests and sometimes also to non-residents. A minimum charge is frequently demanded for sending a fax (for example, the price of a three-minute phone call). Larger hotels offer an office service in the Business Center, where business travellers especially will find all the modern means of communication.

Time

Central Indonesian Time

Indonesia has three time zones from west to east. Bali and Lombok are on Central Indonesian Time (= GMT + 8 hours). There is no daylight saving time.

Toilets

Especially away from the towns, there are still squat toilets, whose use demands a certain degree of physical agility. To clean oneself (using the left hand, which is why it is regarded as »unclean« there is very seldom any toilet paper to hand; mostly one will find a bucket of water with a ladle. Public toilets can be recognized by the inscription »Kamar Kecil«: »Gents« is »Laki« and »Ladies« is »Perempuan«.

Transport

FERRIES

Ferry terminal

Car ferries and jetfoils ply regularly (several times daily) between Bali and Java and between Bali and Lombok. The terminals in Bali for ferries to Java (Ketapang, most easterly port) are in Gilimanuk on the western tip of the island. The ferries to Lombok leave from the port of Benoa (south of Denpasar). Boats to Bali's smaller islands of Lembongan and Penida leave from Benoa, Sanur, Kusamba and Padang Bai. The terminals in Lombok are in Lembar (south of the island's capital, Mataram), on Lembongan near Jungutbatu and on Penida near Toyapakeh. Reservations can be made in all travel agencies, in the terminals, or directly with the ferry companies themselves.

FERRY CONNECTIONS
Bali – Lombok
Lombok Network
Jl. Karika Plaza 97, Kuta
Tel. 03 61 8 75 79 04
www.lombok-network.com
Public ferry from Padang Bai to Lembar
10× daily, crossing time 4 to 5 hours

Bali – Penida
▶p. 210

Bali – Lembongan
▶p. 210;
The 34 m luxury catamaran »Bali Hai«
plies regularly between Benoa Harbour
and Nusa Lembongan.

Bookings for day tours or evening
»Dinner Cruises« (2.5 hrs.) at:
Bali Hai Cruises
Benoa Harbour
Tel. 03 61 72 03 31
www.balihaicruises.com

RENTAL CARS
Golden Bird Bali
Denpasar Airport
Arrival hall
Tel. 03 61 70 11 11
www.bluebirdgroup.com

Indorent
Denpasar Airport
Arrival hall
Tel. 03 61 7 44 11 41
www.indorent.co.id

BY ROAD

Hire cars

It is possible to explore Bali as well as Lombok by hire car. Particularly in Bali there are a large number of car rental companies. The cars for hire are usually Japanese (mostly Suzuki) four-wheel drive vehicles. The car rental agencies are less interested in seeing an international driving licence than the Balinese police, who will impose fines if the necessary papers are not in order. The driver must be at least 21 years of age. North American drivers especially should be prepared for unaccustomed driving conditions (they drive on the left!) and everyone must expect a local driving style that occasionally borders on the anarchic. Take no chances! Avoid driving at night. In fact, many consider it sensible when hiring a car to hire a local driver as well. They do not cost much, know their way around and, most important, possess the Balinese driving mentality. When hiring a car, check the vehicle's roadworthiness (above all, brakes, condition of tyres, lights) and be sure to look for signs of previous accidents. It goes without saying that the vehicle should be adequately covered with third-party liability insurance. If in doubt, rely on vehicles from well-known car rental companies.

Breakdowns

There are no breakdown services in Bali as there are in Western countries; you will also search in vain for emergency telephones along the roads. Stranded drivers are dependent on the help of other road users. In case of a breakdown, it is best to try to get attention by waving. Towing to the next garage is allowed. The situation can become more difficult at night, especially outside the tourist areas or inland, where it often takes a long time before someone will agree to help. This is one good reason to avoid driving at night. Be sure to ask the car rental agency for a directory of reliable garages, or what else to do in case of a breakdown.

Motorcycles Renting a motorcycle is only recommended to people with a lot of driving experience. But even so, the best driver can often find him or herself in a tricky situation. The miserable condition of many roads, especially in the interior, holds great potential danger (potholes, sudden changes in road surface, lack of traction after a shower, etc.). Another risk factor is the driving style of the natives. Innumerable accidents occur annually, often resulting in prolonged hospital stays or even death. H**elmets are mandatory**!

Behaviour in traffic Asians have a fundamentally different relationship to their car and to traffic than central and northern Europeans, and it is no different in Bali and Lombok. To put it somewhat crudely, behaviour in traffic here is based on the relatively simple principle that the five drivers in front of your car, the five behind and the seventeen bicyclists or motorcyclists or pedestrians to the right and left are supposed to act just as you expect and do nothing silly. Traffic regulations are there to be broken more than followed; speed limits appear to be understood as more of a challenge to coax the last bit out of just barely roadworthy vehicles.

Incidentally, **driving on the left** is the rule in Indonesia. With the exception of the four-lane »Jalan Bypass« between Denpasar and Nusa Dua, there are no expressways or highways on Bali. Particularly in rural regions, the condition of even vital overland roads is precarious. Hazards such as potholes, ruts and soft shoulders are often recognized too late. The islanders make abundant use of their horns, especially when passing through villages – a habit that even visitors quickly adopt. **Traffic signs**, for the most part, follow the customary international system. The roads in Bali are not systematically numbered, not even on the roadmaps available everywhere. Even if only a few locals keep to it, the **speed limit** in built-up areas is 25mph/40kmh. Out of town, 50mph/80kph for cars and 30mph/50kph for buses and lorries is allowed.

Various forms of transport There are ample **taxis** in Denpasar and the south of Bali equipped with taximeters (recognizable by their blue and yellow paint job). In addition, there are a great number of unofficial taxis. In these, the price for the trip must be settled beforehand by bargaining with the driver. The meter is usually turned on during the day and in the early evening hours; but in the late evening and at weekends, when there are not many taxis, the driver will often just name a price that can either be accepted or rejected in the hope of getting a better price from the next driver. Taxi drivers are more inclined to agree on a set price for longer trips. When the taximeter is turned on, the trip is very cheap (5000 Rp. base rate, 4500 Rp. per kilometre (7200 Rp. per mile). In the other parts of the island, there are mostly only unofficial taxis, i.e. drivers with private cars. The price must be negotiated in advance, and is two to three times the taximeter price.

A trip on a **bus** in Bali can be a special kind of experience. For the islanders, the bus is the cheapest form of transport for covering both shorter and longer distances. Taking the bus is extremely popular and the price quite cheap; moreover, it is set and does not have to be bargained over. On the other hand, there are no timetables. The bus driver usually waits in the bus terminal, to be found in every town, until he has collected enough passengers to make the trip worth his while. Minibuses are sometimes called »**colts**«. A widespread form of passenger transport is the minibus called a »**bemo**«, which is a converted delivery van fitted out with benches. They tend to become uncomfortable on longer trips, which is why buses should be given preference. A ride on a »**dokar**« (called a »cidomo« on Lombok), a two-wheeled, one-horse carriage, can be comfortable and peaceful – if you don't happen to take one in Denpasar. This is the islanders' favourite form of transport for short distances. The (modest) fare must be negotiated before the start of the trip.

A modicum of courage is required to entrust your life to one of the ever increasing number of motorcycle taxis (»**ojek**«). Although the drivers usually possess the expertise necessary to deal with the prevailing chaotic traffic conditions, a large number of ojek drivers confuse Bali's streets with (poorly prepared) racetracks. In any case, demand a helmet; once again, a price must be agreed upon beforehand.

Travellers with Disabilities

Large tour operators provide information about travel possibilities for the disabled. Public transport adapted to meet the needs of disabled travellers is the exception rather than the rule in Bali, but the friendly assistance of the locals can be counted on. Most of the sights, especially the temple complexes, can be viewed from a wheelchair. The major hotels in particular are equipped for the needs of disabled guests.

When to Go

High season   For those used to a central or northern European climate, the most pleasant time to travel to Bali is from May through to September. The lowest rainfall is recorded in this period: there are six rainy days on average. The reason for these conditions is the southeast monsoon blowing in from Australia, bringing daily highs of about 30°C/86°F. The Balinese consider the months of June and July to be »cool«; the thermometer then climbs on average up to »only« 26°C/79°F during the day. Hot days are best spent in the cooler hilly country, where pleasant winds make the temperatures tolerable. Peak season in Bali is the period from June to the beginning of September. Many tourists also come to Bali over the Christmas holidays (especially from neighbouring countries).

Low season   The west monsoon blows from October through April / May, bringing, rainfall with it, sometimes abundant, although the customary term for these months, the »rainy season«, is often falsely understood. It does not rain all day but mostly in the night or in the early morning, and then really heavily. Afterwards the clouds quickly clear, revealing blue skies again. The considerably quieter off season also means that there are sufficient vacancies in the hotels on Bali and Lombok; it is sometimes possible to negotiate a price reduction by asking at the hotel reception.

Glossary

Terms from mythology, religion, art and everyday life. We hope that the following list of terms will help you on your visit to Bali. Unfortunately we could only choose a few from the many expressions that occur frequently in life on Bali.

Adat Traditional common law

Aling-Aling Protective wall against demons. This kind of half wall usually stands behind a Covered Gate (►Candi Korung); it is meant to keep demons and evil spirits away.

Atap Palm leaf roof

Bade Coffin for transporting corpses. A Bade is used to transport a dead body to the place of cremation.

Bahasa Indonesia Indonesia's national language

Bale Pavilion-like building within a farm or temple compound. A Bale is usually open on all sides and the roof is supported by pillars. In a temple compound there are usually several Bales.

Bale Agung Pavilion where the elders or married men of a village gather to meet.

Bale Banjar Pavilion where the members of a ►Banjar meet.

Bale Gong Large pavilion in the middle courtyard of the (usually) three temple courtyards. The ►Gamelan play here during temple festivals; musical instruments are kept her too.

Bale Pesamyangan Pavilion within a temple. The gods are welcomed here at the beginning of a temple festival. Since believers never know how many gods will come to visit the Bale Pesamyangan in most temples is usually very large.

Bale Pesimpangan Place where the gods, who do not live in a temple, stay when they come to visit (►Gedong Penimpanan).

Bale Piasan Pavilion where offerings are prepared or set up.

Bali Aga Ancient Balinese

Banjar Part of a village (►Desa). All married men in that part of a village are members of a Banjar. During the regular meetings all of the important things that affect the Banjar are discussed and decided (including conflicts among members). The decisions, usually made by the majority of the members, are binding on all members.

Banyan Expansive trees with aerial roots

Baris Ritual war-like community dance for men

Barong Imaginary creature from Hindu mythology. Unlike witches ►Rangda embodies the Barong, the healing of the world.

Basuki Snake god of the underworld

Bayu Indian deity (god of wind)

Bedawang Turtle as a symbol of the underworld; one of the ten manifestations of the god Vishnu. One or two snakes are wrapped around it; it is always the plinth of a lotus throne (►Padmasana).

Bemo Public minibus

Brahma Creator of the world, one of the three ►Trimurti

Buddha Siddharta Gautama Shakya, founder of Buddhism; »Enlightened One«, who recognized the meaninglessness of the world on his own strength.

Bukit Hill

Candi Gate

Candi Bentar Divided Gate. Its origins go back to the following legend: When the Indian mountain of the gods Mahameru was transported to the island of Bali it fell into two pieces, the Gunung Agung and the Gunung Batur. The Divided Gate symbolizes these holy mountains on Bali. Its shape, which gets narrower toward the top, is reminiscent of a mountain that was divided down the middle into two parts of equal sizes.

Candi Korung Covered Gate. It usually forms the entrance to the inner temple area and is richly decorated. There are often guarding witches and faces of demons (▶Raksasa) attached to the sides of a Candi Korung or Kori Agung, which are supposed to keep the spirits of the underworld away. The Covered Gate also symbolizes the three passages of life for Hindus: birth – death – rebirth.

Chakra Disc, symbol of Vishnu; wheel of Buddha's teaching

Cidomo Two-wheeled horse-drawn carriage

Cili Fertility symbol for the rice goddess ▶Dewi Sri; usually made of flowers or grains of rice, or painted

Danau Lake

Desa Village community. A Desa consists of several ▶Banjar.

Dewi Danu Guardian goddess of water

Durga Hindu mother goddess in various forms (mostly benevolent und punishing)

Dewi Sri Guardian goddess of rice plants

Eka dasa rudra Largest and brightest festival on Bali; held every 100 years in Besakih as a purification ritual for the universe.

Gamelan Orchestra with up to 40 musicians. Mainly gongs and rhythm instruments are used to make music, sometimes also flutes and stringed instruments.

Ganesha Hindu god with the head of an elephant; son of Shiva

Garuda Sun bird, Vishnu's riding animal; also heraldic animal of Indonesia and of the state airline

Gedong Unfenced pavilion

Gedong Agung Building to honour the ancestors

Gedong Penimpanan Small building, where everything is stored that gods and deities can use for shelter when they come to earth.

Goa Cave

Ganung Mountain, volcano

Hanuman (Hanoman) Son of the wind gods, ape from the Ramayana

Ikat Type of weaving, that is resist dyed in warp or weft; tied off parts are not dyed. When warp and weft Ikat are woven together they form double Ikat.

Indra Indian deity (god of wind)

Jaba First court of a temple compound

Jaba Tengah Second court of a temple compound

Jalan (Jl.) Street

Jeroan Third, innermost court of a temple compound

Jukung Catamaran

Kali Awesome appearance of ▶Devi

Kampong Farm; actually one-story straw hut of Javanese people

Karma Sum of all good and bad deeds; effects of fate

Kecak Dance performance of Ramayana in the middle of a choir in a circle around it

Kori Agung ►Candi Korung

Kris Mythical dagger

Krishna Eighth incarnation of Vishnu

Kulkui Bell tower. Wooden clappers are used as »bells« (often hollowed out tree trunks). A Kulkul is not just used to call believers to a temple festival or an important meeting; it is also part of a sophisticated alarm system. it is used to warn against fire among other things.

Laut Ocean

Legong Classical dance performed by three young girls and considered to be the epitome of grace.

Linga(m) Phallus-shaped symbol made of stone or wood. The word comes from Sanskrit and means »sign«. The Lingam symbolizes the god ►Shiva.

Losmen Inexpensive accommodation; guest house

Lumbung Rice storage

Mahabharata Indian epic. A kind of chivalric poem in 110,000 doublets; relates the story of the battle of the Pandavas and the Kauravas for the rulership of the area around modern Delhi.

Meru World mountain; pagoda on a plinth with roofs over one another in stories.

Nyepi Balinese new year's festival (►MARCOPOLO Insight p. 98)

Odalan Temple anniversary

Oggo-Oggo Monster made of paper machee, used during the new year's festival to drive away evil spirits (►MARCOPOLO Insight p. 98).

Padmasana Lotus throne, where the god Shiva sits in his manifestation as the sun god Surya. The back of a Padmasana always faces Gunung Agung; the plinth is the underworld turtle ►Bedawang.

Padur Raksa Special form of ►Candi Korung

Panca Sila Five Principles, which form the socio-political basis of the Republic of Indonesia (faith, nationalism, democracy, humanity, a just and wealthy society).

Pelinggih Shrine for a deity that lives permanently in a temple. Gods that only come to visit can stay in the ►Bale Pesimpangan.

Prasada A special form of ►Candi. A Prasada is similar to a pagoda and is a symbol for honouring the ancestry of a noble dynasty.

Puputan Ritual suicide

Pura Temple (Sanskrit)

Pura Dalem, Pura Desa, Pura Puseh The three temples of a village. The Pura Dalem is dedicated to the god Shiva, the Pura Desa to the god Vishnu and the Pura Puseh to the creator god Brahma. The Pura Desa (temple of life) is the most important temple. In the Pura Dalem, the underworld temple (or temple of the ancestors), the ceremonies of cremation take place.

Pura Subak Small temple. Place of offering for members of a ►Subak.

Puri Palace of a noble family

Raja King, prince

Raksasa Demon figure, demon mask

Rama One of the main goddesses of Hinduism and the seventh incarnation of the god Vishnu. Rama is considered to be the most ideal of all rulers because of his moral and ethical perfection.

Ramayana Indian epic. The »Ramayana« (= »in honour of Rama«) was probably already created in the third century B.C. and tells in 24,000 quadruplets the story of the god ▶Rama.

Rangda Witch figure. She embodies the principle of destruction and is a manifestation of the world destroyer Shiva.

Saka Balinese calendar, based on the lunar year.

Samsara Cycle of existence, cycle of becoming and passing away (rebirth)

Sangyang Basuki Snake of the underworld

Sangyang Widi The highest divine principle. Originated in the course of Hinduism on Bali changing into monotheism, belief in only one god, who bears in himself the characteristics of all gods of Hinduism.

Sarong Wrap made of batik cloth

Sawah Irrigated rice fields, mostly arranged in terraces

Shiva Destroyer of the world, one of the three ▶Trimurti

Selendang Wrap that is worn around the hips or the shoulders when visiting a temple.

Subak Association similar to a cooperative. The Subak is an association of rice farmers whose fields are all irrigated from the same main canal. The Subak is supposed to organize the fieldwork and to maintain the irrigation system. Profits made in a Subak are divided equally among the members and an amount is reserved for hard times.

Sungai River

Taman Park, garden

Tirt(h)a Sacred water

Trimurti Divine trinity of the three highest Hindu gods ▶Brahma, ▶Vishnu and ▶Shiva

Tumpang Step in the top of a pagoda, roof

Vishnu Keeper of the world, one of the three ▶Trimurti

Wada Coffin for transporting corpses. Like the ▶Bade the Wada also serves to transport the dead body to the cremation site, but it is reserved for the members of the rice farmer caste Jaba.

Waringin tree Sacred tree (usually within a temple)

Warung Café, restaurant, drug store, grocery store

Wayang Drama, theatre

Wayang Kulit Shadow figure theatre. The player sits or kneels behind a backlit cloth screen and works with up to ten figures at the same time (▶MARCOPOLO Insight p. 74).

Wayang Topeng Masked drama. The actors wear wooden masks that they change several times during the dramas (which often come from the times when Bali was still ruled by nobility).

Wetu Telu Religion Islamic religion with Hindu and animistic influences; has many adherents on Lombok.

Yoni Symbol of the vagina; counterpart to the ▶Lingam

Yonilingam ▶Lingam with ▶Yoni; in the form of a basin with a drain for the offering water

Index

List of Maps and Illustrations

Photo Credits

Publisher's Information

2nd Edition 2019
Worldwide Distribution: Marco Polo
Travel Publishing Ltd
Pinewood, Chineham Business Park
Crockford Lane, Chineham
Basingstoke, Hampshire RG24 8AL,
United Kingdom.

Photos, illustrations, maps::
113 photos, 23 maps and and illustra-
tions, one large map
Text:
Heiner F. Gstaltmayr,
Birgit Müller-Wöbcke (revision)
Editing:
John Sykes, Robert Taylor, Michael
Scuffil
Translation: David Andersen, Barbara
Schmidt-Runkel, John Sykes, Robert
Taylor, Michael Scuffil
Cartography:
Franz Huber, Munich;
MAIRDUMONT Ostfildern (large map)
3D illustrations:
jangled nerves, Stuttgart
Infographics:
Golden Section Graphics GmbH, Berlin
Design:
independent Medien-Design, Munich
Editor-in-chief:
Rainer Eisenschmid, Mairdumont
Ostfildern

Printed in China

Despite all of our authors' thorough
research, errors can creep in. The pub-
lishers do not accept any liability for thi
Whether you want to praise, alert us to
errors or give us a personal tip Please
contact us by email or post:

MARCO POLO Travel Publishing Ltd
Pinewood, Chineham Business Park
Crockford Lane, Chineham
Basingstoke, Hampshire RG24 8AL
United Kingdom
Email: sales@marcopolouk.com

MIX
Paper from
responsible sources
FSC
www.fsc.org   FSC® C124385